EatingWell™
ONE-POT Meals

Easy, healthy recipes for
100+ delicious dinners

Jessie Price & the EATINGWELL Test Kitchen | Photography by Ken Burris

Library of Congress Cataloging-in-Publication Data
has been applied for.

ISBN 978-0-88150-936-6

Published by The Countryman Press,
P.O. Box 748, Woodstock, VT 05091

4746 3426 11/11

Distributed by W.W. Norton & Company, Inc.,
500 Fifth Avenue, New York, NY 10110
Printed in China by R.R. Donnelley

Photography by Ken Burris
Front cover: Red Curry Bison Short Ribs
with Baby Bok Choy (*page 195*)

1 2 3 4 5 6 7 8 9 10

AUTHORS | Jessie Price & the EATINGWELL Test Kitchen

TEST KITCHEN
TEST KITCHEN MANAGER | Stacy Fraser
ASSOCIATE EDITOR | Hilary Meyer
RECIPE DEVELOPER & TESTER | Carolyn Casner
RECIPE DEVELOPER & FOOD STYLIST | Katie Webster
FOOD STYLISTS | Patsy Jamieson, Susan Herr, Ellen Falsgraf
FOOD STYLING ASSISTANT | Elizabeth Neily
RECIPE TESTER | Patti Cook

PRODUCTION
ART DIRECTOR | Amanda Coyle
PHOTOGRAPHER | Ken Burris
MANAGING EDITOR | Wendy S. Ruopp
ASSISTANT MANAGING EDITOR | Alesia Depot
PRODUCTION MANAGER | Jennifer B. Brown
CONTRIBUTING WRITER | Jim Romanoff
NUTRITION EDITOR | Brierley Wright, M.S., R.D.
DIETITIAN & NUTRITION ADVISOR | Sylvia Geiger, M.S., R.D.
RESEARCH EDITOR | Anne Bliss
INDEXER | Amy Novick, BackSpace Indexing

EATINGWELL MEDIA GROUP
CEO | Tom Witschi
EDITORIAL DIRECTOR | Lisa Gosselin

Contents

Jamaican Curried Shrimp & Mango Soup (*p. 151*)

SIMPLE, EASY
ONE-POT MEALS

There was no counter in the kitchen of my first apartment in San Francisco. I chopped everything on a wooden cutting board balanced across two burners of the stove, a 1940s Wedgewood (the California stove manufacturer, not the British china). Most weekends in that tiny apartment I would pull out my Dutch oven (one of the few pots I owned) and make a big steaming cauldron of soup. Everything went into the one pot. I'd start by dicing onions, carrots and celery on the cutting board on half the stove. Then I'd cook the vegetables with a little olive oil on the other half of the stove. When I was done, all I had to clean was my cutting board and that pot. It was so simple, but the soups were satisfying, healthy and delicious.

The one-pot dinner recipes in this book share that simplified approach to cooking. Each recipe is made in just one pot so it's easy and streamlined. But we're not just talking Dutch ovens—a one-pot recipe can be made in a skillet, a slow cooker, a wok or even a roasting pan. Our one rule: no other cooking vessels are used. A salad bowl even counts as a "pot" in this book. After all, the salad bowl certainly meets the most important criteria—it works for making an easy dinner with little cleanup.

Today I have plenty of counter space and all the pots and pans and kitchen doodads I could hope for, but what I lack most often is time. Cooking a meal all in one pot is perfect for anyone who is busy and wants to get a healthy dinner on the table with little fuss. Many of the recipes in this book take less than 30 minutes start to finish. Some take longer, but the cooking is done almost completely unattended—take the whole chapter of slow-cooker recipes starting on page 128, for example.

All the recipes have been tested by different cooks in the EatingWell Test Kitchen, multiple times, on both gas and electric stoves. The result is recipes that you can trust to work every time you make them in your home kitchen. And you can feel good about sharing these meals with family and friends knowing that each recipe has been reviewed by our team of nutritionists to ensure that calories, saturated fat and sodium are kept in check. The recipes follow the simple approach to healthy cooking that we've been practicing for years: use plenty of fruits and vegetables, go for whole foods over processed, eat lean meats and seafood in moderation, opt for whole grains over refined and choose healthy oils like olive and canola.

We've worked with many of the best cookbook authors and chefs around, such as Perla Meyers, Deborah Madison and Bruce Aidells, to develop the recipes in this book. Some of my favorites include Red-Cooked Lamb with Sweet Potatoes made in a Dutch oven (*page 199*), Pad Thai cooked in a wok (*page 32*) and Easy Paella with Shrimp & Mussels (*page 51*), which feels like a special event but only takes 40 minutes start to finish, all in one skillet. Throw together a salad while the paella cooks, and you're ready for guests. With the recipes in this book you can get a great, healthy dinner on the table without breaking a sweat and with barely any dishes to do. Before you get started, turn the page for some tips to make your cooking easy and efficient.

—*Jessie Price*

9 ways to be a better cook

1 Get the right equipment

The seven essential types of pots for one-pot meals include skillets, Dutch ovens, woks, roasting pans, casserole dishes, slow cookers and salad bowls. (Each chapter is devoted to one of these types of pots, so turn to their respective chapters for more information on what to look for.) Besides those pots, a well-stocked kitchen includes a saucepan or two and at least two cutting boards, one for meat and fish and one for everything else. And ideally you should have a third board for fruit, so that it doesn't end up tasting like garlic. We recommend using the biggest cutting boards your space will accommodate—the bigger the board, the more room you have for quickly prepping ingredients. You should also have a set of mixing bowls, dry and wet measuring cups and measuring spoons.

2 Organize your work space

Create a well-lit, clutter-free prep space in your kitchen that has space for your cutting board, ingredients and a bowl or two. Keep knives close by. And position a garbage can, trash bowl or compost bin within arm's reach so you can get carrot peels, onions skins and so forth out of the way. (Of course, your space may be constrained, if you live in a tiny apartment, for instance, so improvise where necessary!)

3 Shop smart

Half the battle of getting dinner on the table quickly is making sure you don't have to go to the supermarket every other day. The best approach is to make a weekly plan of what you're going to cook, consult your recipes and write a detailed shopping list. You can make your trip to the store as quick as possible if you organize your list by aisle. Try breaking it into these sections: produce, meat & seafood, dry goods, freezer, dairy, refrigerator, bakery & deli.

4 Keep a well-stocked pantry

When you're making a shopping list, and as you cook and use up ingredients, keep your pantry in mind. If every time you reach the bottom of a bottle of soy sauce you always jot it down on your list, you won't come up empty-handed the next time you're about to throw your ingredients in a wok for a stir-fry. For a complete list of what to stock in a healthy pantry, turn to page 211.

5 Use the power of herbs and spices

Herbs and spices are essential for making great-tasting food that's healthy too. They let you create bright, aromatic, vibrant-tasting dishes without loading them up with salt, sugar, butter or cream. So keep a well-organized array of dried herbs and spices, preferably close to your work space. Keep in mind that herbs and spices do lose potency the longer they sit on your shelves. After they've been there a year or two, replace them. And if you have space, plant an herb garden or, if you live in a colder climate, a small planter that you can bring inside in the winter.

6 Read your recipe

When you're ready to cook, take a moment and read your recipe. Though you may want to dive right in without reading, you'll save time in the end, and probably do a better job, if you know what to expect. Of course, we're the first to say that you should have fun and experiment in the kitchen; try using different ingredients, add more of something you like or skip something you don't. But for a sure success, follow the recipe and keep in mind the subtle conventions of recipe writing.

The most important convention (that's probably the least obvious) is that the commas in the ingredient list really matter. For example, when we say "1 pound chicken thighs, trimmed" we mean that you should buy 1 pound of thighs and then trim the fat off them. If, on the other hand, we call for "1 pound trimmed chicken thighs" you would need to either purchase trimmed thighs or buy more than the 1 pound that we want you to cook. Does it really matter? In some cases no, but those small differences will impact the nutrition profile of a dish, and might even affect how something cooks. For instance, if you put too much meat in a stir-fry, you run the risk of overcrowding the wok, causing your meat to stew instead of getting the desired sear. We try to call for ingredients in terms of what you would buy at the market (e.g., 1 small onion rather than 1 cup diced onion). When we call for measures of an ingredient instead of the amount you buy at the market, it's typically because the amount of that ingredient has a big impact on the way the dish will turn out.

7 Cook like a pro

If you've ever watched line cooks in a restaurant then you know that the secret to how they churn out all those plates of food so quickly is that all their ingredients are prepared, organized and ready to go when they get an order. Chefs call this idea of having all the ingredients ready *mise en place*. Translated literally, it means everything in place. This is a great way to approach cooking at home, too—once you've read your recipe, head to the refrigerator and cupboards, pull out all the ingredients you'll need and set them up next to your work space. If it's going to take you a little while to chop and prep, then leave your meat in the refrigerator until closer to when you're ready to put it in a pan. As you prepare ingredients, if you don't have enough room to keep them organized in little piles on your cutting board, transfer them to small bowls. We like to use the glass ramekins that you can pick up at most supermarkets for prepped ingredients.

    The other thing you may notice as you watch line cooks at a sauté station is that they use metal tongs for everything. Metal tongs are like an extension of the professional cook's arm. Try them: a decent pair is inexpensive and you will never want to cook without them once you do. (If you cook with a nonstick skillet a lot, you should also get silicone-coated tongs.)

8 Chop quickly

Nothing slows you down more in the kitchen than dull knives. Invest in a good chef's knife and paring knife. Then buy an inexpensive handheld knife sharpener—these can cost under $10—and take just a couple swipes of the knife through the little V groove before you get to work. You'll be slicing through the skin of ripe tomatoes like it's nothing. Also, if your chopping skills are slow and clunky, spend some time watching the pros on TV and mimic how they do it. You may not get as quick as them, but you can certainly pick up some of their technique, speed things up and be safer.

9 Develop a repertoire of effortless sides

When it comes to rounding out a meal, think *easy*. Many of the recipes in this book deliver a complete meal. But you may want to serve a homey soup like Swedish Cabbage Soup with Meatballs (*page 159*) with a crusty piece of whole-grain bread or a light green salad. Boil up some whole-wheat egg noodles to serve with Marsala Chicken Stew (*page 186*). And it's always smart to add more veggies to your meal, so learn some basic ways to cook them. Turn to the Resources section (*page 200*) for handy vegetable and whole-grain cooking guides plus simple ways to season the results. Check the "serve with" suggestions that accompany each recipe if you need a little help with inspiration.

Now that you know our favorite ways to make cooking easy and enjoyable, it's time to turn to the 100-plus recipes in this book and make dinner. If you want to use your wok or plug in your slow cooker (while you're at work), turn to the chapters for those pots, pages 24 and 128 respectively. If, on the other hand, you know you're in the mood for shrimp, check the comprehensive index starting on page 215, where you'll find all the recipes organized by their main ingredient (among other things). Whatever you decide to cook, here's to many happy, healthy meals. Cheers!

Curried Salad with Egg & Cashews

SALAD BOWL

For looks, invest in a lovely wooden salad bowl, but for utility, a metal one does the trick just fine—and doubles as a mixing bowl for baking. The only essential thing to keep in mind when you're picking a salad bowl is that bigger really is better. There's no reason to complicate tossing a salad by insisting on using a too-small bowl. The bigger the bowl, the less likely you are to fling lettuce and vegetables on your counter and floor when you make a salad.

Southwestern Salad with Black Beans

ACTIVE TIME: 20 minutes
TOTAL: 20 minutes
TO MAKE AHEAD: Cover and refrigerate dressing for up to 3 days.

MAKES: 4 servings

H✂W   H↑F   H♥H
PER SERVING: 235 calories; 4 g fat (1 g sat, 2 g mono); 0 mg cholesterol; 43 g carbohydrate; 0 g added sugars; 13 g protein; 13 g fiber; 307 mg sodium; 1,325 mg potassium.
NUTRITION BONUS: Vitamin A (108% daily value), Vitamin C (80% dv), Folate (77% dv), Potassium (38% dv), Iron (27% dv), Magnesium (21% dv), Calcium (18% dv).

SERVE WITH:

A quick quesadilla made by melting shredded cheese on a whole-wheat tortilla, along with a few spoonfuls of salsa, in a hot skillet

Here we top salad greens with black beans, sweet corn and grape tomatoes and bring it all together with a tangy avocado-lime dressing for a Mexican-inspired salad. If you want to take this salad along for lunch, pack the greens, salad toppings and dressing in separate containers and toss them together just before eating.

CREAMY CILANTRO-AVOCADO DRESSING

- 1/2 **ripe avocado**
- 3/4 **cup packed fresh cilantro**
- 1/2 **cup nonfat plain yogurt**
- 2 **scallions, chopped**
- 1 **clove garlic, quartered**
- 1 **tablespoon lime juice**
- 1/2 **teaspoon sugar**
- 1/2 **teaspoon salt**

SALAD

- 12 **cups mixed greens**
- 2 **cups black beans, canned (rinsed) *or* cooked**
- 2 **cups corn kernels, fresh (*see Note*) *or* frozen (thawed)**
- 2 **cups grape tomatoes, halved**

1. **To prepare dressing:** Place avocado, cilantro, yogurt, scallions, garlic, lime juice, sugar and salt in a blender; blend until smooth.
2. **To prepare salad:** Place greens in a salad bowl; toss with ½ cup of the dressing. (Refrigerate the remaining ½ cup dressing for another use.) Top the greens with black beans, corn and tomatoes.

NOTE: Stand an **ear of corn** on one end and slice the kernels off with a sharp knife. One ear will yield about ½ cup kernels.

Hoisin-Sesame Salad with Baked Tofu

ACTIVE TIME: 15 minutes
TOTAL: 15 minutes
TO MAKE AHEAD: Cover and refrigerate dressing for up to 5 days.

MAKES: 4 servings

H✂W   H⬆F   H♥H

PER SERVING: 336 calories; 21 g fat (2 g sat, 9 g mono); 0 mg cholesterol; 23 g carbohydrate; 0 g added sugars; 17 g protein; 8 g fiber; 383 mg sodium; 836 mg potassium.
NUTRITION BONUS: Vitamin A (305% daily value), Vitamin C (100% dv), Folate (57% dv), Iron (26% dv), Calcium & Potassium (24% dv), Magnesium (17% dv).

SERVE WITH:

Baked sweet potato wedges tossed with soy sauce, sesame seeds and toasted sesame oil

This Asian-inspired salad is made satisfying with savory baked tofu; carrots and snap peas add crunch. If you find mixed greens labeled "Asian," which typically include mizuna and other spicy greens, choose them for this recipe.

HOISIN-SESAME DRESSING

- ⅓ **cup canola oil**
- 3 **tablespoons rice vinegar**
- 2 **tablespoons hoisin sauce (*see Note*)**
- 1 **tablespoon toasted sesame oil**
- 1 **tablespoon sesame seeds, toasted (*see Note, page 213*)**
- 1 **scallion, minced**

SALAD

- 12 **cups mixed greens**
- 3 **cups cubed baked tofu (12 ounces)**
- 2 **cups carrot matchsticks *or* slices**
- 2 **cups sliced snap peas**

1. **To prepare dressing:** Place canola oil, vinegar, hoisin sauce, sesame oil, sesame seeds and scallion in a bowl or a jar with a tight-fitting lid; whisk or shake until well combined.

2. **To prepare salad:** Place greens in a salad bowl; toss with ½ cup of the dressing. (Refrigerate the remaining ¼ cup dressing for another use.) Top the greens with tofu, carrots and snap peas.

NOTE: **Hoisin sauce** is a dark brown, thick, spicy-sweet sauce made from soybeans and a complex mix of spices. Look for it in the Asian section of your supermarket and in Asian markets.

Curried Salad with Egg & Cashews

ACTIVE TIME: 15 minutes

TOTAL: 15 minutes

TO MAKE AHEAD: Cover and refrigerate dressing for up to 5 days.

MAKES: 4 servings

H⬆F

PER SERVING: 368 calories; 16 g fat (4 g sat, 7 g mono); 190 mg cholesterol; 48 g carbohydrate; 21 g added sugars; 13 g protein; 7 g fiber; 432 mg sodium; 900 mg potassium.

NUTRITION BONUS: Vitamin C (207% daily value), Vitamin A (142% dv), Folate (66% dv), Magnesium & Potassium (26% dv), Iron (25% dv), Zinc (18% dv), Calcium (17% dv).

SERVE WITH:

Whole-grain crackers with a spread of goat cheese

Here we toss fresh salad greens with a light and creamy dressing, then top with chopped hard-boiled egg, crunchy bell pepper, dried cranberries and toasted cashews for a satisfying vegetarian salad. (Photograph: page 8.)

CREAMY CURRY DRESSING

- 1/2 **cup nonfat plain yogurt**
- 1/2 **cup low-fat mayonnaise**
- 3 **tablespoons lemon juice**
- 2 **tablespoons water**
- 1 **tablespoon honey**
- 1 **teaspoon curry powder**
- 1/4 **teaspoon salt**
- 1/4 **teaspoon freshly ground pepper**

SALAD

- 12 **cups mixed greens**
- 2 **cups diced *or* sliced red bell pepper**
- 1 **cup dried cranberries**
- 4 **hard-boiled eggs (*see Note, page 212*), chopped**
- 1/2 **cup toasted cashews (*see Note, page 212*)**

1. **To prepare dressing:** Place yogurt, mayonnaise, lemon juice, water, honey, curry powder, salt and pepper in a bowl or a blender; whisk or blend until smooth.
2. **To prepare salad:** Place greens in a salad bowl; toss with ½ cup of the dressing. (Refrigerate the remaining ½ cup dressing for another use.) Top the greens with bell pepper, cranberries, egg and cashews.

Mediterranean Tuna Antipasto Salad

The convenience and superb nutritional profile of canned beans make them a pantry essential. Here they are combined with similarly virtuous canned tuna, fresh herbs, mixed greens and crunchy vegetables to create a meal in a salad bowl that can be on the table in a flash. For an extra kick, add a pinch of crushed red pepper or cayenne.

1   15- to 19-ounce can beans, such as chickpeas, black-eyed peas *or* kidney beans, rinsed
2   5- to 6-ounce cans water-packed chunk light tuna, drained and flaked (*see Note*)
1   large red bell pepper, finely diced
1/2   cup finely chopped red onion
1/2   cup chopped fresh parsley, divided
4   teaspoons capers, rinsed
1 1/2   teaspoons finely chopped fresh rosemary
1/2   cup lemon juice, divided
4   tablespoons extra-virgin olive oil, divided
  Freshly ground pepper to taste
1/4   teaspoon salt
8   cups mixed salad greens

1. Combine beans, tuna, bell pepper, onion, parsley, capers, rosemary, 1/4 cup lemon juice and 2 tablespoons oil in a medium bowl. Season with pepper.
2. Combine the remaining 1/4 cup lemon juice, 2 tablespoons oil and salt in a large bowl. Add salad greens; toss to coat. Divide the greens among 4 plates. Top each with the tuna salad.

NOTE: **Chunk light tuna**, like most fish and shellfish, contains some mercury. According to the FDA and EPA, women who are or might become pregnant, nursing mothers and young children should limit their consumption to 12 ounces a week of fish with lower mercury, including canned "light" tuna. Consumption of albacore tuna (which is labeled "white") should be limited to no more than 6 ounces a week. And, if you're looking for an environmentally sustainable canned tuna option, check the label—tuna that was caught by troll or pole-and-line is considered the best choice, according to Monterey Bay Aquarium's Seafood Watch program. Or look for the blue Certified Sustainable Seafood label from the Marine Stewardship Council.

ACTIVE TIME: 25 minutes
TOTAL: 25 minutes

MAKES: 4 servings

H✂W   H↑F   H♥H

PER SERVING: 290 calories; 16 g fat (2 g sat, 11 g mono); 12 mg cholesterol; 24 g carbohydrate; 0 g added sugars; 17 g protein; 9 g fiber; 505 mg sodium; 638 mg potassium.
NUTRITION BONUS: Vitamin C (157% daily value), Vitamin A (100% dv), Folate (43% dv), Potassium (18% dv), Iron (16% dv).

SERVE WITH:

Toasted slices of whole-grain Italian bread, brushed with extra-virgin olive oil and rubbed with the cut side of a garlic clove

Smoky Artichoke-Sardine Salad

Smoked paprika and sherry vinegar add Spanish flair to the dressing of this artichoke-and-sardine salad. If tomatoes are in season, slice a few fresh wedges to add to this salad.

SMOKED PAPRIKA VINAIGRETTE

- ½ **cup extra-virgin olive oil**
- 3 **tablespoons sherry vinegar**
- 1 **large shallot, minced**
- 1 **teaspoon Dijon mustard**
- ¾ **teaspoon smoked paprika (*see Note*)**
- ¼ **teaspoon salt**
- ¼ **teaspoon freshly ground pepper**

SALAD

- 12 **cups mixed greens**
- 2 **cups canned artichoke hearts, rinsed and quartered**
- 8 **ounces canned sardines**
- 1 **cup sliced red onion**

1. **To prepare vinaigrette:** Place oil, vinegar, shallot, mustard, paprika, salt and pepper in a blender or a jar with a tight-fitting lid; blend or shake until well combined.

2. **To prepare salad:** Place greens in a salad bowl; toss with ½ cup of the dressing. (Refrigerate the remaining ¼ cup dressing for another use.) Top the greens with artichoke hearts, sardines and onion.

NOTE: **Smoked paprika** is made from smoke-dried red peppers and adds earthy, smoky flavor. It can be used in many types of savory dishes. Look for different types of paprika at some large supermarkets or at *tienda.com* or *penzeys.com*.

ACTIVE TIME: 15 minutes
TOTAL: 15 minutes
TO MAKE AHEAD: Cover and refrigerate dressing for up to 5 days.

MAKES: 4 servings

H↑F   H♥H

PER SERVING: 383 calories; 26 g fat (4 g sat, 17 g mono); 81 mg cholesterol; 19 g carbohydrate; 0 g added sugars; 21 g protein; 8 g fiber; 832 mg sodium; 809 mg potassium.
NUTRITION BONUS: Vitamin A (102% daily value), Vitamin C (70% dv), Folate (51% dv), Calcium (32% dv), Potassium (23% dv), Iron (22% dv), Magnesium (17% dv).

SERVE WITH:

Mixed olives and warmed pita bread, along with store-bought hummus

Orange-Walnut Salad with Chicken

Orange segments, toasted walnuts and tangy goat cheese brighten up this simple salad. If you don't have cooked chicken for this salad, try it with smoked tofu or smoked turkey breast.

ORANGE-WALNUT VINAIGRETTE

- ⅓   cup walnut oil
- ⅓   cup orange juice
- 1   tablespoon red-wine vinegar
- 1   clove garlic, minced
- 1   teaspoon freshly grated orange zest
- 1   teaspoon reduced-sodium soy sauce
- ¼   teaspoon salt
- ¼   teaspoon freshly ground pepper

SALAD

- 12   cups mixed greens
- 2   cups diced or shredded cooked chicken breast (see Notes)
- 4   oranges, cut into segments (see Notes)
- ½   cup crumbled goat cheese
- ½   cup toasted walnuts (see Note, page 212)

1. **To prepare vinaigrette:** Place oil, orange juice, vinegar, garlic, orange zest, soy sauce, salt and pepper in a bowl or a jar with a tight-fitting lid; whisk or shake until well combined.
2. **To prepare salad:** Place greens in a salad bowl; toss with ½ cup of the dressing. (Refrigerate the remaining ¼ cup dressing for another use.) Top the greens with chicken, orange segments, goat cheese and walnuts.

NOTES:

If you don't have **cooked chicken**, you can quickly poach some for this recipe. Place about 1 pound boneless, skinless chicken breast in a medium skillet or saucepan. Add lightly salted water (or chicken broth) to cover and bring to a boil. Cover, reduce heat to low and simmer gently until the chicken is cooked through and no longer pink in the middle, 10 to 15 minutes. (1 pound raw boneless, skinless chicken breast makes about 2½ cups diced or shredded.)

To segment citrus, slice both ends off the fruit. Using a sharp knife, remove the peel and white pith; discard. Working over a bowl, cut the segments from their surrounding membranes. Squeeze juice into the bowl before discarding membrane, if desired.

ACTIVE TIME: 20 minutes
TOTAL: 20 minutes
TO MAKE AHEAD: Cover and refrigerate dressing for up to 5 days.

MAKES: 4 servings

H✂W   H⬆F   H❤H
PER SERVING: 466 calories; 29 g fat (6 g sat, 6 g mono); 71 mg cholesterol; 24 g carbohydrate; 0 g added sugars; 31 g protein; 8 g fiber; 294 mg sodium; 1,060 mg potassium.
NUTRITION BONUS: Vitamin C (173% daily value), Vitamin A (101% dv), Folate (63% dv), Potassium (30% dv), Magnesium (26% dv), Calcium & Iron (21% dv).

SERVE WITH:

Pita chips

Chicken & White Bean Salad

ACTIVE TIME: 25 minutes
TOTAL: 25 minutes
TO MAKE AHEAD: Prepare through Step 2 (omitting basil), cover and refrigerate for up to 2 days. Stir in chopped basil just before serving.

MAKES: 4 servings, about 2 cups each

H⧖W   H↑F   H♥H

PER SERVING: 428 calories; 23 g fat (5 g sat, 15 g mono); 79 mg cholesterol; 24 g carbohydrate; 0 g added sugars; 34 g protein; 8 g fiber; 667 mg sodium; 648 mg potassium.
NUTRITION BONUS: Vitamin C (47% daily value), Vitamin A (30% dv), Folate (21% dv), Potassium (19% dv).

SERVE WITH:

Slices of crunchy whole-grain baguette

Diced cooked chicken breast and convenient canned beans give this simple salad a satisfying double punch of protein. We think the slight bitterness of escarole and radicchio works best with the fresh flavors in this dish, but any type of salad greens will do.

VINAIGRETTE

1	medium clove garlic
¼	teaspoon salt, plus more to taste
5	tablespoons extra-virgin olive oil
6	tablespoons fresh orange juice, plus more to taste
¼	cup white-wine vinegar *or* red-wine vinegar
1	tablespoon Dijon mustard

SALAD

1	15-ounce can cannellini *or* other white beans, rinsed
2½	cups diced cooked chicken breast (*see Notes, page 19*)
2	cups diced zucchini *and/or* summer squash (about 2 small)
1½	cups diced celery
¼	cup finely diced ricotta salata, halloumi (*see Note*) *or* feta cheese
⅓	cup chopped, well-drained, oil-packed sun-dried tomatoes (optional)
1	cup coarsely chopped fresh basil, plus whole basil leaves for garnish
	Salt & freshly ground pepper to taste (optional)
2	cups torn escarole *or* romaine lettuce
2	cups torn radicchio leaves

1. **To prepare vinaigrette:** Peel the garlic and smash with the side of a chef's knife. Using a fork, mash the garlic with ¼ teaspoon salt in a small bowl to form a coarse paste. Whisk in oil. Add 6 tablespoons orange juice, vinegar and mustard; whisk until well blended. Taste and whisk in up to 4 tablespoons more juice to mellow the flavor; season with more salt, if desired.

2. **To prepare salad:** Combine beans, chicken, zucchini (and/or summer squash), celery, cheese and sun-dried tomatoes (if using) in a large bowl until well blended. Add chopped basil and ¾ cup of the vinaigrette; toss until combined. Taste and season with salt and/or pepper, if desired.

3. Toss the remaining vinaigrette with escarole (or romaine) and radicchio in a medium bowl. Serve the salad on the greens, garnished with fresh basil leaves.

NOTE: **Ricotta salata** and **halloumi** are both firm, salted cheeses that can be found at large supermarkets and cheese shops.

Ken Burris

I had always wanted

a bowl like that, a

bowl that still said

"I am a tree."

—*Lisa Gosselin*

Dinner in a Bowl
Gather everything you need for a wonderful salad

I t took me years to find the salad bowl. I finally saw it, at a farmers' market where a bearded man with rough hands was turning a block of wood on a lathe. He hollowed out what had once been a trunk of a maple tree, leaving bits of bark along the rim, carving down toward the center through a ringed history of freezes and thaws, bare winter branches and dappled forest summers.

I had always wanted a bowl like that, a bowl that still said "I am a tree." For some reason, that sturdy bowl seemed, and still seems, like the only fitting way to serve the delicate greens—spicy arugula, crisp Boston lettuce and sharp kale—that shoot from the dark earth of the garden. It was not an inexpensive bowl, but it was one I knew would last—a solid piece that would not crack at the seams. I thought of it as furniture for my kitchen.

I took it home and began the seasoning process, rubbing it first with mineral oil, then letting the bowl take on a flavor of its own. (I believe in the early years it tasted a tad bit of maple, too, but I probably just imagined that.)

It was light enough so I brought it with me to the garden in the early evenings, using it to gather tender shoots of greens like parsley, chives and cilantro and blooms from nasturtium and pansies.

It was wide and shallow, so a heavier item—a steamed shrimp, a chunk of feta—that I might toss in later would not disappear into the fathoms. It welcomed the colors and shapes I'd layer in—shaved carrots, slivers of red and green peppers, sections of clementines or melons—and splayed their colors like a painter's palette.

And it carried the vague memories of every dressing—creamy cilantro, a vinaigrette with Dijon and smoked paprika—exhaling scents of ginger, walnut oil and orange zest.

For years, I lived alone and the salad bowl, for much of the year, was my dinner bowl. I could fill it half full and still feel good about what I was eating. I loved the feel of wood in my hands, the bright colors of fruits and vegetables tucked in among the leaves of greens. Leftovers, which might look pathetic in little sealed ramekins in my fridge, took on new glory when I tossed them into the bowl. And magically, when I had friends for dinner, I seemed to be able to pile it high to near overflowing—and it would serve six or seven.

Gradually, what had once been rooted in the ground has taken on a new life, feeding other lives. 🥣

Lisa Gosselin is the editorial director of EatingWell Media Group and editor-in-chief of EatingWell *Magazine.*

Broccoli, Ham & Pasta Salad

A great pasta salad is as versatile as it is satisfying—an easy make-ahead meal good for lunch, suppers and potlucks. In this lightened version, plenty of crunchy vegetables balance out whole-wheat pasta and the sweet-and-savory flavor combo of raisins and smoky ham. This recipe calls for cooked pasta—boil extra pasta on a night when you have it for dinner so you can have leftovers ready for this salad later in the week.

ACTIVE TIME: 20 minutes
TOTAL: 50 minutes
TO MAKE AHEAD: Prepare through Step 2, cover and refrigerate for up to 2 days.

MAKES: 5 servings, about 2 cups each

CREAMY HERBED DRESSING

- 1/2 cup low-fat mayonnaise
- 1/3 cup nonfat plain yogurt
- 1/4 cup reduced-fat sour cream
- 3 tablespoons rice vinegar *or* white-wine vinegar
- 1 tablespoon Dijon mustard
- 1 tablespoon honey, or more to taste
- 1 1/2 teaspoons dried minced onion *or* dried chopped chives
- 1 1/4 teaspoons dried tarragon *or* dill
- 1/2 teaspoon onion salt *or* celery salt *or* 1/4 teaspoon of each
  White pepper to taste

SALAD

- 3 cups cooked whole-wheat fusilli *or* similar pasta (about 6 ounces dry)
- 4 cups chopped broccoli florets (about 1 1/2 large heads)
- 1 1/2 cups diced ham (8 ounces), preferably reduced-sodium
- 1 large red *or* yellow bell pepper (*or* a combination), diced
- 1/4 cup diced red onion, plus slices for garnish
- 1/3 cup raisins
  Freshly ground pepper to taste
- 4 cups spinach leaves
- 1 cup torn radicchio leaves

H✂W   H⬆F   H❤H
PER SERVING: 306 calories; 7 g fat (2 g sat, 2 g mono); 31 mg cholesterol; 46 g carbohydrate; 4 g added sugars; 19 g protein; 6 g fiber; 838 mg sodium; 696 mg potassium.
NUTRITION BONUS: Vitamin C (167% daily value), Vitamin A (85% dv), Folate (24% dv), Potassium (20% dv), Magnesium (18% dv), Zinc (17% dv), Iron (16% dv).

SERVE WITH:

Whole-grain breadsticks wrapped in paper-thin slices of a low-fat Swiss cheese, such as Jarlsberg Lite

1. **To prepare dressing:** Combine mayonnaise, yogurt, sour cream, vinegar, mustard, honey, dried onion (or chives), tarragon (or dill) and onion salt (and/or celery salt) in a large bowl until well blended. Season with white pepper. Taste and adjust seasonings, if desired.
2. **To prepare salad:** Add pasta, broccoli, ham, bell pepper, diced onion and raisins to the bowl. Toss with the dressing until evenly incorporated. Cover and refrigerate to blend the flavors for at least 30 minutes and up to 2 days.
3. Serve on a bed of spinach and radicchio, garnished with slices of red onion.

Beef & Red Pepper Stir-Fry

WOK

For as little as $30 you can get a great wok that will last for years. Choose a carbon-steel wok with a flat bottom—they're light, easy to hold and move, and the flat bottom allows them to sit directly on the burner of your stove, so they get hot enough. Avoid non-stick woks—most nonstick cookware should not be used over high heat, and many wok stir-fries require high heat for the best results. *(For tips on how to season a wok, turn to page 208.)*

Farmers' Market Fried Rice

ACTIVE TIME: 30 minutes
TOTAL: 30 minutes

MAKES: 4 servings, about 1½ cups each

H↑F   H♥H

PER SERVING: 400 calories; 13 g fat (3 g sat, 6 g mono); 93 mg cholesterol; 60 g carbohydrate; 0 g added sugars; 11 g protein; 7 g fiber; 471 mg sodium; 541 mg potassium.
NUTRITION BONUS: Vitamin C (53% daily value), Magnesium (29% dv), Vitamin A (20% dv), Folate (17% dv), Potassium (15% dv).

SERVE WITH:

Mesclun greens tossed with shredded carrots, toasted sesame seeds and scallions dressed with sesame oil, rice vinegar and ginger dressing

This fresh take on fried rice includes thinly sliced Brussels sprouts and diced parsnips. Substitute other vegetables, such as snap peas, carrots or corn, when they're in season. Cook the egg pancake before prepping any of the other ingredients so it has some time to cool. Always use cold cooked rice. If the rice is freshly cooked, the fried rice will be gummy and sticky. If you know you want to have fried rice for dinner, make a pot of rice the previous night so it's cool and ready to use the next day.

2	teaspoons plus 2 tablespoons peanut oil *or* canola oil, divided
2	large eggs, beaten
2	tablespoons minced garlic
½	cup thinly sliced shallots
1	cup diced peeled and cored parsnips (*see Notes*)
4	medium Brussels sprouts, trimmed and sliced ¼ inch thick
4	cups cold cooked brown rice (*see Notes*)
12	cherry tomatoes, halved or quartered (if large)
2	tablespoons reduced-sodium soy sauce
¼	cup finely chopped fresh cilantro
¼	teaspoon salt
¼	teaspoon ground white pepper

1. Heat a 14-inch flat-bottomed wok over high heat until a bead of water vaporizes within 1 to 2 seconds of contact. Swirl 2 teaspoons oil into the wok, making sure the bottom gets completely coated. Add beaten eggs and cook, tilting the pan to cover the surface as thinly as possible with egg to make a pancake. When the bottom is just beginning to brown and the pancake is just set, about 30 seconds to 1 minute, flip the pancake using a metal spatula and allow it to set for about 5 seconds. Transfer to a cutting board and let cool. Cut the pancake into bite-size pieces.
2. Swirl 1 tablespoon oil into the wok, add garlic and shallots and stir-fry, using a metal spatula, until fragrant, 10 seconds. Add parsnips and Brussels sprouts, reduce the heat to medium-high and stir-fry until the vegetables are nearly cooked through, about 2 minutes. Swirl in the remaining 1 tablespoon oil, add rice, tomatoes and soy sauce and stir-fry, breaking up the rice, until it is heated through, 2 minutes. Sprinkle with cilantro, salt and pepper; add the egg pieces and toss to combine.

NOTES:
To peel parsnips, remove the peel with a vegetable peeler, then quarter the parsnip lengthwise and cut out the woody core with a paring knife before dicing.

To make 4 cups cooked brown rice, bring 4 cups water and 2 cups brown rice to a boil in a large saucepan. Reduce heat to low, cover and simmer at the lowest bubble until the water is absorbed and the rice is tender, about 40 minutes. Let stand, covered, for 10 minutes. (Or, to save time, prepare 4 cups instant brown rice according to package directions.) To cool, spread the cooked rice out on a large baking sheet and let stand until room temperature, then refrigerate until cold.

Scallop Scampi with Peppers

Use a mixture of bell peppers for a colorful stir-fry. When stir-frying scallops be sure to pat them dry before cooking. If the scallops are wet they will spatter when added to the wok and cause the stir-fry to turn into a braise.

- **1** pound dry sea scallops (*see Note*), patted dry
- **2** tablespoons peanut oil *or* canola oil, divided
- **1** tablespoon minced garlic
- **½** teaspoon crushed red pepper
- **2** medium bell peppers (mixed colors, if desired), cut into ¼-by-2-inch strips
- **1** tablespoon capers, rinsed
- **¼** teaspoon salt
- **¼** teaspoon freshly ground pepper
- **3** tablespoons dry white wine

1. Cut any larger scallops in half so all the pieces are about the same thickness.
2. Heat a 14-inch flat-bottomed wok over high heat until a bead of water vaporizes within 1 to 2 seconds of contact. Swirl 1 tablespoon oil into the wok, carefully add the scallops and spread them in one layer. Cook undisturbed, letting the scallops begin to sear, for 1 minute. Add garlic and crushed red pepper and stir-fry until the scallops are opaque but not cooked through, about 1 minute. Transfer the scallop mixture to a plate.
3. Swirl the remaining 1 tablespoon oil into the wok, add bell peppers and stir-fry until they begin to soften, about 1 minute. Return the scallops and any accumulated juice to the wok. Sprinkle with capers, salt and pepper; swirl in wine. Stir-fry until the scallops are just cooked through and the peppers are tender-crisp, 1 to 2 minutes.

NOTE: Be sure to buy **"dry" sea scallops**. "Wet" scallops, which have been treated with sodium tripolyphosphate (STP), are mushy and less flavorful. Some scallops will have a small white muscle on the side; remove it before cooking.

ACTIVE TIME: 25 minutes
TOTAL: 25 minutes

MAKES: 4 servings, about 1 cup each

H✂W   H♥H
PER SERVING: 170 calories; 8 g fat (1 g sat, 3 g mono); 27 mg cholesterol; 9 g carbohydrate; 0 g added sugars; 15 g protein; 1 g fiber; 616 mg sodium; 382 mg potassium.
NUTRITION BONUS: Vitamin C (128% daily value), Vitamin A (39% dv).

SERVE WITH:

Whole-wheat linguine and roasted broccoli tossed with lemon and sea salt

Steven Mark Needham

For over 2,000 years the wok has been the essential tool in the Chinese kitchen—it is the original natural nonstick pan.

—Grace Young

The Wok Evangelist

One author's mission to save this pot from extinction

My mother was raised in Shanghai and my father in Guangzhou, but by the time they started their life together in America, in 1949, they did not cook with a wok. Round-bottomed woks, the only kind they could find, didn't get hot enough for stir-frying on their all-American electric range. So they resorted to a stainless-steel skillet for Chinese cooking. My father lamented as he served his exquisite, fragrant dishes that the food hadn't been "properly" stir-fried, meaning in a wok. It wasn't until years later when I discovered the carbon-steel flat-bottomed wok and made my first successful wok stir-fry, a simple cashew chicken, that I understood my father's concern. I still remember it vividly.

The moment I swirled the peanut oil into the preheated wok, it shimmered. With the minced ginger, my wok hummed and crackled, releasing a perfume of aromatics. The marinated chicken lent the wok music a steady sizzle. After searing undisturbed for a minute, the chicken to my amazement yielded to the metal spatula without a hint of sticking, and after a quick stir-fry, achieved a perfect golden hue. Growing hungrier and happier, I added a touch more oil along with sugar snaps, carrots and roasted cashews. Within a few strokes of the spatula, the sugar snaps turned bright green. I added a couple spoonfuls of rich chicken broth, a splash of rice wine and soy sauce. Stir-frying the mixture until the vegetables were crisp and tender, I could feel myself bonding not only with my wok, but with the hundreds of years of stir-frying tradition that had produced such a simple, healthy and elegant cooking technique. The chicken that evening possessed the concentrated caramelized flavor and seared aroma known as *wok hei* that the Chinese prize. The vegetables were exquisitely sweet and crunchy.

To this day I marvel at the natural nonstick quality of a seasoned carbon-steel wok, which is what makes it indispensable for stir-frying. For over 2,000 years the wok has been the essential tool in the Chinese kitchen—it is the *original* natural nonstick pan. Once seasoned, just as with a cast-iron skillet, its surface acquires a nonstick patina. The more it is used, the less oil the carbon-steel wok requires. Nutritionally, a carbon-steel wok imparts dietary iron into food and cooking quickly at high heat preserves such delicate nutrients as vitamin C and folic acid. But what home cooks praise the most is that a carbon-steel wok imparts the coveted *wok hei* into stir-fries.

Despite all those benefits, the carbon-steel wok is becoming increasingly difficult to find in Chinatowns throughout the U.S. On a recent visit to Philadelphia's Chinatown in search of a carbon-steel wok, I found only nonstick cookware. In fact, the only place that had one was a cookware store in the Italian section of town. And in China, too, in urban centers, I've observed that "modern" nonstick cookware has usurped carbon-steel and cast-iron woks nearly into obsolescence. But nonstick is just not the same; it's not safe to use traditional Teflon-based nonstick pans over high heat. Food stir-fried in a nonstick pan is devoid of the coveted browning a carbon-steel wok imparts. As a Chinese American I am dismayed at the looming extinction of the carbon-steel wok.

I've been called the wok evangelist, the stir-fry guru and the wok doctor. When I travel, I carry my wok onto flights, and I am subject to the enhanced scrutiny of Homeland Security. But when I lecture and teach, my wok is at my side—or on the flame. After all, my mission is to educate people everywhere about the magic of the wok and the beauty of a "properly" cooked stir-fry. 🥄

Cookbook author Grace Young's most recent book, Stir-Frying to the Sky's Edge *(Simon & Schuster, 2010), won a 2011 James Beard Award and was a finalist for the IACP International Cookbook Award. She lives in New York City.*

Spicy Tofu with Shrimp

This dish is saucy and full of bold flavor from fresh garlic, ginger and scallions. For a vegetarian version, use vegetable broth instead of chicken broth, omit the shrimp and double the tofu.

1   14- to 16-ounce package firm tofu, cut into 1-inch slabs
8   ounces raw shrimp, peeled and deveined (*see Note, page 213*), chopped
2   tablespoons Shao Hsing rice wine (*see Note, page 213*) *or* sake, divided
6   teaspoons reduced-sodium soy sauce, divided
½   teaspoon sesame oil
5   tablespoons minced scallions (about 4), divided
1½ tablespoons minced garlic
1½ tablespoons minced fresh ginger
1   teaspoon chile-garlic sauce (*see Note, page 212*)
2   cups reduced-sodium chicken broth
2   tablespoons canola oil, divided
1   tablespoon cornstarch mixed with 1 ½ tablespoons water

1. Press tofu (*see Note*). Cut into ½-inch cubes. Set aside.
2. Combine shrimp, 1 tablespoon rice wine (or sake), 2 teaspoons soy sauce and sesame oil in a medium bowl. Combine 3 tablespoons scallions, garlic, ginger and chile-garlic sauce in a small bowl. Combine broth, the remaining 1 tablespoon rice wine (or sake) and the remaining 4 teaspoons soy sauce in another medium bowl.
3. Heat a 14-inch flat-bottom wok over high heat until a bead of water vaporizes within 1 to 2 seconds of contact. Swirl in 1 tablespoon canola oil. Add the shrimp mixture and stir-fry until opaque, 30 to 40 seconds. Remove the shrimp with a slotted spoon and set aside, covered.
4. Add the remaining 1 tablespoon canola oil and the scallion mixture and stir-fry until fragrant, 10 to 15 seconds. Add the broth mixture and bring to a boil.
5. Add the tofu, reduce heat to maintain a simmer and cook until the sauce is reduced by about one-fourth, about 20 minutes.
6. Add the cornstarch-water mixture and cook, stirring, until the sauce boils and thickens, 30 seconds to 1 minute. Add the shrimp, toss to coat, and heat through. Serve garnished with the remaining 2 tablespoons scallions.

NOTE: To press tofu, cut it to the thickness specified in the recipe. Fold a clean kitchen towel and place it on a cutting board or large plate. Set tofu on the towel. Put another folded clean towel over the tofu and place a flat, heavy weight (such as a skillet) on top; drain for 30 minutes.

ACTIVE TIME: 50 minutes
TOTAL: 50 minutes

MAKES: 4 servings

H✖W   H♥H
PER SERVING: 220 calories; 12 g fat (2 g sat, 6 g mono); 71 mg cholesterol; 9 g carbohydrate; 0 g added sugars; 19 g protein; 1 g fiber; 912 mg sodium; 393 mg potassium.
NUTRITION BONUS: Calcium (25% daily value).

SERVE WITH:

Brown or jasmine rice and steamed snow peas seasoned with rice vinegar and a sprinkle of sea salt

Pad Thai

ACTIVE TIME: 25 minutes
TOTAL: 45 minutes

MAKES: 3 servings, about
1 1/3 cups each

H ♥ H

PER SERVING: 354 calories; 9 g fat
(2 g sat, 4 g mono); 157 mg
cholesterol; 50 g carbohydrate;
8 g added sugars; 19 g protein;
3 g fiber; 1,392 mg sodium;
321 mg potassium.
NUTRITION BONUS: Vitamin C (22%
daily value), Folate (21% dv).

SERVE WITH:

Steamed broccoli tossed with
shallots, ginger, rice vinegar,
salt and pepper

The classic dish Pad Thai has such complex flavor that it's easy to forget it's really just a simple noodle stir-fry that gets its characteristic flavors from a combo of chile-garlic and fish sauces. You can have this version on the table in well under an hour (with a side), which makes it an excellent weeknight alternative to takeout.

4	ounces wide rice noodles, preferably brown-rice noodles (*see Notes*)
2	teaspoons peanut oil
3	cloves garlic, minced
1	large egg, lightly beaten
8	ounces small shrimp, peeled and deveined (70-90 per pound; *see Note, page 213*)
2	cups mung bean sprouts
1/2	cup sliced scallion greens
3	tablespoons rice vinegar
2	tablespoons fish sauce (*see Note, page 212*)
2	tablespoons sugar
1	teaspoon chile-garlic sauce (*see Notes*)
2	tablespoons chopped dry-roasted peanuts

1. Place rice noodles in a large bowl and cover with warm water; soak until limp, about 20 minutes.
2. Heat oil over high heat in a wok until very hot. Add garlic and stir-fry until golden, about 10 seconds. Add egg and cook, stirring, until scrambled, about 30 seconds. Add shrimp and stir-fry until they curl and turn pink, about 2 minutes.
3. Drain the noodles and add to the wok, tossing with tongs until they soften and curl, about 1 minute. Add bean sprouts, scallion greens, vinegar, fish sauce, sugar and chile-garlic sauce; toss until the shrimp are fully cooked and the noodles are heated through, 1 to 2 minutes. Sprinkle with peanuts and serve immediately.

NOTES:
Look for dried **wide rice noodles**, sometimes called "Pad Thai noodles" or "straight-cut," in the Asian-food section at most supermarkets and natural-foods stores. Annie Chun's brand now makes brown rice noodles that are becoming more widely available. We like to use them in place of regular rice noodles because they have 4 grams of fiber per serving versus 0 grams in noodles made with white rice.

Chile-garlic sauce is a blend of ground chiles, garlic and vinegar. It can be found in the Asian section of large supermarkets. Refrigerate for up to 1 year.

Saucy Coconut-Chicken Stir-Fry

ACTIVE TIME: 35 minutes
TOTAL: 35 minutes

MAKES: 4 servings, about
1½ cups each

H❌W   H❤H

PER SERVING: 254 calories; 11 g fat
(3 g sat, 4 g mono); 63 mg
cholesterol; 12 g carbohydrate;
2 g added sugars; 28 g protein;
3 g fiber; 678 mg sodium;
627 mg potassium.
NUTRITION BONUS: Vitamin C (42%
daily value), Vitamin A (35% dv),
Folate (22% dv), Potassium
(18% dv).

SERVE WITH:

Steamed jasmine rice mixed
with chopped peanuts

This Thai-themed, coconut- and basil-scented stir-fry calls for napa cabbage, but you could use bok choy instead. If you prefer milder foods, skip the jalapeño, or if you like, use Thai bird chiles to really turn up the heat.

4	**teaspoons canola oil, divided**
1	**pound chicken tenders, cut into bite-size pieces**
1	**jalapeño pepper, minced (optional)**
1	**bunch scallions, sliced, whites and greens separated**
2	**cups sliced shiitake mushroom caps**
1	**tablespoon minced fresh ginger**
3/4	**cup "lite" coconut milk**
2	**tablespoons fish sauce (*see Note*)**
4	**teaspoons lime juice**
1	**tablespoon brown sugar**
6	**cups sliced napa cabbage**
3/4	**cup chopped fresh basil**

1. Heat 2 teaspoons oil in a wok over medium-high heat. Add chicken and cook, stirring often, until cooked through and lightly browned, about 5 minutes. Transfer the chicken to a plate.
2. Heat the remaining 2 teaspoons oil in the wok. Add jalapeño (if using), scallion whites, mushrooms and ginger and cook, stirring, until fragrant and the mushrooms start to soften, 30 seconds to 1 minute. Stir in coconut milk, fish sauce, lime juice and brown sugar; bring to a simmer. Cook, stirring occasionally, until the mushrooms are tender, 2 to 3 minutes. Stir in cabbage, the chicken and scallion greens; cook, stirring constantly, until the cabbage is slightly wilted, 2 to 3 minutes. Stir in basil just before serving.

NOTE: **Fish sauce** is a pungent Southeast Asian condiment made from salted, fermented fish. Find it in the Asian-food section of large supermarkets and in Asian specialty markets. We use Thai Kitchen fish sauce (1,190 mg sodium per tablespoon) in our recipe testing and analyses.

Chicken with Peppers

ACTIVE TIME: 45 minutes
TOTAL: 45 minutes

MAKES: 4 servings, about
1½ cups each

H✖W   H♥H

PER SERVING: 323 calories; 11 g fat
(2 g sat, 6 g mono); 63 mg
cholesterol; 25 g carbohydrate;
8 g added sugars; 26 g protein;
3 g fiber; 791 mg sodium;
469 mg potassium.
NUTRITION BONUS: Vitamin C (135%
daily value), Vitamin A (41% dv),
Potassium (18% dv).

SERVE WITH:

Fresh Chinese-style noodles or
whole-wheat spaghetti

A quick marinade in soy sauce, sake and sesame oil turns chicken breast into the flavor-packed star of this easy stir-fry. The hoisin-based sauce adds complex flavor and a deep mahogany color that's well suited to this dish but would also be at home coating steamed vegetables.

4   **tablespoons reduced-sodium soy sauce, divided**
4   **tablespoons Shao Hsing rice wine (*see Note, page 213*) or sake, divided**
1   **teaspoon toasted sesame oil**
1   **pound boneless, skinless chicken breasts, cut into ¾-inch pieces**
⅓   **cup water**
3   **tablespoons hoisin sauce (*see Note*)**
1½   **tablespoons sugar**
1   **tablespoon cornstarch**
2   **tablespoons canola oil, divided**
5   **cloves garlic, minced**
1   **tablespoon minced fresh ginger**
2   **medium red bell peppers, cut into thin strips**
1   **8-ounce can sliced water chestnuts, rinsed**
4   **scallions, green part only, sliced into ½-inch lengths**

1. Combine 2 tablespoons soy sauce, 1½ tablespoons rice wine (or sake) and sesame oil in a medium bowl. Add chicken and toss lightly to coat. Cover and refrigerate for 30 minutes.
2. Combine the remaining 2 tablespoons soy sauce and 1½ tablespoons rice wine (or sake) with water, hoisin sauce, sugar and cornstarch in a small bowl.
3. Heat a wok over high heat until a bead of water vaporizes within 1 to 2 seconds of contact. Swirl in 1 tablespoon canola oil. Add the chicken and its marinade; stir-fry until just cooked through, 3 to 5 minutes. Remove with a slotted spoon and set aside.
4. Add the remaining 1 tablespoon canola oil to the pan and heat until very hot. Add garlic and ginger and stir-fry until fragrant, 10 to 15 seconds. Add bell peppers and the remaining 1 tablespoon rice wine (or sake) and stir-fry until the peppers are slightly tender, about 2 minutes. Add water chestnuts and stir-fry until heated through, about 1 minute. Pour in the reserved sauce mixture and cook, stirring constantly, until thickened, about 1 minute. Return the chicken to the pan and toss lightly until heated through. Add scallions and toss.

NOTE: **Hoisin sauce** is a dark brown, thick, spicy-sweet sauce made from soybeans and a complex mix of spices. Look for it in the Asian section of your supermarket and in Asian markets.

Pork Stir-Fry with Vietnamese Flavors

Fresh ginger, chiles, garlic, cilantro and pungent fish sauce are hallmark flavors of Vietnamese cooking. Here they are combined with slices of quick-cooking, lean pork tenderloin to create an exotic stir-fry that can be ready to serve in about a half hour.

ACTIVE TIME: 25 minutes
TOTAL: 35 minutes

MAKES: 4 servings

H✂W   H♥H
PER SERVING: 225 calories; 6 g fat
(1 g sat, 3 g mono); 74 mg
cholesterol; 16 g carbohydrate;
3 g added sugars; 26 g protein;
2 g fiber; 660 mg sodium; 536
mg potassium.
NUTRITION BONUS: Vitamin C (32%
daily value), Potassium (18% dv),
Zinc (16% dv).

2	tablespoons finely chopped fresh ginger
2	serrano *or* jalapeño peppers, seeded and finely chopped
4	cloves garlic, finely chopped
2	tablespoons fish sauce (*see Note, page 212*), divided
2	tablespoons orange juice, divided
1	teaspoon cornstarch
½	teaspoon freshly ground pepper
1	pound pork tenderloin, cut into ¼-inch-thick slices
1	tablespoon sugar
3	teaspoons canola oil, divided
2	cups finely sliced onions
¼	cup sliced fresh cilantro leaves

1. Combine ginger, peppers, garlic, 1 tablespoon fish sauce, 1 tablespoon orange juice, cornstarch and pepper in a shallow dish. Add pork and toss to coat. Set aside to marinate for 10 to 20 minutes.
2. Mix sugar, the remaining 1 tablespoon fish sauce and 1 tablespoon orange juice in a small bowl.
3. Heat a wok over high heat. Swirl in 1 teaspoon oil. Add onions and cook, stirring, until limp and caramelized, about 5 minutes. Transfer the onions to a plate. Wipe out the wok.
4. Add the remaining 2 teaspoons oil to the wok and increase heat to high. Slowly drop in the pork and cook, stirring, until browned and just cooked through, 2 to 3 minutes. Add the reserved fish sauce mixture and the onions; toss until the pork is coated with sauce. Sprinkle with cilantro.

SERVE WITH:

Vermicelli rice noodles tossed
with sliced cucumber, scallions
and shredded carrots

Mu Shu Pork

ACTIVE TIME: 1 hour

TOTAL: 1 hour

MAKES: 4 servings, about
1½ cups each

H✄W   H♥H

PER SERVING: 298 calories; 13 g fat
(2 g sat, 7 g mono); 148 mg
cholesterol; 20 g carbohydrate;
1 g added sugars; 24 g protein;
4 g fiber; 527 mg sodium;
783 mg potassium.

NUTRITION BONUS: Vitamin C (55%
daily value), Potassium (22% dv),
Zinc (20% dv), Folate (19% dv),
Magnesium (15% dv).

SERVE WITH:

Brown rice studded with baby
green peas and some flecks of
chopped ham or Canadian bacon

Who would have thought that this Chinese restaurant favorite could be prepared so easily at home? This version is heady with the aromas of ginger, garlic and smoky black mushrooms. You can eat it like a stir-fry or enjoy it the classic way: spoon it into warmed whole-wheat flour tortillas or store-bought crepes spread with a little hoisin sauce, roll up and eat.

MARINADE & PORK

2	tablespoons reduced-sodium soy sauce
1½	tablespoons Shao Hsing rice wine (*see Note, page 213*) *or* sake
1	teaspoon sesame oil
12	ounces pork tenderloin, trimmed, cut into 1½-inch matchstick shreds

SAUCE

3	tablespoons reduced-sodium chicken broth
2	tablespoons Shao Hsing rice wine *or* sake
1	tablespoon reduced-sodium soy sauce
1	tablespoon cornstarch
½	teaspoon sugar
¼	teaspoon freshly ground pepper

MU SHU FILLING

10	dried Chinese black mushrooms *or* shiitake mushrooms
2	tablespoons canola oil, divided
2	large eggs, lightly beaten
6	cloves garlic, minced
1½	tablespoons minced fresh ginger
4	cups shredded green cabbage (about ⅓ small cabbage)
8	scallions, green part only, cut into 1-inch lengths

1. **To marinate pork:** Combine 2 tablespoons soy sauce, 1½ tablespoons rice wine (or sake) and sesame oil in a medium bowl. Add pork and toss lightly to coat. Cover and refrigerate for 30 minutes.
2. **To prepare sauce:** Combine broth, 2 tablespoons rice wine (or sake), 1 tablespoon soy sauce, cornstarch, sugar and pepper in a small bowl.
3. **To prepare mu shu filling:** Place dried mushrooms in a bowl, cover with hot water and let soak for 20 minutes. Drain, discard the stems and thinly slice the caps.
4. Heat a 14-inch flat-bottomed wok over high heat until a bead of water vaporizes within 1 to 2 seconds of contact. Swirl in 1 tablespoon canola oil. Add the pork and stir-fry until cooked through, about 2 minutes. Remove with a slotted spoon; set aside. Cook down any remaining juices to a glaze, about 2 minutes, and add to the pork.
5. Add another ½ tablespoon canola oil to the wok and heat until very hot. Add eggs and stir-fry, scrambling them until just dry. Remove and set aside. Add the remaining ½ tablespoon oil and heat until very hot. Add garlic and ginger and stir-fry until fragrant, 10 to 15 seconds. Add cabbage and the mushroom caps and stir-fry until tender, about 2 minutes. Pour in the reserved sauce and stir constantly until thickened, 30 seconds to 1 minute. Return the pork and eggs to the pan and toss until heated through. Stir in scallions.

Beef & Red Pepper Stir-Fry

The secret to great flavor in a stir-fry is all in the sauce. Here, Shao Hsing rice wine and pungent, sea-scented oyster sauce give this simple beef-and-vegetable dish its amazing (and effortless) flavor. (Photograph: page 24.)

- ⅓ cup oyster sauce (*see Note*)
- ¼ cup water
- 2 tablespoons Shao Hsing rice wine *or* dry sherry (*see Note, page 213*)
- 1 tablespoon reduced-sodium soy sauce
- ⅓ cup plus 2 tablespoons finely chopped scallions, divided
- 2 large cloves garlic, minced
- 2 tablespoons minced fresh ginger
- ¼ teaspoon crushed red pepper
- 3 teaspoons peanut oil *or* canola oil, divided
- 12 ounces sirloin tip, cut into ⅛-by-3-inch strips
- 2 medium red bell peppers, cut into 1-inch pieces
- 12 ounces bok choy, stems and leaves separated, cut into 1-inch pieces (4 cups)
- 1 8-ounce can baby corn, rinsed

1. Combine oyster sauce, water, rice wine (or sherry) and soy sauce in a small bowl; set aside.
2. Combine ⅓ cup scallions, garlic, ginger and crushed red pepper in another small bowl.
3. Heat a 14-inch flat-bottomed wok over high heat until a bead of water vaporizes within 1 to 2 seconds of contact. Swirl in 1 teaspoon oil. Add 1 tablespoon of the scallion mixture and sirloin; stir-fry until only a trace of pink remains in the meat, 1 to 2 minutes. Transfer to a bowl and set aside.
4. Heat the remaining 2 teaspoons oil in the wok and add the remaining scallion mixture. Stir-fry until fragrant, about 30 seconds. Add bell peppers and bok choy stems and stir-fry for 2 minutes. Add bok choy greens and stir-fry until the vegetables begin to wilt, about 1 minute more.
5. Add corn and the reserved oyster sauce mixture; stir until the sauce simmers, about 2 minutes. Add the reserved sirloin and toss until heated through, about 30 seconds. Serve immediately, sprinkled with the remaining 2 tablespoons scallions.

NOTE: **Oyster sauce** is a richly flavored Chinese condiment made from oysters and brine. Vegetarian oyster sauces substitute mushrooms for the oysters. Both can be found in large supermarkets or at Asian specialty markets.

ACTIVE TIME: 35 minutes
TOTAL: 35 minutes

MAKES: about 8 cups, for 4 servings

H✖W   H♥H

PER SERVING: 226 calories; 8 g fat (2 g sat, 3 g mono); 45 mg cholesterol; 18 g carbohydrate; 0 g added sugars; 21 g protein; 3 g fiber; 852 mg sodium; 800 mg potassium.
NUTRITION BONUS: Vitamin C (170% daily value), Vitamin A (113% dv), Zinc (25% dv), Potassium (23% dv), Folate (22% dv), Iron (15% dv).

SERVE WITH:

Cooked whole-grain spaghetti quickly stir-fried until lightly browned in 1 to 2 teaspoons toasted sesame oil. (You can wipe out your wok after you make the beef stir-fry, then quickly cook the noodles.)

Sweet & Sour Pork

ACTIVE TIME: 45 minutes
TOTAL: 45 minutes

MAKES: 4 servings, about
1¼ cups each

H✖W

PER SERVING: 312 calories; 17 g fat
(5 g sat, 8 g mono); 65 mg
cholesterol; 21 g carbohydrate;
3 g added sugars; 19 g protein;
2 g fiber; 419 mg sodium;
465 mg potassium.
NUTRITION BONUS: Vitamin C (77%
daily value), Vitamin A (60% dv),
Zinc (24% dv).

SERVE WITH:

Brown rice noodles tossed with
chopped watercress and scallion

This is a bright, light take on sweet & sour pork that's studded with plenty of pineapple, carrots and wedges of tomato. If the acid from this dish removes some of the patina of your wok, reseason it after you wash it. (See page 208 for how to season a wok.)

1	tablespoon minced fresh ginger
4	teaspoons reduced-sodium soy sauce, divided
2	teaspoons plus 1 tablespoon Shao Hsing rice wine (*see Note, page 213*) *or* dry sherry, divided
1½	teaspoons plus 2 teaspoons cornstarch, divided
¼	teaspoon salt
⅛	teaspoon ground white pepper
1	pound trimmed boneless pork shoulder *or* butt (*see Note*), cut into ¼-inch-thick bite-size slices
1	teaspoon sesame oil
2	tablespoons pineapple juice *or* juice from can of pineapple
2	tablespoons distilled white vinegar
1	tablespoon ketchup
1½	teaspoons light brown sugar
2	tablespoons peanut oil *or* canola oil, divided
½	cup sliced carrot (¼ inch thick)
1	small tomato, thinly sliced into wedges
¼	cup finely chopped scallions
2	cups chopped fresh pineapple (bite-size pieces) *or* drained canned pineapple chunks

1. Combine ginger, 2 teaspoons soy sauce, 2 teaspoons rice wine (or sherry), 1½ teaspoons cornstarch, salt and pepper in a medium bowl. Stir in pork and sesame oil until well combined.
2. Combine pineapple juice, vinegar, ketchup and brown sugar in a small bowl. Stir in the remaining 2 teaspoons soy sauce, 1 tablespoon rice wine (or sherry) and 2 teaspoons cornstarch.
3. Heat a 14-inch flat-bottomed wok over high heat until a bead of water vaporizes within 1 to 2 seconds of contact. Swirl 1 tablespoon peanut (or canola) oil into the wok. Carefully add the pork and spread in one layer. Cook undisturbed, letting the pork begin to sear, for 1½ minutes. Then, using a metal spatula, stir-fry until the pork is lightly browned but not cooked through, 1 minute. Transfer the pork to a plate.
4. Swirl the remaining 1 tablespoon oil into the wok, add carrot and stir-fry for 30 seconds. Return the pork with any juices to the wok. Add tomato and scallions and stir-fry for 30 seconds. Swirl in the pineapple juice mixture, add pineapple and stir-fry until the pork is just cooked through and the sauce is lightly thickened, 1 to 2 minutes more.

NOTE: Pork shoulder or butt is available both bone-in or boneless and typically sold in portions significantly larger than 1 pound—3 to 5 pounds. To get the amount you need for this recipe, ask the butcher to start with 1½ to 1¾ pounds before trimming to make sure you get 1 pound of trimmed boneless pork shoulder or butt. Or buy a larger portion and freeze the rest for another use.

Beef Chow Fun

The recipe for beef chow fun works equally well with tofu for a vegetarian meal or with boneless, skinless chicken breast. To keep it quick, we call for a bag of prepared stir-fry veggies, which you can find in the produce department of many supermarkets. If you prefer, chop up your own blend of whatever is best at the moment—anything from peppers and onions to carrots, broccoli and bok choy will work.

8 ounces wide rice noodles, preferably brown-rice noodles (*see Notes*)
½ cup Shao Hsing rice wine *or* dry sherry (*see Note, page 213*)
4 teaspoons black bean-garlic sauce (*see Notes*)
1 tablespoon reduced-sodium soy sauce
2 teaspoons light brown sugar
2 teaspoons cornstarch
4 teaspoons canola *or* peanut oil, divided
1 teaspoon minced ginger
1 small onion, thinly sliced
1 12-ounce bag fresh Asian stir-fry vegetables (about 5½ cups)
½ cup water, divided
8 ounces sirloin steak, cut into thin slices

1. Fill a large wok with water and bring to a boil. Add noodles and cook, stirring frequently, until just tender, 4 to 6 minutes or according to package directions. Drain, rinse with cold water and transfer to a large bowl. Wipe the pan dry.
2. Combine rice wine (or sherry), black bean-garlic sauce, soy sauce, brown sugar and cornstarch in a small bowl; set aside.
3. Heat 2 teaspoons oil in the wok over medium-high heat. Reduce heat to medium. Add ginger and cook, stirring, for 30 seconds. Add onion and cook, stirring, until softened, 1 to 3 minutes. Add vegetables and ¼ cup water; cover and cook, stirring occasionally, until the vegetables are tender-crisp, 2 to 4 minutes. Transfer the vegetables to the bowl with the noodles. Wipe the pan dry.
4. Heat the remaining 2 teaspoons oil in the wok over medium-high heat. Add steak and cook, stirring, until browned, 1 to 3 minutes. Stir the reserved sauce and add to the pan; cook, stirring, until the sauce has thickened slightly, 1 to 2 minutes.
5. Return the noodles and vegetables to the wok along with the remaining ¼ cup water; cook, tossing to coat with the sauce, until heated through, about 2 minutes more.

NOTES:

Look for dried **wide rice noodles**, sometimes called "Pad Thai noodles" or "straight-cut," in the Asian-food section at most supermarkets and natural-foods stores. Annie Chun's brand now makes brown rice noodles that are becoming more widely available. We like to use them in place of regular rice noodles because they have 4 grams of fiber per serving versus 0 grams in noodles made with white rice.

Black bean-garlic sauce, a savory, salty sauce used in Chinese cooking, is made from fermented black soybeans, garlic and rice wine. Find it in the Asian-foods section of most supermarkets or at Asian markets. Refrigerate for up to 1 year.

ACTIVE TIME: 30 minutes
TOTAL: 30 minutes

MAKES: 4 servings, about 1½ cups each

PER SERVING: 381 calories; 8 g fat (1 g sat, 4 g mono); 30 mg cholesterol; 57 g carbohydrate; 1 g added sugars; 15 g protein; 3 g fiber; 723 mg sodium; 223 mg potassium.
NUTRITION BONUS: Vitamin C (37% daily value), Vitamin A (30% dv).

SERVE WITH:

Sliced cucumbers tossed with rice vinegar and a pinch of salt

Easy Paella with Shrimp & Mussels

SKILLET

Stock your kitchen with three types of large (12-inch) skillets—stainless steel, nonstick and cast-iron. Nonstick lets you use less oil and still cook delicate food like eggs without sticking. Cast-iron skillets are a great alternative because you can cook with them over high heat and put them in the oven safely. *(See pages 208-209 for tips on using nonstick and cast-iron skillets.)* And a stainless skillet made out of heavy material, which conducts heat evenly and will last for years, is a worthwhile investment. It's your go-to pan for everything from quick sautéed vegetables to seared pork chops.

Barley Hoppin' John

ACTIVE TIME: 20 minutes
TOTAL: 40 minutes

MAKES: 4 servings, 1½ cups each

H✂W   H⬆F   H❤H
PER SERVING: 320 calories; 5 g fat
(1 g sat, 3 g mono); 0 mg
cholesterol; 57 g carbohydrate;
0 g added sugars; 12 g protein;
11 g fiber; 677 mg sodium;
529 mg potassium.
NUTRITION BONUS: Vitamin C (58%
daily value), Folate & Vitamin A
(24% dv), Potassium (15% dv).

SERVE WITH:

Green salad and some crusty
bread on the side, or if you want
to extend the Dixie theme,
some sautéed collards greens
or kale.

Our fast version of this Southern favorite gets an outstanding toothsome texture from quick-cooking barley rather than the traditional rice. The beans make the dish perfect for a meatless night, but if you prefer, add some ham or Canadian bacon when you cook the peppers, onions and celery.

1	tablespoon extra-virgin olive oil
1	medium onion, chopped
1	small red bell pepper, chopped
2	stalks celery, chopped
2	cloves garlic, minced
1	14-ounce can vegetable broth
1	cup quick-cooking barley
1	tablespoon chopped fresh thyme *or* 1 teaspoon dried
2	teaspoons lemon juice
¼	teaspoon crushed red pepper
¼	teaspoon salt
2	15-ounce cans black-eyed peas, rinsed

Heat oil in a large nonstick skillet over medium heat. Add onion, bell pepper and celery. Cook until the vegetables soften, 3 to 4 minutes. Add garlic and cook 1 minute. Add broth, barley, thyme, lemon juice, crushed red pepper and salt; bring to a boil. Reduce heat, cover and simmer until the barley is done, 15 to 20 minutes. Remove from the heat and stir in black-eyed peas. Cover and let stand for 5 minutes. Serve hot.

Black Bean Quesadillas

A hot skillet is all it takes to get dinner on the table in about a quarter of an hour. We've used black beans to make these satisfying quesadillas, but pinto beans work well too. For some nice spice, be sure to use pepper Jack cheese in the filling and add a dollop of plain yogurt or sour cream for cooling balance.

- **1   15-ounce can black beans, rinsed**
- **½   cup shredded Monterey Jack cheese, preferably pepper Jack**
- **½   cup prepared fresh salsa (*see Note*), divided**
- **4   8-inch whole-wheat tortillas**
- **2   teaspoons canola oil, divided**
- **1   ripe avocado, diced**

1. Combine beans, cheese and ¼ cup salsa in a medium bowl. Place tortillas on a work surface. Spread ½ cup filling on half of each tortilla. Fold tortillas in half, pressing gently to flatten.
2. Heat 1 teaspoon oil in a large nonstick skillet over medium heat. Add 2 quesadillas and cook, turning once, until golden on both sides, 2 to 4 minutes total. Transfer to a cutting board and tent with foil to keep warm. Repeat with the remaining 1 teaspoon oil and quesadillas. Serve the quesadillas with avocado and the remaining salsa.

NOTE: Look for **prepared fresh salsa** in the supermarket refrigerator section near other dips and spreads.

ACTIVE TIME: 15 minutes
TOTAL: 15 minutes

MAKES: 4 servings

H↑F
PER SERVING: 375 calories; 16 g fat (4 g sat, 8 g mono); 13 mg cholesterol; 45 g carbohydrate; 0 g added sugars; 13 g protein; 10 g fiber; 599 mg sodium; 486 mg potassium.
NUTRITION BONUS: Calcium (24% daily value), Folate (22% dv), Iron (18% dv).

SERVE WITH:

Frozen white and gold corn kernels sautéed with a can of diced green chiles plus a splash of fresh lime juice at the end

Braised Squash with Peppers & Hominy

ACTIVE TIME: 15 minutes

TOTAL: 1 hour

MAKES: 6 servings, 1 1/3 cups each

H✕W   H↑F   H♥H

PER SERVING: 153 calories; 3 g fat
(0 g sat, 2 g mono); 0 mg
cholesterol; 31 g carbohydrate;
0 g added sugars; 3 g protein;
8 g fiber; 546 mg sodium;
653 mg potassium.

NUTRITION BONUS: Vitamin A (385%
daily value), Vitamin C (97% dv),
Potassium (19% dv), Magnesium
(17% dv).

SERVE WITH:

Baby spinach salad and refried
black beans

Think of canned hominy as mega corn kernels with a little more starchiness and attitude. Here the underused ingredient adds a distinctive, earthy flavor to this spice-warmed winter squash stew that takes only 15 minutes to get simmering.

1	tablespoon canola oil
2	medium onions, chopped
1	butternut squash (2 1/2 pounds), peeled, seeded and cut into 1 1/4-inch chunks
1	medium red bell pepper, cut into large dice
2	teaspoons sweet paprika
1/2	teaspoon ground cumin
1/4	teaspoon caraway seeds
1 1/2	teaspoons all-purpose flour
1	teaspoon salt
1/4	teaspoon freshly ground pepper, plus more to taste
	Pinch of cayenne pepper
1	15-ounce can hominy (*see Note*), rinsed
2 1/2-3	cups water
4	tablespoons chopped fresh parsley *or* cilantro, divided
2	tablespoons tomato paste
6	lime wedges

1. Heat oil in a large straight-sided skillet or Dutch oven over high heat. Add onions, squash, bell pepper, paprika, cumin and caraway seeds. Cook, stirring, until the onions and squash are browned in places, about 10 minutes. Add flour, salt, pepper and cayenne; cook, stirring, for 1 minute more.
2. Stir in hominy, 2 1/2 cups water, 3 tablespoons parsley (or cilantro) and tomato paste. Bring to a boil. Reduce heat to low, cover and simmer until the squash is tender, 25 to 30 minutes. (Add the remaining 1/2 cup water if the vegetables look dry.) Garnish with the remaining 1 tablespoon parsley (or cilantro). Serve with lime wedges.

NOTE: **Hominy** is white or yellow corn treated with lime to remove the tough hull and germ. Canned cooked hominy can be found in the Latin section of large supermarkets—near the beans—or at Latin markets.

Zucchini-Ricotta Frittata with Tomato Garnish

Making a warm, eggy frittata is one of the best uses there is for a nonstick skillet. For this light version, we traded the fat in a few egg yolks (that we omitted) for the rich-tasting and satisfying addition of part-skim ricotta and freshly grated Parmesan cheese.

FRITTATA

1½	pounds zucchini (about 3 medium), coarsely grated
1⅛	teaspoons salt, divided
2	tablespoons extra-virgin olive oil, divided
4	large eggs
4	large egg whites
¼	teaspoon freshly ground pepper
½	cup grated Parmesan *or* aged Monterey Jack cheese
1	tablespoon chopped fresh marjoram
⅔	cup part-skim ricotta cheese

TOMATO GARNISH

2½	cups chopped tomatoes (2-3 medium)
1	small shallot, minced
1	small clove garlic, minced
2	teaspoons chopped fresh marjoram
2	teaspoons extra-virgin olive oil
1	teaspoon balsamic vinegar
⅛	teaspoon freshly ground pepper
	Pinch of salt

ACTIVE TIME: 1 hour
TOTAL: 1 hour

MAKES: 6 servings

H)(W
PER SERVING: 220 calories; 14 g fat (5 g sat, 7 g mono); 138 mg cholesterol; 10 g carbohydrate; 0 g added sugars; 14 g protein; 2 fiber; 718 mg sodium; 620 mg potassium.
NUTRITION BONUS: Vitamin C (52% daily value), Vitamin A (25% dv), Calcium (20% dv), Potassium (18% dv), Folate (15% dv).

SERVE WITH:

Spicy arugula or mesclun salad and toasted whole-grain bread brushed with garlic-infused olive oil

1. **To prepare frittata:** Toss zucchini with 1 teaspoon salt in a medium bowl. Transfer to a colander set over a large bowl; let drain for 20 to 30 minutes. Rinse briefly under cool water and squeeze to dry.
2. Preheat oven to 400°F.
3. Heat 1 tablespoon oil in a large nonstick ovenproof skillet (*see Note, page 209*) over medium-high heat. Add the zucchini and cook, stirring frequently, until the moisture in the pan has evaporated, 5 to 6 minutes. Transfer to a bowl. Wipe out the pan.
4. Whisk eggs and egg whites with pepper and the remaining ⅛ teaspoon salt in a large bowl until combined. Stir in the zucchini, Parmesan (or Monterey Jack) and marjoram. Heat the remaining 1 tablespoon oil in the pan over medium-high heat. Add the egg mixture and reduce heat to medium-low. Distribute dollops of ricotta on top of the eggs and cook until the eggs are mostly set, tilting the pan and lifting the edges of the frittata to allow the uncooked egg to flow underneath, 5 to 7 minutes. (The top of the frittata will still be a little wet.) Transfer the pan to the oven and bake until cooked through and lightly brown on top, 6 to 8 minutes.
5. **To prepare tomato garnish:** Toss tomatoes with shallot, garlic, marjoram, oil, vinegar, pepper and salt in a medium bowl.
6. To serve, slide the frittata onto a serving plate and cut into 6 slices. Serve warm or cold, topped with the tomato garnish.

Crispy Potatoes with Green Beans & Eggs

ACTIVE TIME: 35 minutes
TOTAL: 40 minutes

MAKES: 4 servings

H✛W   H↑F   H♥H

PER SERVING: 318 calories; 12 g fat
(3 g sat, 7 g mono); 186 mg
cholesterol; 42 g carbohydrate;
0 g added sugars; 12 g protein;
5 g fiber; 381 mg sodium;
1,100 mg potassium.
NUTRITION BONUS: Vitamin C (35%
daily value), Potassium (31% dv),
Iron (17% dv), Magnesium
(16% dv).

SERVE WITH:

Boston lettuce and tomato
salad with buttermilk dressing

This one-skillet meal is easiest to make with precooked or leftover potatoes and beans, but can be made from raw in only a few minutes more. Best of all, the eggs cook nestled in among all the vegetables so the flavors commingle in a divine way.

1	cup cooked *or* fresh green beans, cut into 1-inch pieces
2	tablespoons extra-virgin olive oil
2	pounds boiling potatoes, peeled and cut into ½-inch dice, *or* 5 cups diced cooked potatoes
2	cloves garlic, minced
⅛	teaspoon crushed red pepper
½	teaspoon salt
	Freshly ground pepper to taste
4	large eggs
	Pinch of paprika (optional)

1. If using fresh green beans, place in a medium microwave-safe bowl with ¼ cup water. Cover and microwave on High until crisp-tender, about 4 minutes. Drain and refresh under cold running water.
2. Heat oil in a large nonstick or cast-iron skillet over medium heat until hot enough to sizzle a piece of potato. Spread potatoes in an even layer and cook, turning every few minutes with a wide spatula, until tender and browned, 15 to 20 minutes for raw potatoes, 10 to 12 minutes for cooked. Stir in the green beans, garlic, crushed red pepper, salt and pepper.
3. Crack each egg into a small bowl and slip them one at a time into the pan on top of the vegetables, spacing evenly. Cover and cook over medium heat until the whites are set and the yolks are cooked to your taste, 3 to 5 minutes. Sprinkle the eggs with paprika, if desired, and serve immediately.

Easy Paella with Shrimp & Mussels

Traditional paella is made in a special wide pan with short-grain rice, but our quick version uses instant brown rice as a shortcut and cooks in your standard 12-inch skillet. Studded with mussels and shrimp and scented with golden saffron, this dish makes up with flavor and convenience what it lacks in authenticity. (Photograph: page 44.)

ACTIVE TIME: 40 minutes
TOTAL: 40 minutes

MAKES: 4 servings

PER SERVING: 365 calories; 7 g fat (1 g sat, 3 g mono); 155 mg cholesterol; 45 g carbohydrate; 0 g added sugars; 28 g protein; 5 g fiber; 941 mg sodium; 408 mg potassium.
NUTRITION BONUS: Vitamin C (53% daily value), Vitamin A (31% dv), Magnesium (27% dv), Zinc (20% dv), Folate (18% dv), Iron (16% dv).

- **1 tablespoon extra-virgin olive oil**
- **½ cup chopped onion**
- **½ cup chopped red bell pepper**
- **2 cloves garlic, minced**
- **2 cups instant brown rice**
- **1⅓ cups reduced-sodium chicken broth**
- **½ teaspoon dried thyme**
- **¼ teaspoon freshly ground pepper**
- **l large pinch saffron (*see Notes*)**
- **1 pound peeled and deveined raw shrimp (21-25 per pound; *see Note, page 213*)**
- **1 cup frozen green peas, thawed**
- **1 pound mussels, scrubbed well (*see Notes*)**
- **4 lemon wedges (optional)**

1. Heat oil in a large skillet over medium heat. Add onion, bell pepper and garlic and cook, stirring occasionally, until the vegetables are softened, about 3 minutes. Add rice, broth, thyme, pepper and saffron and bring to a boil over medium heat. Cover and cook for 5 minutes.
2. Stir in shrimp and peas. Place mussels on top of the rice in an even layer. Cover and continue cooking until the mussels have opened and the rice is tender, about 5 minutes more. Remove from the heat and let rest, covered, until most of the liquid is absorbed, about 5 minutes. Serve with lemon wedges, if desired.

NOTES:

The dried stigma from *Crocus sativus*, **saffron** adds flavor and golden color to a variety of Middle Eastern, African and European foods. Find it in the spice section of supermarkets, gourmet shops or at tienda.com. It will keep in an airtight container for several years.

To clean mussels, rinse very well under cold running water and use a stiff brush to remove any barnacles or grit from the shell. Discard any mussels with broken shells or any whose shells remain open after you tap them lightly. Pull off any fibrous "beard" that might be pinched between the shells; the "beards" of most cultivated mussels are already removed.

Pan-Fried Trout with Red Chile Sauce

ACTIVE TIME: 30 minutes
TOTAL: 30 minutes

MAKES: 4 servings

H♥H

PER SERVING: 383 calories; 20 g fat (4 g sat, 7 g mono); 90 mg cholesterol; 19 g carbohydrate; 0 g added sugars; 32 g protein; 3 g fiber; 508 mg sodium; 787 mg potassium.
NUTRITION BONUS: Vitamin A (29% daily value), Potassium (25% dv), Magnesium (22% dv).

SERVE WITH:

A side of brown rice dotted with corn and diced tomatoes

This quick fish dish is all about the spice. A chile powder and buttermilk dip adds tang and heat while providing sticking power to create a nice cornmeal crust on the trout. More chile powder goes in after the golden fillets come out, to create a pan sauce that is assertive, but light enough to let the delicate trout shine through. It's worth seeking out real New Mexican chile powder for this recipe. It's made just from dried red New Mexican chiles (as opposed to the blends of spices called "chili powder" at most supermarkets) and it has a subtle earthy, smoky, spicy flavor that's addictively delicious.

½ cup buttermilk
2   tablespoons chile powder, preferably New Mexican, mild to medium-hot, divided
½ teaspoon salt
¾ cup cornmeal
4   trout fillets (about 5 ounces each), skin on
4   teaspoons canola oil, divided
2   teaspoons butter
1   medium shallot, minced
1   cup reduced-sodium chicken broth
1¼ teaspoons Worcestershire sauce
2   tablespoons pine nuts, toasted (*see Note*)

1. Combine buttermilk, 1½ tablespoons chile powder and salt in a shallow bowl. Place cornmeal in another shallow dish. Dip each trout fillet in the buttermilk mixture, coating both sides, then dredge both sides in the cornmeal.
2. Heat 2 teaspoons oil in large nonstick or cast-iron skillet over medium heat. Cook 2 fillets until golden brown, 3 to 4 minutes per side (it's OK if the pan is crowded). Transfer to a plate and keep warm. Repeat with the remaining oil and fillets.
3. Add butter and shallot to the pan; cook, stirring, for 1 minute. Stir in the remaining ½ tablespoon chile powder. Increase heat to medium-high. Add broth and Worcestershire; cook until the sauce is reduced by about one-third, 2 to 3 minutes. Pour the sauce over the trout and sprinkle with pine nuts.

NOTE: **To toast pine nuts**, place in a small dry skillet and cook over medium-low heat, stirring constantly, until fragrant and lightly browned, 2 to 4 minutes.

Five-Spice Tilapia

When you taste the layers of flavor in this simple tilapia sauté you'll be amazed that it comes from just four ingredients—Chinese five-spice powder, soy sauce, brown sugar and scallions. You'll need a skillet that is 12 inches or larger to accommodate the pound of tilapia fillets— if you don't have one large enough, use 2 smaller skillets instead or cook them in two separate batches, using more oil as necessary. You don't want to overcrowd the fish in the pan.

1. pound tilapia fillets (*see Note, page 213*)
1. teaspoon Chinese five-spice powder (*see Note*)
¼ cup reduced-sodium soy sauce
3. tablespoons light brown sugar
1. tablespoon canola oil
3. scallions, thinly sliced

1. Sprinkle both sides of tilapia fillets with five-spice powder. Combine soy sauce and brown sugar in a small bowl.
2. Heat oil in a large nonstick skillet over medium-high heat. Add the tilapia and cook until the outer edges are opaque, about 2 minutes. Reduce heat to medium, turn the fish over, stir the soy mixture and pour into the pan. Bring the sauce to a boil and cook until the fish is cooked through and the sauce has thickened slightly, about 2 minutes more. Add scallions and remove from the heat. Serve the fish drizzled with the pan sauce.

NOTE: **Five-spice powder** is a blend of cinnamon, cloves, fennel seed, star anise and Szechuan peppercorns. Look for it in the spice section at the market or with other Asian ingredients.

ACTIVE TIME: 15 minutes
TOTAL: 15 minutes

MAKES: 4 servings

PER SERVING: 180 calories; 6 g fat (1 g sat, 3 g mono); 57 mg cholesterol; 9 g carbohydrate; 9 g added sugars; 24 g protein; 0 g fiber; 596 mg sodium; 411 mg potassium.

SERVE WITH:

Brown rice and sautéed baby bok choy drizzled with a bit of toasted sesame oil or oyster sauce

Tuna-Pimiento Burgers

Turn a couple cans of tuna into a zesty tuna burger with this quick recipe. If you can't find good whole-wheat hamburger buns, whole-wheat English muffins are a great substitute. The burger mixture might seem a little soft going into the pan, but once the first side is cooked, you'll be able to flip them easily.

- **2** **5- to 6-ounce cans chunk light tuna (*see Note*), drained**
- **½** **cup coarse dry whole-wheat breadcrumbs (*see Note, page 212*)**
- **½** **cup low-fat mayonnaise, divided**
- **1** **4-ounce jar chopped pimientos, drained, *or* ⅓ cup chopped roasted red peppers, divided**
- **¼** **cup finely chopped celery**
- **¼** **cup finely chopped onion**
- **½** **teaspoon Old Bay seasoning, divided**
- **1** **tablespoon extra-virgin olive oil**
- **4** **whole-wheat hamburger buns *or* English muffins, toasted**
- **4** **lettuce leaves**
- **4** **slices tomato**

1. Combine tuna, breadcrumbs, ¼ cup mayonnaise, half of the pimientos (or roasted red peppers), celery, onion and ¼ teaspoon Old Bay seasoning in a medium bowl, breaking up any larger pieces of tuna until the mixture is uniform and holds together.
2. Combine the remaining ¼ cup mayonnaise, the remaining pimientos (or peppers) and ¼ teaspoon Old Bay seasoning in a bowl.
3. Heat oil in a large nonstick skillet over medium heat. Using a generous ⅓ cup each, form the tuna mixture into four 3-inch burgers. Cook until heated through and golden brown, about 2 minutes per side.
4. Spread the top half of each bun (or English muffin) with pimiento mayonnaise and place a burger, lettuce and tomato on the bottom half.

NOTE: **Chunk light tuna**, like most fish and shellfish, contains some mercury. According to the FDA and EPA, women who are or might become pregnant, nursing mothers and young children should limit their consumption to 12 ounces a week of fish with lower mercury, including canned "light" tuna. Consumption of albacore tuna (which is labeled "white") should be limited to no more than 6 ounces a week. And, if you're looking for an environmentally sustainable canned tuna option, check the label—tuna that was caught by troll r pole-and-line is considered the best choice, according to Monterey Bay Aquarium's Seafood Watch program. Or look for the blue Certified Sustainable Seafood label from the Marine Stewardship Council.

ACTIVE TIME: 30 minutes
TOTAL: 30 minutes

MAKES: 4 servings

PER SERVING: 321 calories; 12 g fat (2 g sat, 5 g mono); 20 mg cholesterol; 39 g carbohydrate; 5 g added sugars; 17 g protein; 5 g fiber; 656 mg sodium; 365 mg potassium.
NUTRITION BONUS: Vitamin C (40% daily value), Vitamin A (29% dv).

SERVE WITH:

Celery and carrot sticks with light blue cheese dressing

Baked Cod Casserole

ACTIVE TIME: 20 minutes
TOTAL: 40 minutes

MAKES: 4 servings

PER SERVING: 361 calories; 17 g fat
(6 g sat, 8 g mono); 85 mg
cholesterol; 14 g carbohydrate;
0 g added sugars; 28 g protein;
4 g fiber; 640 mg sodium;
444 mg potassium.
NUTRITION BONUS: Calcium
(35% daily value), Zinc (18% dv),
Magnesium (17% dv).

SERVE WITH:

A mild green, such as chard or
fresh spinach, sautéed in olive
oil with a touch of garlic, salt and
freshly ground black pepper

Here's a simple, homey fish casserole that starts out on the stovetop and ends up baked in the oven to create a cheese-laced breadcrumb crust. We first had this dish with local fish from Vermont's lakes, but any freshwater or saltwater, white-fleshed fish will do just fine.

- 2 tablespoons extra-virgin olive oil, divided
- 2 medium onions, very thinly sliced
- 1 cup dry white wine
- 1¼ pounds Pacific cod (*see Notes*), cut into 4 pieces
- 2 teaspoons chopped fresh thyme
- ½ teaspoon kosher salt
- ½ teaspoon freshly ground pepper
- 1½ cups finely chopped whole-wheat country bread (about 2 slices)
- ½ teaspoon paprika
- ½ teaspoon garlic powder
- 1 cup finely shredded Gruyère *or* Swiss cheese

1. Preheat oven to 400°F.
2. Heat 1 tablespoon oil in a large ovenproof skillet (*see Notes*) over medium-high heat. Add onions and cook, stirring often, until just starting to soften, 5 to 7 minutes. Add wine, increase heat to high and cook, stirring often, until the wine is slightly reduced, 2 to 4 minutes.
3. Place cod on the onions and sprinkle with thyme, salt and pepper. Cover the pan tightly with foil; transfer to the oven and bake for 12 minutes.
4. Toss bread with the remaining 1 tablespoon oil, paprika and garlic powder in a medium bowl. Spread the bread mixture over the fish and top with cheese. Bake, uncovered, until the fish is opaque in the center, about 10 minutes more.

NOTES:
U.S.-caught **Pacific cod**, a.k.a. Alaska cod, is considered a good choice for the environment because it is sustainably fished and has a larger, more stable population.

Stainless-steel skillets with metal handles or cast-iron skillets are good **ovenproof skillets**. If your skillet has a plastic or wood handle, wrap the handle in foil before transferring to the oven to prevent melting or overheating.

Cast-Iron Chef

A versatile pan to be passed down through generations

When I spotted the black cast-iron skillet at a yard sale in the late 1960s it was love at first sight. Having arrived from Europe (I grew up in Barcelona) a few months earlier, I had never been to a tag sale. My then boyfriend, now my husband, and I were on our way to visit friends in Pennsylvania Dutch Country when we came across a sale at a stone farmhouse flanked by two sugar maples in full autumn regalia. There, on a long table covered with farm tools, was the skillet. Three dollars later, it was mine.

I had always cooked with copper and light carbon-steel pans and this solid piece of cookware was a happy discovery for me. I soon found that it was the perfect tool for cooking everything from a simple side of sautéed cabbage to a whole roasted chicken. Although many people shy away from iron skillets because of their weight, they conduct heat beautifully, and go from stovetop to oven with no problem. Plus, they never buckle; you don't have to worry about the finish being scraped off; and after decades of use, they are as good as new. Their high straight sides are great for one-dish meals, which means less to wash. Plus, consider the health benefits: food cooked in a cast-iron skillet, especially acidic foods like tomato sauce, has increased iron content, in some cases up to 20 times as much.

Of course, you have to treat these skillets right. When I bought my first iron skillet, I asked the farmer's wife how she cared for it. She told me how to season it—making the pan virtually nonstick. For years I have passed her method on to students in cooking classes I teach at my home in Connecticut and across the country: Cover the bottom of the pan with a thick layer of kosher salt. Add at least half an inch of cooking oil and place over high heat. When the oil starts to smoke, pour it into a bowl together with the salt. Using a fat ball of paper towels, rub the inside of the pan until it is smooth. The skillet is now seasoned.

Today, most cast-iron skillets are preseasoned when you buy them. With any cast-iron skillet, you may occasionally get hot spots and some sticking. To eliminate that, reseason the offending area by rubbing it with coarse salt and a little oil. And, the farmer's wife never used soap. She simply scrubbed her skillet with a stiff brush and hot water and made sure to dry it completely.

Admittedly, iron skillets are not the only skillets I use. I find, for instance, that modern coated nonstick skillets are better suited for sautéing fish fillets and for egg dishes.

But if I could have only one piece of cookware it would be a cast-iron skillet. Chicken and scallops sear up golden. Over lower heat leeks gently wilt. And a whole chicken turns brown and crisp when you start it on the stovetop then finish it in the oven in a single pan. Whatever you whip up in this classic skillet will cook perfectly, and that is what counts.

The latest book by award-winning food writer Perla Meyers is How to Peel a Peach: And 1001 Other Things Every Good Cook Needs to Know *(Wiley & Sons, 2005).*

If I could have only one piece of cookware it would be a cast-iron skillet.

—Perla Meyers

Quick Coq au Vin

The classic French red wine-braised chicken-and-vegetable stew Coq au Vin need not take half a day and half your pots and pans to make. Our quick, one-skillet version calls for bone-in chicken breast (although you can use thighs if you like) and can be on the table in well under an hour, perfect for a touch of weeknight sophistication.

¼ cup all-purpose flour
2 bone-in chicken breasts (about 12 ounces each), skin removed, trimmed
½ teaspoon salt, divided
½ teaspoon freshly ground pepper, divided
¼ cup water
2 tablespoons extra-virgin olive oil, divided
4 ounces mushrooms, quartered (about 1 ½ cups)
2 large carrots, thinly sliced
1 small onion, halved and sliced
1 teaspoon crumbled dried rosemary
1 14-ounce can reduced-sodium chicken broth
½ cup dry red wine, preferably Zinfandel
1 tablespoon tomato paste
2 tablespoons chopped fresh parsley

1. Place flour in a shallow dish. Cut each chicken breast in half on the diagonal to get 4 portions about equal in weight. (Two will be smaller but thicker, the other two larger but thinner.) Sprinkle the chicken with ¼ teaspoon each salt and pepper and dredge in the flour. Whisk water with 2 tablespoons of the leftover flour in a small bowl; set aside.

2. Heat 1 tablespoon oil in a large nonstick skillet over medium-high heat. Reduce heat to medium and add the chicken. Cook, turning once or twice, until lightly browned on all sides, 5 to 7 minutes total. Transfer to a plate.

3. Add the remaining 1 tablespoon oil to the pan; reduce heat to medium-low. Add mushrooms, carrots, onion and rosemary and cook, stirring occasionally, until the vegetables are softened and browned in spots, about 5 minutes. Add broth, wine, tomato paste and the remaining ¼ teaspoon each salt and pepper. Stir until the tomato paste is dissolved. Bring to a simmer.

4. Return the chicken and any accumulated juice to the pan. Cover, reduce the heat to maintain a simmer and cook, stirring once or twice, until an instant-read thermometer inserted into the thickest part of the breast registers 165°F, 15 to 20 minutes. Transfer the chicken to a serving plate.

5. Increase the heat under the sauce to medium-high. Stir the water-flour mixture, add it to the pan and cook, stirring, until the sauce is thickened, about 1 minute. Serve the chicken with the sauce, sprinkled with parsley.

ACTIVE TIME: 45 minutes
TOTAL: 45 minutes

MAKES: 4 servings, ½ breast & ¾ cup sauce each

PER SERVING: 288 calories; 10 g fat (2 g sat, 6 g mono); 68 mg cholesterol; 14 g carbohydrate; 0 g added sugars; 29 g protein; 2 g fiber; 641 mg sodium; 624 mg potassium.
NUTRITION BONUS: Vitamin A (125% daily value), Potassium (19% dv).

SERVE WITH:

Green beans and boiled baby red potatoes tossed with a bit of olive oil and freshly chopped parsley

Lemon-Rosemary Turkey Meatballs

ACTIVE TIME: 50 minutes
TOTAL: 50 minutes

MAKES: 4 servings, 3 meatballs &
about ¼ cup sauce each

H❯❮W

PER SERVING: 346 calories; 15 g fat
(5 g sat, 3 g mono); 78 mg
cholesterol; 20 g carbohydrate;
0 g added sugars; 29 g protein;
2 g fiber; 641 mg sodium;
446 mg potassium.

SERVE WITH:

Whole-wheat noodles tossed
with a touch of olive oil and a
salad of baby romaine lettuce
leaves

If you like Swedish meatballs then you'll love these lemon- and rosemary-flavored turkey meatballs, which have a similarly velvety-rich sauce. This is a perfect make-ahead-and-freeze kind of dish, so you can have a supper or toothpick-ready appetizers ready in the flash of a microwave.

1	medium onion, cut into chunks
2	large cloves garlic, smashed and peeled
2	teaspoons freshly grated lemon zest
2	tablespoons chopped fresh rosemary *or* 1¼ teaspoons dried, divided
1	pound 93%-lean ground turkey
¾	cup fresh breadcrumbs, preferably whole-wheat (*see Note*)
⅓	cup freshly grated Parmesan cheese
¾	teaspoon kosher salt, divided
¼	teaspoon freshly ground pepper, plus more to taste
¼	cup all-purpose flour
2	teaspoons extra-virgin olive oil
½	cup dry white wine (*or* substitute more chicken broth)
1	14-ounce can reduced-sodium chicken broth
4	teaspoons lemon juice
1	tablespoon butter

1. Place onion, garlic and lemon zest in a food processor. Add 1 tablespoon fresh rosemary (or 1 teaspoon dried) and pulse just until the mixture is finely and evenly chopped (but not mushy).
2. Transfer the mixture to a medium bowl and gently mix in turkey, breadcrumbs, Parmesan, ½ teaspoon salt and pepper until combined. Use a generous 2 tablespoons each to shape the mixture into 12 meatballs (about 1½ inches in diameter). Place flour in a shallow dish and roll the meatballs in it to lightly coat. (Reserve the remaining flour.)
3. Heat oil in a large nonstick skillet over medium-high heat. Reduce heat to medium, add meatballs and cook, turning once, until brown, 3 to 5 minutes total. Transfer to a plate.
4. Add wine (or ½ cup broth) to the pan, increase heat to medium-high and cook, scraping up any browned bits, until almost evaporated, 1 to 3 minutes. Add the can of broth and bring to a boil. Reduce heat to maintain a simmer and return the meatballs to the pan along with the remaining 1 tablespoon fresh rosemary (or ¼ teaspoon dried). Cover and cook until the meatballs are cooked through, 8 to 10 minutes. Remove the meatballs to a serving bowl.
5. Bring the sauce to a boil over medium-high heat and cook until reduced to 1 cup, 4 to 8 minutes. Whisk lemon juice and 1 tablespoon of the reserved flour in a small bowl (discard any remaining flour); whisking constantly, add the flour mixture to the sauce along with butter and the remaining ¼ teaspoon salt. Simmer, whisking, until slightly thickened, 1 to 2 minutes. Strain the sauce through a fine-mesh sieve. Serve the sauce over the meatballs.

NOTE: **To make your own fresh breadcrumbs,** trim crusts from whole-wheat bread. Tear bread into pieces and process in a food processor until coarse crumbs form. One slice of bread makes about ½ cup fresh breadcrumbs.

Quick Chicken Tikka Masala

ACTIVE TIME: 40 minutes
TOTAL: 40 minutes

MAKES: 4 servings, 1½ cups each

H✂W   H♥H

PER SERVING: 320 calories; 14 g fat
(5 g sat, 6 g mono); 85 mg
cholesterol; 22 g carbohydrate;
0 g added sugars; 27 g protein;
3 g fiber; 641 mg sodium;
676 mg potassium.
NUTRITION BONUS: Vitamin C
(38% daily value), Iron & Potassium
(19% dv).

SERVE WITH:

Nutty-flavored brown basmati
rice and roasted cauliflower
(*see page 202*)

Usually involving a laborious regimen of marinating and grilling, the wildly popular Indian dish chicken tikka masala is simplified here into a one-skillet operation. We lightened it considerably by increasing the vegetables, omitting the butter and using only a splash of cream.

4	teaspoons garam masala (*see Note*)
½	teaspoon salt
¼	teaspoon turmeric
½	cup all-purpose flour
1	pound chicken tenders
4	teaspoons canola oil, divided
6	cloves garlic, minced
1	large sweet onion, diced
4	teaspoons minced fresh ginger
1	28-ounce can plum tomatoes, undrained
⅓	cup whipping cream
½	cup chopped fresh cilantro for garnish

1. Stir together garam masala, salt and turmeric in a small dish. Place flour in a shallow dish. Sprinkle chicken with ½ teaspoon of the spice mixture and dredge in the flour. (Reserve the remaining spice mix and 1 tablespoon of the remaining flour.)
2. Heat 2 teaspoons oil in a large skillet over medium-high heat. Cook the chicken until browned, 1 to 2 minutes per side. Transfer to a plate.
3. Heat the remaining 2 teaspoons oil in the pan over medium-low heat. Add garlic, onion and ginger and cook, stirring often, until starting to brown, 5 to 7 minutes. Add the reserved spice mix and cook, stirring, until fragrant, 30 seconds to 1 minute. Sprinkle with the reserved 1 tablespoon flour and stir until coated. Add tomatoes and their juice. Bring to a simmer, stirring and breaking up the tomatoes with a wooden spoon. Cook, stirring often, until thickened and the onion is tender, 3 to 5 minutes.
4. Stir in cream. Add the chicken and any accumulated juices to the pan. Bring to a simmer and cook over medium-low heat until the chicken is cooked through, 3 to 4 minutes. Garnish with cilantro.

NOTE: **Garam masala,** a blend of spices used in Indian cooking, usually includes cardamom, black pepper, cloves, nutmeg, fennel, cumin and coriander. It is available in the spice section of most supermarkets.

Cornmeal-Crusted Chicken Nuggets with Blackberry Mustard

Our tasty chicken nuggets are a healthy and kid-friendly alternative to fast food. Instead of giving them a trip to the deep fryer, we toss chunks of chicken tenders with cornmeal and crisp them in a skillet using only a little bit of oil. Blackberries (or raspberries, if you prefer) combined with whole-grain mustard make for a sweet-and-savory dipping sauce, which will top off what is sure to be a happy meal for all involved.

1	cup fresh blackberries *or* raspberries, finely chopped
1½	tablespoons whole-grain mustard
2	teaspoons honey
1	pound chicken tenders, cut in half crosswise (*see Note*)
½	teaspoon salt
¼	teaspoon freshly ground pepper
3	tablespoons cornmeal
1	tablespoon extra-virgin olive oil

1. Mash blackberries (or raspberries), mustard and honey in a small bowl until it looks like a chunky sauce.
2. Sprinkle chicken tenders with salt and pepper. Place cornmeal in a medium bowl, add the chicken and toss to coat (discard any leftover cornmeal).
3. Heat oil in a large nonstick skillet over medium-high heat. Reduce heat to medium and cook the chicken, turning once or twice, until browned and just cooked through, 6 to 8 minutes total (thinner nuggets will cook faster than thicker ones). Serve the chicken nuggets with the berry mustard.

NOTE: **Chicken tenders** are the lean strips of rib meat typically found attached to the underside of chicken breasts. They can also be purchased separately. Four 1-ounce tenders will yield a 3-ounce cooked portion. Tenders are perfect for quick stir-fries, chicken satay or kid-friendly breaded "chicken nuggets."

ACTIVE TIME: 20 minutes
TOTAL: 20 minutes

MAKES: 4 servings

H)(W   H♥H

PER SERVING: 201 calories; 7 g fat (1 g sat, 4 g mono); 63 mg cholesterol; 9 g carbohydrate; 3 g added sugars; 24 g protein; 2 g fiber; 459 mg sodium; 259 mg potassium.

SERVE WITH:

Steamed cauliflower (*see page 204*) smashed with a touch of butter, salt and pepper

Chicken Breasts Stuffed with Pimiento Cheese

ACTIVE TIME: 25 minutes
TOTAL: 40 minutes

MAKES: 4 servings

H✳W   H♥H

PER SERVING: 200 calories; 10 g fat
(3 g sat, 5 g mono); 76 mg
cholesterol; 1 g carbohydrate;
0 g added sugars; 26 g protein;
0 g fiber; 445 mg sodium;
234 mg potassium.

SERVE WITH:

Long-grain brown rice and
kale sautéed with two slices
of crumbled cooked bacon

Down South, pimiento cheese would likely be made with something processed like Velveeta, so we've taken a bit of liberty here by using flavorful smoked Gouda. Our cheese blend is stuffed, along with fresh scallions, into boneless, skinless chicken breasts, which are browned on the stovetop and then transferred (in the same skillet) to the oven to finish.

- ½ **cup shredded Gouda cheese, preferably smoked**
- 2 **tablespoons chopped scallion**
- 1 **tablespoon sliced pimientos, chopped**
- 1 **teaspoon paprika, divided**
- 4 **small boneless, skinless chicken breasts (1¼-1½ pounds total), trimmed and tenders removed (*see Note*)**
- ½ **teaspoon salt, divided**
- ½ **teaspoon freshly ground pepper, divided**
- 1 **tablespoon extra-virgin olive oil**

1. Preheat oven to 400°F.
2. Combine Gouda, scallion, pimientos and ½ teaspoon paprika in a small bowl.
3. Cut a horizontal slit along the thin, long edge of each chicken breast, nearly through to the opposite side, and open like a book. Sprinkle the breasts with ¼ teaspoon each salt and pepper. Divide the cheese filling among the breasts, placing it in the center of each. Close the breast over the filling, pressing the edges firmly together to seal. Sprinkle the breasts with the remaining ½ teaspoon paprika, ¼ teaspoon salt and pepper.
4. Heat oil in a large ovenproof skillet (*see Note, page 209*) over medium-high heat. Add the chicken and cook until browned on one side, about 2 minutes. Turn the chicken over and transfer the skillet to the oven. Bake until the chicken is no longer pink in the center and an instant-read thermometer inserted into the thickest part registers 165°F, about 15 minutes.

NOTE: It can be difficult to find an **individual chicken breast** small enough for one portion. Removing the thin strip of meat from the underside of a 5-to-6-ounce breast—the "tender"— removes about 1 ounce of meat and yields a perfect individual portion. Wrap and freeze the tenders to use later.

Chicken Sausage with Potatoes & Sauerkraut

Here's our weeknight version of choucroute garni, "dressed sauerkraut," made with chicken sausage. The flavor of the dish will vary depending on what type of chicken sausage you choose. We like the taste of roasted garlic sausage or sweet apple sausage in this recipe. And although any type of sauerkraut can be used, we prefer the crisp texture of refrigerated kraut over canned.

ACTIVE TIME: 30 minutes
TOTAL: 30 minutes

MAKES: 4 servings, about 1 ½ cups each

H✗W   H♥H
PER SERVING: 295 calories; 9 g fat (1 g sat, 3 g mono); 60 mg cholesterol; 24 g carbohydrate; 0 g added sugars; 14 g protein; 4 g fiber; 562 mg sodium; 545 mg potassium.
NUTRITION BONUS: Vitamin C (45% daily value), Potassium (16% dv).

- **1** tablespoon extra-virgin olive oil
- **12** ounces (4 links) cooked chicken sausage, halved lengthwise and cut into 2- to 3-inch pieces
- **1** medium onion, thinly sliced
- **3** medium Yukon Gold potatoes, halved and cut into ¼-inch slices
- **1 ½** cups sauerkraut, rinsed
- **1 ½** cups dry white wine
- **½** teaspoon freshly ground pepper
- **¼** teaspoon caraway seeds
- **1** bay leaf

SERVE WITH:

Roasted carrots and mustard to spread on the sausage

Heat oil in a large skillet over medium heat. Add sausage and onion and cook, stirring frequently, until beginning to brown, about 4 minutes. Add potatoes, sauerkraut, wine, pepper, caraway seeds and bay leaf; bring to a simmer. Cover and cook, stirring occasionally, until the potatoes are tender and most of the liquid has evaporated, 10 to 15 minutes. Remove the bay leaf before serving.

Chicken with Tarragon Cream Sauce

ACTIVE TIME: 50 minutes
TOTAL: 50 minutes

MAKES: 6 servings

H)(W
PER SERVING: 251 calories; 11 g fat
(6 g sat, 3 g mono); 88 mg
cholesterol; 11 g carbohydrate;
0 g added sugars; 26 g protein;
1 g fiber; 258 mg sodium; 286 mg
potassium.

SERVE WITH:

Steamed asparagus spears and
oven-roasted new potatoes

For this elegant but easy dish, a modest amount of cream is simmered with the dynamic flavor duo of lemon and tarragon to make a pan sauce that elevates simple sautéed chicken breasts. Who needs dinner out at a restaurant?

	Juice of 1 lemon
1/3	**cup heavy cream**
1/2	**teaspoon kosher salt, divided**
1	**teaspoon plus 1/2 cup all-purpose flour, divided**
1	**teaspoon plus 1 tablespoon butter, divided**
3	**boneless, skinless chicken breasts (about 1 1/2 pounds total), trimmed**
1/4	**teaspoon ground white pepper**
1	**teaspoon peanut *or* canola oil**
1	**cup reduced-sodium chicken broth, divided, plus more as needed**
1/2	**cup frozen peas, thawed**
3	**tablespoons finely minced fresh tarragon *or* dill, plus sprigs for garnish**

1. Combine lemon juice and cream in a small bowl. Season with 1/4 teaspoon salt. Mash 1 teaspoon flour and 1 teaspoon butter in another small bowl until a paste forms. Set both bowls aside.

2. Dry chicken thoroughly with paper towels. Season with the remaining 1/4 teaspoon salt and white pepper. Dredge lightly in the remaining 1/2 cup flour, shaking off any excess. (Discard leftover flour.)

3. Heat the remaining 1 tablespoon butter and oil in a 12-inch cast-iron skillet over medium-high heat. Add the chicken—do not crowd the pan. Cook, turning once, until nicely browned on both sides, about 10 minutes total. Add 1/2 cup broth, reduce the heat and cover. Simmer until the chicken is cooked through, 4 to 6 minutes. (Check to make sure the pan juices don't run dry. If necessary, add more broth, a tablespoonful at a time, to prevent scorching.) Transfer the chicken to a clean cutting board and tent with foil.

4. Add the remaining 1/2 cup broth to the pan and bring to a boil over high heat. Cook until reduced to about 1/4 cup, 2 to 4 minutes. Reduce heat to medium, add the reserved lemon cream and bring to a simmer. Gradually whisk in the reserved butter-flour paste, a few bits at a time, until the sauce coats the spoon, 1 to 2 minutes. Stir in peas.

5. Reduce the heat to low and return the chicken to the pan along with minced tarragon (or dill). Turn to coat with the sauce and cook until heated through, 1 to 2 minutes. Slice the chicken and serve with the sauce, garnished with sprigs of tarragon (or dill), if desired.

Pan-Roasted Chicken & Gravy

ACTIVE TIME: 25 minutes
TOTAL: 1 1/4 hours

MAKES: 6 servings

H✕W   H♥H

PER SERVING (WITHOUT SKIN): 208
calories; 9 g fat (3 g sat, 3 g mono);
89 mg cholesterol; 1 g
carbohydrate; 0 g added sugars;
29 g protein; 0 g fiber; 314 mg
sodium; 290 mg potassium.

SERVE WITH:

Boiled Yukon Gold potatoes
mashed with a little extra-virgin
olive oil, salt, freshly ground
black pepper and, if you have
it, a splash of buttermilk or a
little plain yogurt

Roasted chicken. What pair of words in the food lexicon so instantly brings such comfort to the soul? And for all its curative powers it's easy to forget that it takes but one pan and scarcely more than an hour to get this meal (gravy included) from refrigerator to table.

1	**large clove garlic, minced**
1/2	**teaspoon kosher salt**
1/4	**teaspoon ground white pepper**
1 1/2	**teaspoons fresh thyme leaves**
1	**3 1/2-pound chicken, giblets removed**
1	**teaspoon peanut *or* canola oil**
2	**teaspoons butter, softened, divided**
2	**teaspoons all-purpose flour**
1 1/2	**cups reduced-sodium chicken broth**
1	**tablespoon minced flat-leaf parsley for garnish**

1. Preheat oven to 400°F.
2. Mash garlic and salt into a paste in a small bowl, using the back of a spoon. Stir in pepper and thyme.
3. With a sharp knife, remove any excess fat from chicken. Dry the inside with a paper towel. With your fingers, loosen the skin over the breasts and thighs to make pockets, being careful not to tear the skin. Rub the garlic mixture over the breast and thigh meat.
4. Heat oil and 1 teaspoon butter in a 12-inch cast-iron skillet over medium heat. Add the chicken and cook, turning often, until nicely browned on all sides, about 10 minutes.
5. Transfer the pan to the oven and roast the chicken until the internal temperature in the thickest part of the thigh reaches 165°F, 50 minutes to 1 hour. Transfer the chicken to a clean cutting board; tent with foil.
6. Meanwhile, mash the remaining 1 teaspoon butter and flour in a small bowl until a paste forms. Place the pan (use caution, the handle will be hot) over medium-high heat. Add broth and bring to a simmer, stirring to scrape up any browned bits. Gradually whisk in the butter-flour paste a few bits at a time, until the gravy thickens, about 8 minutes. Remove from the heat and let stand for 5 minutes, allowing any fat to rise to the top. Skim off the fat with a spoon. Carve the chicken and serve with the gravy. Garnish with parsley, if desired.

Hamburger Buddy

Our ground-beef-and-noodle skillet meal has a nutritional and flavor helper: some very finely chopped onion, mushrooms and carrots, which—rather than a packet of seasoning and thickeners— form the base for the sauce.

3	cloves garlic, crushed and peeled
2	medium carrots, cut into 2-inch pieces
10	ounces white mushrooms, large ones cut in half
1	large onion, cut into 2-inch pieces
1	pound 90%-lean ground beef
2	teaspoons dried thyme
3/4	teaspoon salt
1/4	teaspoon freshly ground pepper
2	cups water
1	14-ounce can reduced-sodium beef broth, divided
8	ounces whole-wheat elbow noodles (2 cups)
2	tablespoons Worcestershire sauce
2	tablespoons all-purpose flour
1/2	cup reduced-fat sour cream
1	tablespoon chopped fresh parsley *or* chives for garnish

1. Fit a food processor with the steel blade attachment. With the motor running, drop garlic through the feed tube and process until minced, then add carrots and mushrooms and process until finely chopped. Turn it off, add onion, and pulse until roughly chopped.
2. Cook beef in a large straight-sided skillet or Dutch oven over medium-high heat, breaking it up with a wooden spoon, until no longer pink, 3 to 5 minutes. Stir in the chopped vegetables, thyme, salt and pepper and cook, stirring often, until the vegetables start to soften and the mushrooms release their juices, 5 to 7 minutes.
3. Stir in water, 1 1/2 cups broth, noodles and Worcestershire sauce; bring to a boil. Cover, reduce heat to medium and cook, stirring occasionally, until the pasta is tender, 8 to 10 minutes.
4. Whisk flour with the remaining 1/4 cup broth in a small bowl until smooth; stir into the hamburger mixture. Stir in sour cream. Simmer, stirring often, until the sauce is thickened, about 2 minutes. Serve sprinkled with parsley (or chives), if desired.

ACTIVE TIME: 40 minutes
TOTAL: 40 minutes

MAKES: 6 servings, about 1 1/3 cups each

PER SERVING: 321 calories; 9 g fat (4 g sat, 3 g mono); 56 mg cholesterol; 38 g carbohydrate; 0 g added sugars; 23 g protein; 5 g fiber; 558 mg sodium; 583 mg potassium.
NUTRITION BONUS: Vitamin A (70% daily value), Zinc (33% dv), Iron (22% dv), Potassium (17% dv).

SERVE WITH:

Baby peas sautéed with chopped scallions and dried or fresh tarragon

French Onion Beef Tenderloin

In this dish, the best of two bistro-style dishes meet up—pan-seared steak and French onion soup. Medallions of filet mignon get smothered with sweet caramelized onions and topped by a crispy, Swiss cheese–covered crostini. This is nice for a dinner party, so if you have 8 guests double the recipe: use 2 large skillets and prepare one 4-serving recipe in each.

 **ACTIVE TIME:** 45 minutes
TOTAL: 45 minutes

MAKES: 4 servings

PER SERVING: 364 calories; 17 g fat (5 g sat, 8 g mono); 75 mg cholesterol; 20 g carbohydrate; 0 g added sugars; 29 g protein; 3 g fiber; 528 mg sodium; 547 mg potassium.
NUTRITION BONUS: Zinc (33% daily value), Calcium & Potassium (16% dv).

SERVE WITH:

Sautéed broccolini and oven-crisped frozen hash browns

- 1 pound beef tenderloin (filet mignon) *or* sirloin steak, 1-1½ inches thick, trimmed and cut into 4 steaks
- ½ teaspoon minced dried onion
- ½ teaspoon salt, divided
- ½ teaspoon freshly ground pepper
- 2 tablespoons canola oil, divided
- 2 large sweet onions, thinly sliced
- ⅓ cup dry sherry (*see Note*)
- 1 tablespoon all-purpose flour
- 1 cup reduced-sodium beef broth
- 2 teaspoons chopped fresh thyme
- 4 slices whole-grain baguette (½ inch thick), toasted
- ½ cup shredded Swiss cheese

1. Sprinkle steaks with dried onion, ¼ teaspoon salt and pepper. Heat 1 tablespoon oil in a large skillet over medium-high heat. Add the steaks and reduce the heat to medium. Cook, turning once, until desired doneness, 3 to 6 minutes per side for medium-rare. Transfer the steaks to a plate and tent with foil.
2. Position a rack in upper third of oven. Preheat broiler.
3. Add the remaining 1 tablespoon oil to the pan. Add onions and sherry, cover and cook over medium heat, stirring occasionally, until the onions are tender and golden brown and the liquid has evaporated, 10 to 12 minutes. Sprinkle flour over the onions and stir to coat. Add broth, thyme and the remaining ¼ teaspoon salt; cook until bubbling and thickened, about 1 minute more.
4. Remove from the heat and return the steaks and any accumulated juice to the pan. Pile up some of the onions on top of the steaks. Top each steak with a slice of baguette and some cheese. Transfer the pan to the oven and broil until the cheese is melted and bubbling, about 2 minutes. Serve the steaks with the onions and sauce.

NOTE: **Sherry** is a type of fortified wine originally from southern Spain. "Cooking sherry" sold in many supermarkets can be high in sodium. Instead, get dry sherry that's sold with other fortified wines at your wine or liquor store.

Skillet-Roasted Strip Steaks with Pebre Sauce & Avocado

ACTIVE TIME: 30 minutes
TOTAL: 30 minutes
TO MAKE AHEAD: Cover and refrigerate the sauce for up to 2 days. Bring to room temperature before serving.

MAKES: 4 servings

H✖W   H↑F

PER SERVING: 343 calories; 23 g fat (4 g sat, 13 g mono); 61 mg cholesterol; 13 g carbohydrate; 0 g added sugars; 25 g protein; 8 g fiber; 337 mg sodium; 903 mg potassium.
NUTRITION BONUS: Vitamin C (33% daily value), Zinc (32% dv), Potassium (26% dv), Folate (25% dv).

SERVE WITH:

Buttered corn on the cob sprinkled with sea salt, a pinch of chili powder and a squeeze of lime

Pebre salsa is a fresh tomato-and-onion blend often combined with mashed avocado to top a popular Chilean steak sandwich called a churrasco. Here, we recreate those flavors for a pan-seared strip-steak dinner, which takes only about 30 minutes to make. If you have any leftovers, layer them on crunchy baguette the next day to make your own churrasco.

PEBRE SAUCE

- 1/2 cup finely chopped sweet onion, such as Vidalia *or* Walla Walla
- 1 medium-large tomato, seeded and diced
- 1/3 cup chopped fresh cilantro
- 2 tablespoons minced jalapeño *or* serrano pepper
- 2 tablespoons red-wine *or* cider vinegar
- 1 clove garlic, minced
- 1/4 teaspoon kosher salt

STEAK

- 3/4 teaspoon paprika
- 3/4 teaspoon ground cumin
- 3/4 teaspoon dried oregano
- 3/4 teaspoon kosher salt, divided
- 1/2 teaspoon ground pepper
- 2 8- to 10-ounce New York strip (top loin) steaks, trimmed
- 2 teaspoons canola oil
- 2 avocados, pitted and peeled

1. **To prepare sauce:** Place onion in a medium bowl, cover with ice water and let soak for 10 to 20 minutes. Drain. Combine the onion, tomato, cilantro, jalapeño (or serrano), vinegar, garlic and 1/4 teaspoon salt in a medium bowl.
2. Preheat oven to 325°F.
3. **To prepare steak:** Mix paprika, cumin, oregano, 1/2 teaspoon salt and pepper in a small bowl. Rub the spice mixture evenly over both sides of steaks.
4. Heat oil in a large ovenproof skillet (*see Note, page 209*) over medium-high. Add the steaks and cook just until browned, 1 to 2 minutes per side. Transfer the pan to the oven and roast the steaks 5 to 7 minutes for medium-rare, depending on thickness. Transfer to a clean cutting board. Tent with foil and let rest for 5 minutes.
5. Meanwhile, mash avocados with the remaining 1/4 teaspoon salt in a small bowl.
6. Carve the steak into thin slices. Serve with the avocado and sauce.

Seared Strip Steaks with Horseradish-Root Vegetable Slaw

Steaks are often served with hearty accompaniments like mashed potatoes, which can make the whole meal seem heavy. Here we lighten things up by topping pan-seared steaks with a raw slaw dressed with pungent horseradish vinaigrette. We use shredded beets, turnips and carrots, but feel free to change up the combination of vegetables based on what you're pulling from the garden at the moment.

ACTIVE TIME: 40 minutes
TOTAL: 40 minutes

MAKES: 4 servings, 3-4 ounces steak & generous ½ cup slaw each

H✕W H♥H

PER SERVING: 246 calories; 12 g fat (3 g sat, 7 g mono); 62 mg cholesterol; 10 g carbohydrate; 0 g added sugars; 23 g protein; 2 g fiber; 341 mg sodium; 538 mg potassium.

NUTRITION BONUS: Vitamin A (93% daily value), Zinc (29% dv), Potassium (15% dv).

3	cups shredded peeled root vegetables (*see Notes*), such as beets, carrots, celeriac *and/or* turnips
2	teaspoons plus 1 tablespoon extra-virgin olive oil, divided
3	tablespoons chopped fresh dill, divided
¾	teaspoon kosher salt, divided
1	pound strip steak (1-1¼ inches thick), trimmed and cut into 4 portions
¼	teaspoon freshly ground pepper
¼	cup water
¼	cup white balsamic vinegar (*see Notes*) *or* regular balsamic vinegar
2-4	tablespoons prepared horseradish
1	tablespoon reduced-fat sour cream

1. Toss root vegetables, 2 teaspoons oil, 2 tablespoons dill and ½ teaspoon salt in a medium bowl. Set aside.
2. Sprinkle steaks with the remaining ¼ teaspoon salt and pepper. Heat the remaining 1 tablespoon oil in a large skillet over medium-high heat. Reduce heat to medium, add the steaks and cook, turning once and adjusting the heat as necessary to prevent burning, 3 to 5 minutes per side for medium-rare.
3. Remove the pan from the heat and transfer the steaks to a clean plate to rest. Add water, vinegar and horseradish to taste to the pan; scrape up any browned bits. Stir any accumulated juice from the steaks into the pan sauce. Drizzle half the sauce (about ¼ cup) over the vegetable slaw and toss to coat. Stir sour cream and the remaining 1 tablespoon dill into the sauce remaining in the pan. To serve, divide the slaw and steaks among 4 plates and drizzle with the pan sauce.

NOTES:

To prevent nicking your fingers on the sharp holes of a box grater while **shredding round root vegetables**, such as turnips or beets, shred about half the vegetable, then use a clean dish towel to grip the remaining half (and protect your fingers) as you shred. Or, use the shredding blade on your food processor and let the machine do the work for you.

White balsamic vinegar is unaged balsamic made from Italian white wine grapes and grape musts (unfermented crushed grapes). It's milder in flavor than aged, dark-colored balsamic vinegar. Look for it near other vinegars in well-stocked supermarkets or specialty food shops.

SERVE WITH

Roasted Brussels sprouts (*see page 202*) tossed with lemon zest

Pork Chops with Creamy Marsala Sauce

Sweet Marsala plus a little low-fat milk blended with cornstarch are the basis for a pan sauce for these pork chops that is thick and creamy yet deceptively light. Chopped chives add an elegant, fresh finish to this 35-minute skillet entree.

½ cup Marsala (*see Note*), divided
2 teaspoons cornstarch
¼ cup all-purpose flour
4 thin boneless pork loin chops (about 1 pound), trimmed
¼ teaspoon kosher salt
¼ teaspoon freshly ground pepper
2 teaspoons extra-virgin olive oil
4 thin slices prosciutto (2 ounces), chopped
1 small onion, halved and thinly sliced
3 teaspoons chopped fresh oregano *or* 1 teaspoon dried
3 teaspoons chopped fresh chives, divided
1 cup low-fat milk

1. Mix 2 tablespoons Marsala and cornstarch in a small bowl; set aside.
2. Place flour in a shallow dish. Sprinkle pork chops with salt and pepper, then dredge in the flour.
3. Heat oil in a large nonstick skillet over medium-high heat. Reduce heat to medium and add the pork chops. Cook until well browned on both sides, about 2 minutes per side. Transfer to a plate. Add prosciutto to the pan and cook, stirring constantly, until browned, about 1 minute. Add onion and cook, stirring often, until it starts to soften and brown, 2 to 3 minutes. Add the remaining 6 tablespoons Marsala, oregano and 1½ teaspoons chives and bring to a boil, scraping up any browned bits. Add milk and the reserved cornstarch mixture to the pan; adjust the heat to maintain a simmer. Cook, stirring occasionally, until the sauce has thickened and reduced slightly, 4 to 6 minutes.
4. Return the pork chops and any accumulated juice to the pan and simmer, turning to coat, until heated through, 1 to 2 minutes. Serve the chops topped with the sauce and garnished with the remaining 1½ teaspoons chives.

NOTE: **Marsala**, a fortified wine from Sicily, is a flavorful addition to many sauces. Don't use the "cooking Marsala" sold in many supermarkets—it can be surprisingly high in sodium and can make your sauce too salty. Instead, purchase Marsala that's sold with other fortified wines in your wine or liquor store. An opened bottle can be stored in a cool, dry place for months.

ACTIVE TIME: 35 minutes
TOTAL: 35 minutes

MAKES: 4 servings

PER SERVING: 332 calories; 12 g fat (4 g sat, 5 g mono); 78 mg cholesterol; 17 g carbohydrate; 2 g added sugars; 30 g protein; 1 g fiber; 526 mg sodium; 498 mg potassium.
NUTRITION BONUS: Zinc (16% daily value).

SERVE WITH:

Orzo pasta tossed with sautéed cremini mushroom slices and a simple green salad

Thyme, Pork Chop & Pineapple Skillet Supper

ACTIVE TIME: 30 minutes
TOTAL: 30 minutes

MAKES: 4 servings

H✕W   H♥H
PER SERVING: 257 calories; 8 g fat (3 g sat, 3 g mono); 72 mg cholesterol; 25 g carbohydrate; 8 g added sugars; 22 g protein; 2 g fiber; 388 mg sodium; 434 mg potassium.
NUTRITION BONUS: Vitamin C (78% daily value).

SERVE WITH:

Whole-grain rice pilaf and steamed green beans

Thyme adds bright, woodsy flavor to pork and pineapple in this simple dish. If you have leftover thyme (or other woody herbs, such as rosemary or oregano), wrap it in a paper towel, place in a plastic bag and refrigerate.

- 3 tablespoons pineapple *or* apricot preserves *or* jam *or* orange marmalade
- 3 tablespoons orange juice, plus more if needed
- 2 teaspoons stone-ground *or* Dijon mustard
- ½ teaspoon minced fresh ginger
- ½ teaspoon curry powder
- 4 fresh *or* canned pineapple rings (½ inch thick), cut in half, any juice reserved
- 2 teaspoons butter
- 4 4- to 5-ounce boneless pork loin chops (½ inch thick), trimmed
- 2 tablespoons chopped fresh thyme (*see Note*), divided
- ½ teaspoon salt, divided
- ¼ teaspoon freshly ground pepper, divided

1. If the preserves are chunky, chop any large pieces. Combine preserves (or jam or marmalade), 3 tablespoons orange juice, mustard, ginger and curry powder in a small bowl; set aside. Pour pineapple juice into a measuring cup; if necessary, add enough orange juice to equal ⅓ cup total. Set aside.
2. Heat butter in a large nonstick skillet over medium-high heat. Add pork chops, sprinkle with ½ tablespoon thyme, ¼ teaspoon salt and ⅛ teaspoon pepper. Immediately turn them over and sprinkle with another ½ tablespoon thyme and the remaining salt and pepper. Cook the chops, turning occasionally and adjusting the heat as necessary, until browned, 3 to 4 minutes.
3. Add the reserved juice to the pan. Reduce heat to medium and continue cooking until the chops are cooked through, 2 to 3 minutes more. Transfer to a platter and keep warm.
4. Add pineapple, the reserved sauce and the remaining 1 tablespoon thyme to the pan. Cook, stirring, until hot and bubbling, 1 to 2 minutes. To serve, spoon the sauce onto the chops and pineapple.

NOTE: To remove **thyme leaves** from the sprig, hold each sprig at the top with one hand, then run the thumb and finger of the other hand down the stem to strip off the leaves.

Vegetable Stew with Sausage & Chickpeas

ACTIVE TIME: 35 minutes
TOTAL: 45 minutes

MAKES: 4 servings

H✖W   H↑F   H♥H

PER SERVING: 310 calories; 11 g fat (3 g sat, 5 g mono); 16 mg cholesterol; 41 g carbohydrate; 0 g added sugars; 14 g protein; 10 g fiber; 700 mg sodium; 1,073 mg potassium.

NUTRITION BONUS: Vitamin C (205% daily value), Vitamin A (40% dv), Folate (33% dv), Potassium (31% dv), Iron (22% dv), Magnesium (20% dv), Zinc (16% dv).

SERVE WITH:

Chewy-textured barley or short-grain brown rice with baby peas stirred in

Fennel lovers, look no further. This quick and hearty stew gets a double dose of what you're looking for from slices of fresh fennel bulb and some fennel seed as well. Sausage, tomatoes, mixed bell peppers, plenty of garlic and diced zucchini finish off the Italian theme.

4	ounces Italian sausage (about 2 small links)
1½	teaspoons extra-virgin olive oil
1	large red onion, thinly sliced
1	large red bell pepper, thinly sliced
1	large green bell pepper, thinly sliced
1	small bulb fennel, trimmed, quartered and thinly sliced
¼	teaspoon crushed red pepper
5	cloves garlic, minced
2	small zucchini, diced
1	14-ounce can diced tomatoes, with juice
1	tablespoon fresh thyme leaves *or* 1 teaspoon dried
½	teaspoon fennel seed
1	15-ounce can chickpeas, rinsed (1½ cups cooked)
2	tablespoons chopped fresh parsley
¼	teaspoon freshly ground pepper

1. Pierce sausage in several places with a fork. Cook in a large skillet over medium-high heat, turning, until browned on all sides, 5 to 7 minutes. Transfer the sausage to a cutting board and let rest for a few minutes. Slice crosswise into ¼-inch-thick rounds. Wipe out the pan.
2. Heat oil in the pan over medium heat. Add onion, bell peppers, fennel and crushed red pepper; cook, stirring, until the vegetables are tender and the onion is lightly browned, 10 to 15 minutes.
3. Add garlic and cook, stirring, for 1 minute. Add zucchini, tomatoes, thyme, fennel seed and the sausage. Reduce heat to low and simmer, partially covered, until the zucchini is tender and the mixture is slightly thickened, 10 to 15 minutes. Add chickpeas and parsley and heat through. Season with salt and pepper.

Rack of Lamb with a Cilantro-Mustard Seed Crust

The cilantro-mustard seed crust on this rack of lamb makes it special enough that no other sauce or embellishment is necessary.

2	**tablespoons chopped fresh cilantro**
1	**tablespoon Dijon mustard**
1½	**teaspoons mustard seeds**
1	**clove garlic, minced**
1	**rack of lamb, trimmed of fat (8 ribs, about 1½ pounds)**
½	**teaspoon salt**
½	**teaspoon freshly ground pepper**
1	**teaspoon canola oil**

1. Preheat oven to 425°F.
2. Combine cilantro, mustard, mustard seeds and garlic in a small bowl.
3. Season lamb with salt and pepper. Brush oil evenly over a large cast-iron or other ovenproof skillet (*see Note, page 209*). Heat the skillet over medium-high heat. Add the lamb, meat-side down, and cook until browned, 2 to 3 minutes. Remove from the heat and spread the mustard mixture over the browned side. Transfer the skillet to the oven and roast the lamb until an instant-read thermometer inserted into the center registers 140°F for medium-rare, 15 to 20 minutes.
4. Transfer the lamb to a cutting board and let rest for 5 minutes. Carve the rack between the ribs into 8 chops.

ACTIVE TIME: 15 minutes
TOTAL: 40 minutes

MAKES: 4 servings, 2 chops each

H✖W   H♥H
PER SERVING: 174 calories; 8 g fat (3 g sat, 4 g mono); 68 mg cholesterol; 1 g carbohydrate; 0 g added sugars; 22 g protein; 0 g fiber; 441 mg sodium; 291 mg potassium.
NUTRITION BONUS: Zinc (20% daily value).

SERVE WITH:

Quinoa seasoned with cumin and a simple salad of tomato wedges with sliced Spanish onion tossed in red-wine vinegar and olive oil

Lemon & Oregano Lamb Chops

ACTIVE TIME: 30 minutes
TOTAL: 45 minutes

TO MAKE AHEAD: Prepare sauce (Step 3), cover and refrigerate for up to 3 days. Prepare rub and rub onto lamb chops (Step 2) and refrigerate for up to 1 hour.

MAKES: 4 servings, 2 lamb chops & 3 tablespoons sauce each

H✳W

PER SERVING: 283 calories; 17 g fat (4 g sat, 8 g mono); 68 mg cholesterol; 7 g carbohydrate; 0 g added sugars; 25 g protein; 1 g fiber; 429 mg sodium; 429 mg potassium.
NUTRITION BONUS: Vitamin C (27% daily value), Zinc (26% dv).

SERVE WITH:

Cooked large pearl couscous tossed with diced tomato, chopped black olives, some crumbled feta, lemon juice and extra-virgin olive oil

Starting these lemony Middle Eastern-flavored lamb chops on the stovetop gives them a nice brown crust and finishing them in the oven ensures they come out juicy and evenly cooked.

	Freshly grated zest of 2 lemons
1	tablespoon chopped fresh oregano *or* 1 teaspoon dried
1¼	teaspoons kosher salt, divided
	Freshly ground pepper to taste
8	lamb loin chops (1½-1¾ pounds total), trimmed
¼	cup tahini (*see Note*)
¼	cup nonfat plain yogurt, preferably Greek-style
¼	cup diced seeded cucumber, peeled if desired
¼	cup lemon juice
2	cloves garlic, minced
1	tablespoon chopped fresh parsley
1-3	tablespoons water
2	teaspoons extra-virgin olive oil

1. Preheat oven to 400°F.
2. Combine lemon zest, oregano, ¾ teaspoon salt and pepper in a small bowl. Rub the mixture onto both sides of lamb chops and set aside for at least 10 minutes or refrigerate for up to 1 hour.
3. Meanwhile, combine tahini, yogurt, cucumber, lemon juice, garlic, parsley and the remaining ½ teaspoon salt in a small bowl. Whisk in enough water to thin the sauce to desired consistency.
4. Heat oil in a large ovenproof nonstick skillet over medium-high heat. Add the lamb chops and cook until browned on one side, about 2 minutes. Turn them over and transfer the pan to the oven. Roast until an instant-read thermometer inserted horizontally into a chop registers 135°F for medium-rare, 8 to 14 minutes, depending on thickness. Serve the chops with the tahini sauce.

NOTE: **Tahini** is a thick paste of ground sesame seeds. Look for it in large supermarkets in the Middle Eastern section or near other nut butters.

Whole Roasted Lemon-Herb Chicken on a Bed of Vegetables

ROASTING PAN

Choose a roasting pan made of heavy metal so it won't warp. A basic 14-by-16-inch one with sturdy handles is good for most recipes (and will work for your Thanksgiving turkey as well). If you're roasting a small amount of food, use a smaller metal pan, about 9 by 13 inches, to keep the pan from drying out and burning. Even though shiny stainless pans are pretty, we find that darker pans brown foods better and make the morsels on the bottom of the pan more luscious for gravy. Besides a roasting pan, a large rimmed baking sheet is essential. You can make a pizza on it, use it for a freeform meatloaf or roast vegetables for an easy side to serve with dinner. (*Turn to page 202 for our vegetable-roasting guide.*)

Smoked Sausage Pizza

ACTIVE TIME: 30 minutes
TOTAL: 45 minutes

MAKES: 6 servings

H✘W   H♥H

PER SERVING: 172 calories; 6 g fat
(2 g sat, 1 g mono); 11 mg
cholesterol; 25 g carbohydrate;
1 g added sugars; 7 g protein;
2 g fiber; 371 mg sodium;
81 mg potassium.

SERVE WITH:

A romaine salad with chopped
hard-boiled egg and whole-grain
croutons tossed with red-wine
vinegar and olive oil

Smoked turkey sausage is a great, low-fat ingredient for adding quick, garlicky flavor to a pizza because, unlike most Italian sausages, it comes precooked.

	Cornmeal & all-purpose flour for dusting
1	**pound prepared whole-wheat pizza dough** (*see Note*)
1/3	**cup marinara sauce**
1	**small onion, thinly sliced**
1/2	**medium green bell pepper, thinly sliced**
2	**ounces smoked turkey sausage** *or* **turkey kielbasa, thinly sliced**
1/2	**cup shredded Monterey Jack** *or* **part-skim mozzarella cheese (2 ounces)**
1/4	**teaspoon dried oregano**
	Pinch of crushed red pepper (optional)
1/4	**teaspoon salt**
	Freshly ground pepper to taste

1. Position rack in lower third of oven; preheat to 450°F. Coat a large baking sheet with cooking spray and sprinkle with cornmeal to coat evenly.
2. Sprinkle flour over a work surface. Roll out dough to the size of the baking sheet (*see Note, page 94*) and transfer to the prepared baking sheet.
3. Spread marinara sauce evenly over the dough. Scatter onion, bell pepper, sausage and cheese over the top and sprinkle with oregano and crushed red pepper (if using). Sprinkle with salt and pepper.
4. Bake until the crust is crispy and the cheese is melted, 12 to 15 minutes.

NOTE: Look for fresh or frozen balls of **whole-wheat pizza dough** at your supermarket. Check the ingredient list to make sure the dough doesn't contain any hydrogenated oils.

Turkish-Style Pizza

ACTIVE TIME: 30 minutes
TOTAL: 45 minutes

MAKES: 6 servings

H✳w
PER SLICE: 317 calories; 16 g fat
(6 g sat, 5 g mono); 31 mg
cholesterol; 35 g carbohydrate;
1 g added sugars; 13 g protein;
3 g fiber; 421 mg sodium;
233 mg potassium.
NUTRITION BONUS: Vitamin C (33%
daily value), Vitamin A (22% dv),
Calcium (17% dv).

SERVE WITH:

Salad of rinsed white cannellini
beans, chopped bell peppers,
sliced red onion, diced cucumber
and tomatoes tossed with lemon
juice and extra-virgin olive oil

Pizza, the ubiquitous fast (and fast-cooking) food, is considered by many to be an Italian creation, while some people believe that Turkish pide (flatbreads with toppings) may have come first. This recipe, inspired by a pie discovered in the coastal city of Antalya, honors the latter tradition, yet still includes the familiar basics of tomato and cheese.

	Cornmeal & all-purpose flour for dusting
1	pound prepared whole-wheat pizza dough (*see Note, page 92*)
1	teaspoon plus 1 tablespoon extra-virgin olive oil, divided
1½	cups grated fontina *or* Monterey Jack cheese
1½	cups diced tomatoes
1	cup diced sweet onion, such as Vidalia
2	tablespoons minced seeded jalapeño pepper
2	ounces sliced pastrami, diced (½ cup; optional)
	Freshly ground pepper to taste
⅓	cup flat-leaf parsley leaves, torn

1. Position rack in lower third of oven; preheat to 450°F. Coat a large baking sheet with cooking spray and sprinkle with cornmeal to coat evenly.
2. Sprinkle flour over a work surface. Roll out dough to the size of the baking sheet (*see Note*) and transfer to the prepared baking sheet. Turn the edges under to make a slight rim. Brush the rim with 1 teaspoon oil.
3. Sprinkle cheese over the crust, leaving a ½-inch border. Top with tomatoes, onion, jalapeño and pastrami, if using. Season with pepper. Drizzle with the remaining 1 tablespoon oil.
4. Bake until the crust is crispy and the cheese is melted, 10 to 14 minutes. Sprinkle with parsley and serve immediately.

NOTE: **To roll out pizza dough,** turn the dough out onto a lightly floured surface. Dust the top with flour; dimple with your fingertips to shape into a thick, flattened circle—don't worry if it's not perfectly symmetrical. Then use a rolling pin to roll into the desired size. If your dough "resists" being rolled out, let it rest for about 15 minutes, then try rolling it out again.

All in the Pan

Pull out the roasting pan for hearty, healthy meals
everyone will love

Timothy Aguero Photography

I f there's a cardinal rule of cooking I learned from my grandmother, it's that nobody
should ever leave the table hungry. Sadie would have been deeply offended by the
concept of molecular gastronomy with its fussing over olive oil droplets and other
chemical fantasies. When my grandmother had people to feed, they got *fed*. Accom-
plishing this wasn't easy—her kitchen back in Poland didn't even have an oven—but a
roasting pan allowed her to persevere in style. She'd assemble her dinner in the pan,
then lug it down to the local baker's oven to cook. Literally straight from the hearth,
she'd produce a meal of unbelievable deliciousness and abundance. Flanken (short ribs)
nestled in carrots and prunes, chicken rubbed with paprika and smothered in onions
and potatoes, even her moist dark honey cake came out of that battered old pan.

Sadie was a practical gal and so am I. She would have approved of buying good
kitchen gear. I know she would love having a reliable oven, sharp knives, a solid cutting
board and my pretty yellow-enamel roasting pan. Or I should say pans as I have two
roasting pans of enameled cast-iron. One is 8 by 11 inches, the other 10 by 14, because
size really does matter. My smaller pan holds a chicken snugly; the larger one is perfect
for one small turkey or two chickens or a lasagne for 12. When you use a pan too large
for its contents, they dry out, spatter and smoke up the house.

My roasting pans allow me to do so much more than I could with aluminum or
glass pans. I use them on top of the stove to brown meat for a pot roast that will simmer
gently in the oven. I can take them out of the oven and then deglaze the yummy scraps
on the pan right on the stovetop and I never worry that they'll warp or bend. There's no
anxiety about running one of these pans under the broiler to brown a moussaka (which
is dangerous in a glass baking dish, because the broiler can cause it to shatter).

Browning was one of the secrets to my grandmother's tasty cooking. But she also
relied heavily on fatty meats and lots of butter. Grandma Sadie was 200 pounds and
maybe five feet tall—she didn't worry about calories or portion size at all. More was
better. Today we know better: less is more.

My roasting pans are heavy and distribute heat evenly promoting good caramelization.
This helps me cut down on the amount of fat I need without loss of flavor. I try to eat
less meat and prefer it as a flavoring agent. I bulk up meatloaf with bulgur and know
that a slurry will thicken gravy as well as a roux. A drizzle of good olive oil finishes a dish
as well as a swirl of butter and fresh herbs make any meal pop. Grandma stuck to her
own cuisine while I cook dishes from around the globe, using my roasting pans to do
many jobs. I roast and braise in them, make gratins and casseroles in them, I even bake
desserts in them. These versatile pans can do it all. I'm sure she'd like that. 🥄

Ruth Cousineau was test kitchen director, food editor and stylist for more than 10 years at
Gourmet *magazine in New York City before semi-retiring to Seattle.*

I cook dishes from

around the globe,

using my roasting pans

to do many jobs.

—Ruth Cousineau

Roast Salmon with Salsa

ACTIVE TIME: 10 minutes
TOTAL: 25 minutes
TO MAKE AHEAD: Prepare salsa (Step 2), cover and refrigerate for up to 1 day.

MAKES: 6 servings

H✖W   H♥H

PER SERVING: 146 calories; 4 g fat (1 g sat, 2 g mono); 53 mg cholesterol; 2 g carbohydrate; 0 g added sugars; 23 g protein; 1 g fiber; 252 mg sodium; 499 mg potassium.

NUTRITION BONUS: Omega-3s.

SERVE WITH:

Diced hash brown potatoes and a baby arugula salad with a Champagne vinegar, Dijon mustard and extra-virgin olive oil dressing

Here's a zesty roasted salmon recipe that can be in the oven in 10 minutes and on the table in less than half an hour. If that's not fast enough, spoon your favorite jarred tomato salsa onto the salmon, pop it in the oven and preparing dinner becomes a 15-minute affair.

2	medium plum tomatoes, chopped
1	small onion, coarsely chopped
1	clove garlic, peeled and quartered
1	jalapeño pepper, seeded and chopped
2	teaspoons cider vinegar
1	teaspoon chili powder
½	teaspoon ground cumin
½	teaspoon salt
2-4	dashes hot sauce
1 ½	pounds wild salmon fillet, skinned (*see Notes*) and cut into 6 portions

1. Preheat oven to 400°F.
2. Place tomatoes, onion, garlic, jalapeno, vinegar, chili powder, cumin, salt and hot sauce to taste in a food processor; process until finely diced and uniform.
3. Place salmon in a large roasting pan; spoon the salsa on top. Roast until the salmon is flaky on the outside but still pink inside, about 15 minutes.

NOTES:

Wild-caught salmon from the Pacific are more sustainably fished and have a larger, more stable population. For more information, visit Monterey Bay Aquarium Seafood Watch at *seafoodwatch.org*.

To skin a salmon fillet, place it skin-side down and, starting at the tail end, slip a long, sharp knife between flesh and skin, holding the skin down with your other hand. Gently push the blade along at a 30° angle, without cutting through fillet or skin.

Halibut Roasted with Red Bell Peppers, Onions & Russet Potatoes

ACTIVE TIME: 20 minutes

TOTAL: 1 hour

MAKES: 4 servings

H✂W   H♥H

PER SERVING: 343 calories; 10 g fat (2 g sat, 6 g mono); 83 mg cholesterol; 29 g carbohydrate; 0 g added sugars; 35 g protein; 4 g fiber; 417 mg sodium; 1,395 mg potassium.

NUTRITION BONUS: Vitamin C (120% daily value), Potassium (40% dv), Vitamin A (31% dv), Magnesium (19% dv), Folate (17% dv).

SERVE WITH:

Baby spinach and arugula salad

This all-in-one dish—protein and sides—cooks in a single pan, but the potatoes and veggies take longer to roast, so the fish is added only for the final 10 or 15 minutes. The firm flesh of halibut works well with this recipe, but feel free to substitute salmon, cod or any other thick fish. You can also add rosemary, basil or even mint to the gremolata, a classic Italian seasoning of parsley, garlic and lemon zest.

- 2   russet potatoes (about 1 pound), scrubbed, halved lengthwise and cut into ½-inch spears
- 2   tablespoons extra-virgin olive oil
- 1   large red bell pepper, cut into eight ½-inch wedges
- 1   large white onion, peeled and cut into ¼-inch wedges
- ½   teaspoon salt, divided
     Freshly ground pepper to taste
- 2   tablespoons coarsely chopped flat-leaf parsley
- 2   teaspoons coarsely chopped lemon zest
- 1   teaspoon dried oregano
- 1   clove garlic, crushed
- 1 ½   pounds Pacific halibut fillet (about ¾ inch thick; *see Note*), skinned and cut into 4 portions
     Lemon wedges

1. Preheat oven to 400°F. Place potatoes in a large roasting pan or on a large rimmed baking sheet; drizzle with oil and turn to coat evenly. Add bell pepper and onion. Season with ¼ teaspoon salt and pepper.
2. Roast the vegetables, turning the potatoes once or twice and moving the pepper and onion pieces around so they brown evenly, until the potatoes are starting to brown and are almost tender, about 35 minutes.
3. While the vegetables are roasting, finely chop parsley, lemon zest, oregano and garlic together to make gremolata. Season halibut with remaining ¼ teaspoon salt and pepper, then sprinkle with 2 teaspoons gremolata.
4. Remove the pan from the oven. Increase oven temperature to 450°. Push the vegetables to the sides of the pan and place the halibut in the center. Spoon some of the onions and peppers over the halibut. Arrange the potatoes around the edges, turning the browned sides up.
5. Roast until the vegetables are browned and tender and the halibut is opaque in the center, 10 to 15 minutes more, depending on the thickness of the fish. Sprinkle the remaining gremolata on top. Serve with lemon wedges.

NOTE: **Wild-caught halibut** from the Pacific is sustainably fished and has a larger, more stable population, according to the Monterey Bay Aquarium Seafood Watch (*seafoodwatch.org*).

Whole Roasted Lemon-Herb Chicken on a Bed of Vegetables

Roast chicken is always a welcome treat, but here it gets the added bonus of a mixture of vegetables that cook along with it in the pan, absorbing all the luscious drippings. The chicken is seasoned under the skin before roasting, which flavors the meat nicely. (Photograph: page 90.)

- ¼ cup fresh sage leaves, divided
- ¼ cup fresh thyme sprigs, divided
- 2 lemons, divided
- 2 teaspoons minced garlic
- 2 tablespoons extra-virgin olive oil, divided
- 1 teaspoon salt, divided
- ¾ teaspoon freshly ground pepper, divided
- 1 small onion, quartered
- 1 4- to 4½-pound chicken
- 4 large carrots, cut into ½-inch chunks
- 3 medium turnips, peeled (*see Note*) and cut into ½-inch cubes
- 2 celeriac roots (1½-2 pounds total), peeled (*see Note*) and cut into ½-inch cubes

1. Position rack in lower third of oven; preheat to 400°F.
2. Chop 8 sage leaves and place in a bowl with 2 teaspoons thyme leaves. Squeeze the juice from 1 lemon into the bowl. Add garlic, 1 tablespoon oil, ¾ teaspoon salt and ½ teaspoon pepper; mix well.
3. Pierce the remaining lemon all over with a fork. Cram the lemon, onion and the remaining sage and thyme into the chicken cavity.
4. Place the chicken breast-side up on a cutting board. Use your hands to gently loosen the skin covering the breast, thighs and the top end of the drumsticks. Smear the lemon-herb mixture under the skin, covering as much of the meat as possible.
5. Toss carrots, turnips and celeriac in a large bowl with the remaining 1 tablespoon oil and ¼ teaspoon each salt and pepper until well coated.
6. Place the chicken breast-side up in a large roasting pan (but not on a rack). Scatter the vegetables around the chicken. Roast, stirring the vegetables occasionally, until an instant-read thermometer inserted into the thickest part of a thigh without touching bone registers 165°F, 1 to 1¼ hours.
7. Transfer the chicken to a clean cutting board and let rest for 10 minutes before carving. Transfer the vegetables from the roasting pan to a serving dish with a slotted spoon, leaving behind as much of the fat as possible. Serve the chicken with the vegetables.

NOTE: To peel turnips and celeriac (also called celery root), cut off one end of the root to create a flat surface so you can keep it steady on the cutting board. Follow the contour of the vegetable with your knife to remove the skin. Or, if you use a vegetable peeler, be sure to peel around the root at least three times to ensure that all the fibrous skin is removed.

ACTIVE TIME: 40 minutes
TOTAL: 2¼ hours

MAKES: 6 servings, 3-4 ounces chicken & ⅔ cup vegetables each

H✕W   H↑F   H♥H
PER SERVING (WITHOUT SKIN): 343 calories; 13 g fat (3 g sat, 6 g mono); 98 mg cholesterol; 21 g carbohydrate; 0 g added sugars; 35 g protein; 5 g fiber; 669 mg sodium; 914 mg potassium
NUTRITION BONUS: Vitamin A (162% daily value), Vitamin C (50% dv), Potassium (26% dv), Zinc (19% dv), Magnesium (15% dv).

SERVE WITH:

Spinach sautéed with minced garlic and crushed red pepper

Roast Chicken with Pomegranate Glaze

ACTIVE TIME: 30 minutes

TOTAL: 1¹/2 hours

TO MAKE AHEAD: Rub the chicken with the spice mixture (Step 2), cover and refrigerate for up to 1 day. Let stand at room temperature for about 20 minutes before roasting.

MAKES: 6 servings

H✂W   H♥H

PER SERVING (WITHOUT SKIN):
317 calories; 10 g fat (2 g sat, 4 g mono); 98 mg cholesterol; 23 g carbohydrate; 14 g added sugars; 34 g protein; 4 g fiber; 716 mg sodium; 699 mg potassium.

NUTRITION BONUS: Potassium & Vitamin C (20% daily value), Zinc (17% dv).

SERVE WITH:

Whole-wheat couscous studded with chopped dates, dried apricots and shelled pistachios

Sumac and pomegranate give this exotic, Middle Eastern-themed roast chicken a sweet but also tart and citrusy flavor. If you can't get sumac, some grated lemon zest will work with equal effect. For the best results, rub the chicken with the spice mixture earlier in the day, or even the day ahead, so all the flavors can really sink in.

- **1** tablespoon ground sumac (*see Note*) *or* 2 teaspoons lemon zest
- **1** tablespoon kosher salt
- **1** 4-pound chicken
- **6** cups sliced cored fennel (2-3 large bulbs)
- **1** large yellow onion, chopped
- **2** teaspoons extra-virgin olive oil
- **¹/2** cup pomegranate molasses (*see Note, page 212*)
- **2** tablespoons honey
- **1** teaspoon freshly ground pepper
  Pomegranate seeds for garnish (*see Note, page 212*)

1. Preheat oven to 425°F.
2. Combine sumac (or lemon zest) and salt in a small bowl. Remove giblets from chicken (if included) and trim any excess skin; pat dry. Loosen the skin over the breast and thigh meat and rub the salt mixture under the skin plus a little on the skin. Tuck the wings under and tie the legs together with kitchen string, if desired.
3. Combine fennel and onion in a large roasting pan and toss with oil to coat. Place the chicken, breast-side up, on the vegetables.
4. Roast the chicken and vegetables for 20 minutes. Turn the chicken over, stir the vegetables and cook for 20 minutes more.
5. Combine pomegranate molasses, honey and pepper in a small bowl. Transfer half the mixture to a small microwave-safe bowl and set aside to serve with the chicken.
6. Turn the chicken over one more time (so it is breast-side up) and stir the vegetables again. Reduce oven temperature to 400°. Brush the chicken all over with the pomegranate mixture in the bowl. Continue to roast until an instant-read thermometer inserted into a thigh without touching bone registers 165°, 20 to 30 minutes more.
7. Transfer the chicken to a clean cutting board and let rest for 10 minutes. Meanwhile, heat the pomegranate mixture in the microwave on High until heated through, about 45 seconds. Remove the string from the chicken, if necessary, and carve the chicken. Serve with the fennel and onion, drizzled with the warm glaze. Sprinkle with pomegranate seeds, if desired.

NOTE: The tart red berries of the Mediterranean sumac bush add fruity, sour flavor to many regional dishes. Find **ground sumac** in Middle Eastern markets, specialty food shops and online at *penzeys.com*. Or use 2 teaspoons freshly grated lemon zest in place of the sumac.

Orange-Rosemary Glazed Chicken

ACTIVE TIME: 15 minutes
TOTAL: 50 minutes

MAKES: 4 servings

H✕W   H♥H

PER SERVING: 181 calories; 4 g fat
(1 g sat, 2 g mono); 68 mg
cholesterol; 10 g carbohydrate;
8 g added sugars; 25 g protein;
0 g fiber; 213 mg sodium;
213 mg potassium.

SERVE WITH:

Steamed broccoli florets and
wild rice pilaf

Orange marmalade, a touch of sherry vinegar and fresh rosemary create a glaze that dresses up plain baked chicken. If you like, you can use the same glaze for roasted pork tenderloin or even boneless pork loin chops.

- **2** bone-in chicken breast halves (about 12 ounces each), skin removed, trimmed
- **¼** teaspoon salt
  Freshly ground pepper to taste
- **1½** teaspoons chopped fresh rosemary, divided
- **3** tablespoons orange marmalade
- **2** tablespoons sherry vinegar, malt vinegar *or* cider vinegar
- **1** teaspoon extra-virgin olive oil

1. Preheat oven to 400°F. Coat a 9-by-13-inch or similar small roasting pan with cooking spray.
2. Cut each chicken breast in half on the diagonal to get 4 portions about equal in weight. (Two will be smaller but thicker, the other two larger but thinner.) Season chicken on both sides with salt and pepper and place, bone-side up, in the prepared pan. Sprinkle with 1 teaspoon rosemary.
3. Bake the chicken for 20 minutes. Meanwhile, combine the remaining ½ teaspoon rosemary, marmalade, vinegar and oil in a small bowl.
4. Turn the chicken pieces over and top with the marmalade mixture. Bake until the chicken is no longer pink in the center, 15 to 20 minutes more (check after 10 minutes). Serve immediately, spooning the sauce from the pan over the chicken.

Bistro Beef Tenderloin

Dijon mustard and fresh herbs give this simple-to-prepare, yet elegant beef tenderloin a classic Parisian flair. To ensure even roasting and easy carving, be sure to trim off any visible "silver skin"—the translucent, tough membrane lying along the outside curve of the tenderloin.

1	3-pound beef tenderloin, trimmed
2	tablespoons extra-virgin olive oil
1	teaspoon kosher salt
½	teaspoon freshly ground pepper
⅔	cup chopped mixed fresh herbs, such as chives, parsley, chervil, tarragon, thyme
2	tablespoons Dijon mustard

1. Preheat oven to 400°F.
2. Tie kitchen string around tenderloin in three places so it doesn't flatten while roasting. Rub the tenderloin with oil; pat on salt and pepper. Place in a large roasting pan.
3. Roast, turning two or three times during roasting to ensure even cooking, until a thermometer inserted into the thickest part of the tenderloin registers 140°F (*see Note*) for medium-rare, about 45 minutes. Transfer to a cutting board; let rest for 10 minutes. Remove the string.
4. Place herbs on a large plate. Coat the tenderloin evenly with mustard; then roll in the herbs, pressing gently to adhere. Slice and serve.

NOTE: The **internal temperature** of roasted meat rises as it rests—how much depends on the size of the meat, how long it rests and the temperature at which it was cooking. Our rule of thumb is that the internal temperature will rise 5° to 10° per 10 minutes of resting.

ACTIVE TIME: 25 minutes
TOTAL: 1 hour 10 minutes
EQUIPMENT: Kitchen string

MAKES: about 12 servings

H✖W   H♥H

PER 3-OUNCE SERVING: 173 calories; 9 g fat (3 g sat, 4 g mono); 61 mg cholesterol; 0 g carbohydrate; 0 g added sugars; 22 g protein; 0 g fiber; 172 mg sodium; 295 mg potassium.
NUTRITION BONUS: Zinc (27% daily value).

SERVE WITH:

Sliced potatoes, sautéed in extra-virgin olive oil until tender and golden, and steamed asparagus spears

Better Than Mom's Meatloaf

ACTIVE TIME: 20 minutes

TOTAL: 1 hour 25 minutes

MAKES: 8 servings

H✱W   H❤H

PER SERVING: 209 calories; 12 g fat
(4 g sat, 5 g mono); 88 mg
cholesterol; 5 g carbohydrate;
1 g added sugars; 20 g protein;
0 g fiber; 381 mg sodium;
348 mg potassium.
NUTRITION BONUS: Zinc (21% daily
value).

SERVE WITH:

Baked potatoes and baby
lima beans sautéed with diced
tomatoes and frozen corn

A traditional meatloaf is made with ground beef, pork and veal; here we replace the veal with ground turkey for a tender, flavorful and lean result. This is a free-form loaf baked on a baking sheet, but you can also speed up the cooking and make sweet little individual loaves by making this in a muffin tin.

8	ounces lean ground beef
8	ounces lean ground pork
8	ounces ground turkey breast
1	large egg, lightly beaten
¼	cup quick-cooking oats
¼	cup chopped fresh parsley
¼	cup ketchup, divided
3	tablespoons low-fat milk
1	small onion, chopped
¾	teaspoon salt
⅛	teaspoon freshly ground pepper
1½	teaspoons Worcestershire sauce

1. Preheat oven to 375°F. Line a 9-by-13-inch or similar small roasting pan or a rimmed baking sheet with foil and coat the foil with cooking spray.
2. Mix beef, pork, turkey, egg, oats, parsley, 2 tablespoons ketchup, milk, onion, salt and pepper in a large bowl.
3. With dampened hands, form the mixture into a free-form 7-by-4-inch loaf on the prepared pan. Combine the remaining 2 tablespoons ketchup and Worcestershire sauce and spread over the top of the meatloaf.
4. Bake until an instant-read thermometer inserted into the center of the loaf registers 165°F, 50 minutes to 1 hour. Let cool about 10 minutes before slicing.

MINI MEATLOAF VARIATION: To make individual mini meatloaves, you can bake the recipe in a muffin tin instead. Coat 8 standard-size muffin cups with cooking spray. Form the meatloaf mixture into 8 balls and place in the prepared muffin cups. Spread about ½ teaspoon of the ketchup-Worcestershire sauce over each mini loaf. Bake for 25 to 30 minutes.

Garlic-Roasted Pork

Sometimes it only takes a few ingredients to achieve truly mouthwatering results. That's the case with this simple, Puerto Rican-style pork roast, which can be prepped and in the oven in about 10 minutes, and is bursting with garlicky flavor. Leftover slices, layered with pickles, Swiss cheese, mustard and mayo, make an awesome sandwich on crusty baguette.

6   cloves garlic, crushed and peeled
2   tablespoons extra-virgin olive oil
1   tablespoon dried oregano
1   teaspoon paprika
1   teaspoon salt
½   teaspoon freshly ground pepper
1   2-pound boneless pork loin, trimmed

1. Combine garlic, oil, oregano, paprika, salt and pepper in a food processor or blender and puree. Rub pork all over with the seasoning mix and wrap tightly with plastic wrap or place in a large sealable plastic bag. Let marinate in the refrigerator for at least 20 minutes or up to 1 day.
2. Preheat oven to 350°F.
3. Remove the pork from the plastic and place in a 9-by-13-inch or similar small roasting pan. Roast, uncovered, until an instant-read thermometer inserted in the center registers 145°F, 50 minutes to 1 hour. Let rest for 10 minutes, then slice and serve.

ACTIVE TIME: 10 minutes
TOTAL: 1 hour 20 minutes
TO MAKE AHEAD: Prepare through Step 1 up to 1 day ahead.

MAKES: 8 servings

H✕W   H♥H
PER SERVING: 202 calories; 11 g fat (3 g sat, 6 g mono); 64 mg cholesterol; 1 g carbohydrate; 0 g added sugars; 23 g protein; 0 g fiber; 337 mg sodium; 358 mg potassium.

SERVE WITH:

Black beans spiked with lime juice and a salad of sliced summer tomatoes and onions drizzled with olive oil

Molasses-Glazed Pork with Sweet Potatoes

ACTIVE TIME: 20 minutes

TOTAL: 2 1/4 hours (including 1 hour marinating)

TO MAKE AHEAD: Prepare through Step 1 and marinate pork overnight.

MAKES: 6 servings

H✂W   H♥H

PER SERVING: 288 calories; 7 g fat (2 g sat, 3 g mono); 74 mg cholesterol; 31 g carbohydrate; 6 g added sugars; 26 g protein; 4 g fiber; 448 mg sodium; 992 mg potassium.

NUTRITION BONUS: Vitamin A (242% daily value), Vitamin C (37% dv), Potassium (28% dv), Magnesium (25% dv), Folate (21% dv), Zinc (18% dv), Iron (16% dv).

SERVE WITH:

Yellow summer squash, sautéed with chopped onions

The mineral-rich flavor of molasses combined with fresh lime juice, crushed garlic and earthy ground cumin makes a sweet-and-tart glaze that enhances both the pork and the sweet potatoes. The okra puts a taste of the South in this homey dish.

4	cloves garlic, peeled
3/4	teaspoon salt, divided
3 1/2	tablespoons molasses, divided
3 1/2	tablespoons lime juice, divided
2	teaspoons ground cumin
1/2	teaspoon freshly ground pepper, divided
2	12-ounce pork tenderloins, trimmed
3/4	cup reduced-sodium chicken broth
1	tablespoon extra-virgin olive oil
2	medium red onions, cut into 8 wedges each
3	medium sweet potatoes, peeled, halved lengthwise and cut into 1-inch slices
1	10-ounce package frozen whole okra
1	tablespoon chopped fresh thyme *or* 1 teaspoon dried thyme leaves

1. Mash garlic and 1/2 teaspoon salt into a paste with the side of a chef's knife. Transfer to a large shallow dish. Stir in 2 tablespoons molasses, 2 tablespoons lime juice, cumin and 1/4 teaspoon pepper. Add pork and coat well. Cover and marinate in the refrigerator, turning occasionally, for at least 1 hour or overnight.
2. Preheat oven to 450°F.
3. Whisk broth, oil, the remaining 1 1/2 tablespoons each molasses and lime juice in a large roasting pan. Add onions, sweet potatoes, okra and thyme; season with the remaining 1/4 teaspoon each salt and pepper and toss well. Cover tightly with foil.
4. Bake until the sweet potatoes begin to soften, 25 to 30 minutes.
5. Push the vegetables to the sides. Place the tenderloins in the center and pour any remaining marinade over them. Roast, uncovered, until just a trace of pink remains in the center and an instant-read thermometer inserted in the thickest part registers 155°F, 30 to 35 minutes. Transfer the pork to a cutting board and let rest for 5 minutes. Slice thinly on the diagonal. Serve with the vegetables.

Rosemary & Garlic Crusted Pork Loin with Butternut Squash & Potatoes

Yukon Gold potatoes and orange-hued butternut squash soak up all the garlic- and herb-infused flavor of this pork roast to make a gorgeous and savory side dish. If that weren't enough, a quick, roasting-pan gravy made at the end provides the au jus *that ties the whole dish together.*

ACTIVE TIME: 20 minutes
TOTAL: 1 3/4 hours

MAKES: 8 servings

H✂W   H♥H
PER SERVING: 271 calories; 8 g fat (2 g sat, 4 g mono); 49 mg cholesterol; 22 g carbohydrate; 0 g added sugars; 22 g protein; 3 g fiber; 223 mg sodium; 532 mg potassium.
NUTRITION BONUS: Vitamin A (95% daily value), Vitamin C (42% dv), Potassium (15% dv).

SERVE WITH:

Sautéed kale, chard or broccoli rabe

- 3 tablespoons chopped fresh rosemary *or* 1 tablespoon dried
- 4 cloves garlic, minced
- 1 teaspoon kosher salt, divided
- ½ teaspoon freshly ground pepper, plus more to taste
- 1 2-pound boneless center-cut pork loin roast, trimmed
- 1 ½ pounds small Yukon Gold potatoes, scrubbed and cut into 1-inch cubes
- 4 teaspoons extra-virgin olive oil, divided
- 1 pound butternut squash, peeled, seeded and cut into 1-inch cubes
- ½ cup port *or* prune juice
- ½ cup reduced-sodium chicken broth

1. Preheat oven to 400°F.
2. Combine rosemary, garlic and ½ teaspoon each salt and pepper in a mortar; crush with the pestle to form a paste. (*Alternatively, finely chop the ingredients together on a cutting board.*)
3. Coat a large roasting pan with cooking spray. Place pork in the pan and rub the rosemary mixture all over it. Toss potatoes with 2 teaspoons oil and ¼ teaspoon salt in a medium bowl; scatter along one side of the pork. (*See Note.*)
4. Roast the pork and potatoes for 30 minutes. Meanwhile, toss squash with the remaining 2 teaspoons oil, ¼ teaspoon salt and pepper in a medium bowl.
5. Carefully turn the pork over. Scatter the squash along the other side. Continue roasting until an instant-read thermometer inserted in the center of the pork registers 155°F, 30 to 40 minutes more.
6. Transfer the pork to a carving board; tent with foil and let stand for 10 to 15 minutes. If the vegetables are tender, transfer them to a bowl, cover and keep warm. If not, continue roasting until they are browned and tender, 10 to 15 minutes more.
7. After removing the vegetables, place the roasting pan over medium heat and add port (or prune juice); bring to a boil, stirring to scrape up any browned bits. Simmer for 2 minutes. Add broth and bring to a simmer. Simmer for a few minutes to intensify the flavor. Add any juices that have accumulated on the carving board.
8. To serve, carve the pork and serve with the roasted vegetables and pan sauce.

NOTE: By placing the potatoes along one side of the roast and the squash along the other, you have the flexibility of removing one of the vegetables if it is done before the other.

Roast Leg of Lamb, Cauliflower & Shallots

Here we slather lamb with a tarragon-and-parsley rub and roast it with shallots and cool-weather-loving cauliflower. Experiment with colored varieties of cauliflower to wow guests or try it with romanesco—the striking spiral-covered relative of broccoli and cauliflower.

1   **cup fresh tarragon leaves**
1   **cup flat-leaf parsley leaves**
4   **tablespoons extra-virgin olive oil, divided**
2   **tablespoons Dijon mustard**
2   **cloves garlic**
     Zest and juice of 1 lemon, divided
2   **teaspoons salt, divided**
1   **teaspoon freshly ground pepper**
1   **4- to 4½-pound boneless leg of lamb, trimmed**
1   **pound shallots**
2   **medium heads cauliflower *or* romanesco**
1   **tablespoon capers, rinsed**
½   **cup reduced-fat sour cream**

1. Preheat oven to 425°F.
2. Place tarragon and parsley in a food processor. Add 2 tablespoons oil, mustard, garlic, lemon zest, 1 teaspoon salt and pepper and process until fairly smooth. Transfer 3 tablespoons of the mixture to a medium bowl; set aside for Step 6.
3. If your lamb is in the oven-safe netted bag used by most supermarkets, remove the bag. Open the lamb so it's flat. Spread three-fourths of the remaining herb mixture over the surface of the lamb. Roll the lamb closed and tie in several spots with kitchen string so it is about the shape of a large football; transfer to a large roasting pan and spread the remaining herb mixture over the top and sides.
4. (If you prepared the recipe to this point the day before, let the lamb stand at room temperature while you prepare the vegetables.) Leaving the root end intact, peel and halve shallots (quarter larger ones). Trim and cut cauliflower (or romanesco) into 2-inch florets. Combine the shallots and cauliflower in a large bowl with the remaining 2 tablespoons oil and 1 teaspoon salt.
5. Roast the lamb in the center of the oven for 20 minutes. Add the vegetable mixture to the pan around the lamb. Continue to roast, stirring the vegetables every 20 minutes or so, until they are golden brown and an instant-read thermometer inserted into the thickest part of the meat registers 140°F (for medium-rare) to 145° (for medium), 1 hour to 1 hour 20 minutes more. Transfer the lamb to a clean cutting board and let rest for 10 minutes. Stir capers into the vegetables.
6. Add lemon juice and sour cream to the bowl with the reserved herb mixture; stir to combine. Slice the lamb and serve with the vegetables and sauce.

ACTIVE TIME: 1 hour
TOTAL: 2½ hours
TO MAKE AHEAD: Prepare through Step 3, loosely cover with plastic wrap and refrigerate for up to 1 day.
EQUIPMENT: Kitchen string

MAKES: 14 servings, about 3 ounces lamb & ½ cup vegetables each

H✖W   H♥H

PER SERVING: 326 calories; 20 g fat (7 g sat, 10 g mono); 86 mg cholesterol; 11 g carbohydrate; 0 g added sugars; 26 g protein; 2 g fiber; 460 mg sodium; 695 mg potassium.
NUTRITION BONUS: Vitamin C (83% daily value), Zinc (30% dv), Folate (21% dv), Potassium (20% dv), Vitamin A (16% dv), Iron (15% dv).

SERVE WITH:

Boiled red potatoes smashed with buttermilk, parsley, salt and pepper

Mint-Pesto Rubbed Leg of Lamb

ACTIVE TIME: 30 minutes

TOTAL: 2 hours

EQUIPMENT: Kitchen string

MAKES: 12-14 servings

PER SERVING: 250 calories; 17 g fat (6 g sat, 8 g mono); 79 mg cholesterol; 1 g carbohydrate; 0 g added sugars; 22 g protein; 0 g fiber; 247 mg sodium; 293 mg potassium.

NUTRITION BONUS: Zinc (26% daily value).

SERVE WITH:

Orzo pasta tossed with diced cucumber, parsley, olive oil and lemon juice

Forget mint jelly when you can coat your roast lamb in the intense flavor of this fresh mint, pine nut and cheese pesto. The pesto rub is also a terrific dip for fresh vegetables or a sauce for steamed vegetables. For ease of preparation, have your butcher "butterfly" the boneless leg of lamb (that is, open it up to a large, flat cut of meat) and be sure to ask that any visible fat be trimmed off.

- ½ cup packed fresh basil leaves
- ¼ cup packed fresh mint leaves
- ¼ cup packed fresh parsley leaves
- 2 tablespoons toasted pine nuts (*see Note*)
- 2 tablespoons grated Parmigiano-Reggiano cheese
- 2 tablespoons extra-virgin olive oil
- 1 clove garlic, peeled
- 1 teaspoon salt, divided
- ½ teaspoon freshly ground pepper
- 1 3½- to 4-pound boneless leg of lamb, butterflied and trimmed

1. Preheat oven to 350°F.
2. Place basil, mint, parsley, pine nuts, cheese, oil, garlic, ½ teaspoon salt and pepper in a food processor and process until fairly smooth. Sprinkle lamb all over with the remaining ½ teaspoon salt. Reserve 2 tablespoons of the pesto; spread the rest over the top side of the lamb and roll it closed. (It will not be a perfect cylinder.) Tie kitchen string around the roast in five places; do not tie too tightly or the pesto will squeeze out. Rub the reserved pesto over the outside of the lamb and place in a 9-by-13-inch or similar small roasting pan.
3. Roast the lamb until an instant-read thermometer inserted in the thickest part registers 140°F for medium-rare, about 1 hour 20 minutes. Transfer to a cutting board; let rest for 10 minutes. Carve the lamb, leaving the string in place to help hold the roast together.

NOTE: Toast pine nuts in a small dry skillet over medium-low heat, stirring constantly, until fragrant and lightly browned, 3 to 5 minutes.

Southwestern Chile-Cheese Casserole

CASSEROLE

The word "casserole" is used interchangeably to refer both to a cooking vessel as well as the type of food cooked in it. And there's no consensus on what a casserole—the cooking vessel—looks like. (In fact, many people call Dutch ovens, *see page 148*, casseroles.) When we call for a "casserole" we mean a shallow glass or ceramic dish. Sometimes these sorts of dishes have lids, but they are not necessary; you can use foil to cover dishes that need to be cooked covered. If you're only going to get one casserole dish, go for a 9-by-13-inch (or similar-size) one that holds 3 quarts. You may also want a smaller 7-by-11-inch or 2-quart dish. Glass dishes are great because they're inexpensive and available at the supermarket. Spend a little more and you can get a ceramic dish that looks pretty on the table and is safe to use under the broiler.

Southwestern Chile-Cheese Casserole

ACTIVE TIME: 35 minutes

TOTAL: 1 hour 20 minutes

TO MAKE AHEAD: Cover and refrigerate for up to 2 days. Reheat before serving.

MAKES: 12 servings

PER SERVING: 225 calories; 11 g fat (6 g sat, 3 g mono); 90 mg cholesterol; 12 g carbohydrate; 0 g added sugars; 20 g protein; 1 g fiber; 384 mg sodium; 188 mg potassium.

NUTRITION BONUS: Calcium (27% daily value).

SERVE WITH:

Refried black beans and fresh melon cubes tossed with lime juice and a pinch of salt

Home-toasted tortilla strips soak up a cheesy batter, laced with chiles, to create an eggy casserole that's a natural for dinner or brunch. Plus, it's just as good reheated as it is right out of the oven, so it's perfect for easy weekend entertaining. (Photograph: page 112.)

6	corn tortillas
4	large eggs, divided
⅓	cup all-purpose flour
1	teaspoon baking powder
¼	teaspoon salt
6	large egg whites *or* ¼ cup dried egg whites reconstituted according to package directions
2	16-ounce containers low-fat cottage cheese, preferably reduced-sodium
2½	cups shredded extra-sharp Cheddar cheese
4	4-ounce cans chopped mild green chiles
1	cup prepared tomato salsa (optional)

1. Preheat oven to 350°F. Coat a 9-by-13-inch (or similar-size 3-quart) baking dish with cooking spray.
2. Toast tortillas by placing one at a time directly on a burner (gas or electric) set at medium heat and turning frequently with tongs until charred in spots, 30 to 60 seconds. Cut the tortillas into 1-inch-wide strips.
3. Whisk 2 whole eggs in a large bowl until foamy. Add flour, baking powder and salt; whisk until smooth. Add the remaining 2 whole eggs and egg whites and whisk until smooth. Add cottage cheese, Cheddar cheese, chiles and tortilla strips and mix with a rubber spatula. Pour into the prepared baking dish.
4. Bake the casserole until set in the center and golden on top, 40 to 50 minutes. Let cool for 5 to 10 minutes. Cut into squares. Serve with salsa, if desired.

Tex-Mex Summer Squash Casserole

This cheese- and chile-studded squash casserole makes an excellent vegetarian entree, but in small servings can also be a great side for grilled meats and seafood. The jalapeños make this dish quite hot; if you prefer a milder version, use a second can of diced green chiles instead.

2¼ pounds summer squash, quartered lengthwise and thinly sliced crosswise (about 10 cups)

⅔ cup finely chopped yellow onion

1 4-ounce can chopped green chiles

½ cup chopped pickled jalapeños

½ teaspoon salt, or to taste

2¼ cups grated extra-sharp Cheddar cheese, divided

¼ cup all-purpose flour

¾ cup mild salsa

4 scallions, thinly sliced

¼ cup finely chopped red onion

1. Preheat oven to 400°F. Coat a 9-by-13-inch (or similar-size 3-quart) baking dish with cooking spray.
2. Combine squash, onion, chiles, jalapeños, salt and ¾ cup cheese in a large bowl. Sprinkle with flour; toss to coat. Spread the mixture in the prepared baking dish and cover with foil.
3. Bake the casserole until it is bubbling and the squash is tender, 35 to 45 minutes. Spoon salsa over the casserole and sprinkle with the remaining 1½ cups cheese. Bake, uncovered, until golden and heated through, 20 to 30 minutes. Sprinkle with scallions and red onion.

ACTIVE TIME: 20 minutes

TOTAL: 1½ hours

TO MAKE AHEAD: Cover and refrigerate for up to 2 days. Reheat, covered, at 350°F for about 40 minutes. Garnish just before serving.

MAKES: 12 servings

H⨉W

PER SERVING: 123 calories; 7 g fat (5 g sat, 2 g mono); 22 mg cholesterol; 8 g carbohydrate; 0 g added sugars; 7 g protein; 2 g fiber; 110 mg sodium; 337 mg potassium.

NUTRITION BONUS: Vitamin C (37% daily value), Calcium (18% dv).

SERVE WITH:

Salad of cherry tomato halves, diced cucumber and black olives tossed in red-wine vinegar and olive oil, topped with a sprinkle of fresh chopped oregano

Italian White Bean & Polenta Bake

ACTIVE TIME: 35 minutes
TOTAL: 1 hour 50 minutes

MAKES: 10 servings

H)(W   H↑F   H♥H
PER SERVING: 242 calories; 8 g fat
(3 g sat, 3 g mono); 69 mg
cholesterol; 35 g carbohydrate;
0 g added sugars; 13 g protein;
8 g fiber; 633 mg sodium;
475 mg potassium.
NUTRITION BONUS: Folate (29% daily
value), Calcium (20% dv), Zinc
(15% dv).

SERVE WITH:

Roasted broccolini tossed with
salt, pepper and a drizzle of
good balsamic vinegar

This hearty polenta bake is stuffed with artichoke hearts, tomatoes and gooey pockets of Cheddar cheese. Black olives are pretty on top but green olives give it a special tang.

  1   **tablespoon minced garlic**
  1   **teaspoon salt**
  3   **large eggs**
  2   **tablespoons chopped fresh sage**
  1   **teaspoon freshly ground pepper**
  3   **cups water**
  2   **cups stone-ground cornmeal (*see Note*)**
  2   **15-ounce cans *or* one 30-ounce can white beans, rinsed**
  2   **cups diced plum tomatoes**
  1   **9- to 10-ounce package frozen artichoke hearts, thawed and chopped**
  ¾   **cup diced sharp Cheddar cheese**
  ½   **cup chopped pitted olives, divided**
  ½   **cup finely shredded Parmesan cheese**

1. Preheat oven to 400°F. Coat a 9-by-13-inch (or similar-size 3-quart) baking dish with cooking spray.
2. Mash together garlic and salt with the back of a spoon in a large bowl until a paste forms. Add eggs, sage and pepper; whisk until blended. Whisk in water and cornmeal. Add beans, tomatoes, artichokes, Cheddar cheese and ¼ cup chopped olives and stir to combine. Pour into the prepared baking dish.
3. Bake until set in the middle, 45 to 55 minutes. Sprinkle with Parmesan and the remaining ¼ cup olives. Bake until the cheese is melted, 5 to 10 minutes more. Let cool for 20 minutes before serving.

NOTE: Look for whole-grain, stone-ground **cornmeal** in the natural-foods section of super-markets, in natural-foods stores or online at *kingarthurflour.com* and *bobsredmill.com*. It's available in a range of coarseness—fine, medium and coarse grind. For most recipes, any type of grind can be used, but coarse grind will give the finished dish a chewier, grainier texture. If it isn't labeled, it's typically between fine and medium grind.

They're Back...

The return of the casserole, America's favorite comfort food

"Care in cooking, distinction in seasoning and presentation, can make even a tin of tuna memorable" is the reassuring advice on casseroles offered in my *Joy of Cooking* from 1962. As a young working mother in the 1960s with a penchant for entertaining and precious little time, the casserole, along with the electric can opener and the freezer, was my salvation. They were expedient—a one-dish dinner could be assembled in a jiffy, slowly baked in an attractive dish while other chores were done, and whisked to the table with a flourish. Casseroles were perfect at patio parties and buffet brunches, a welcome gift to bring a new neighbor and a family mainstay before fast-food restaurants and takeout changed our eating habits forever.

One-dish dinners, of course, have been on the menu since ancient days; in fact, the French word *casserole* (which refers to both the cooking vessel and the finished dish) was probably derived from the Greek *kyathion*, a small ladle. In this country, as Jean Anderson noted in her book *The American Century Cookbook* (Clarkson Potter, 1997), Americans have been making casseroles since Colonial times—they didn't call them that, but they "scalloped" everything from ham to haddock. Anderson, quoting *Marian Harland's Complete Cook Book* (1903), explains that "the French name 'casserole' has a certain amount of terror for the American housewife… She, a plain, everyday house-keeper, would not dare aspire to the use of a casserole. And yet the casserole itself is no more appalling than a saucepan… Like many other objects of dread this, when once known, is converted into a friend." Harland clearly saw what was coming. Soon, books like *How to Cook in Casserole Dishes* (1912) and *Two Hundred Recipes for Cooking in Casseroles* (1914) were rolling off the presses, fueling the casserole craze.

The economical casserole was a boon during World War I, but perhaps even more so to the burgeoning women's liberation movement of the '20s. *One-Piece Dinners* (1924) by Mary D. Chambers offers a fascinating glimpse into the culture of the period: "The One-piece Dinner, ladies, is like the One-piece Dress. The dress, including waist, skirt, girdle, frills, and draperies, is made in one piece and put on all at once. This saves time, it saves motions, and the dress is as pretty a thing as you could wish to wear. Similarly the One-piece Dinner, including meat, starchy vegetable, green or root vegetable, sauce or gravy, and 'frills,' is put on all at once in the same pot," naturally, she continues, saving time, motion (especially dishwashing) and fuel.

Chambers writes of the advantages of long-cooking casseroles like Duck in Beanpot that they enable the cook to "go off to the matinee, the club, the bridge party or the golf grounds."

Casseroling, though, really reached the recipe hit parade in the '50s with concoctions that invariably included canned soup, oodles of cheese and crunchy toppings, from fried onion bits to corn chips.

Today, mention the word "casserole" in many circles and you'll get a response as horrified as that of those early-20th-century housewives—the result of too many experiences with gloppy dishes hidden under crushed potato chips, along with a modern-day awareness of just what's in all those processed products that composed the post-World War II casserole. Nevertheless, all that's good about the casserole—the make-ahead, feed-a-crowd, one-container convenience—is as relevant to today's cook as it ever has been.

A culinary historian and food journalist, Meryle Evans edited The American Heritage Cookbook, *served as editorial director of the 18-volume* Southern Heritage Cookbook Library *and is a contributing editor at* Food Arts.

> *All that's good about the casserole—the make-ahead, feed-a-crowd, one-container convenience— is as relevant to today's cook as it ever has been.*
>
> *—Meryle Evans*

Mediterranean Roasted Fish & Vegetables

Here's a roasted fish entree plus side dish all in one package. Besides the convenience of one roasting pan, both the fish and the vegetables get the benefit of their flavors mingling as they cook side by side. The recipe calls for a firm white fish, such as striped bass or cod, but salmon would also work beautifully with the fennel, potatoes and tomatoes.

ACTIVE TIME: 30 minutes
TOTAL: 1 ½ hours

MAKES: 6 servings

H✖W   H⬆F   H❤H

PER SERVING: 349 calories; 8 g fat (1 g sat, 4 g mono); 49 mg cholesterol; 43 g carbohydrate; 0 g added sugars; 28 g protein; 7 g fiber; 644 mg sodium; 1,551 mg potassium.
NUTRITION BONUS: Vitamin C (53% daily value), Potassium (44% dv), Magnesium (29% dv), Folate (20% dv), Iron (19% dv).

3	cloves garlic, divided
2	tablespoons extra-virgin olive oil, divided
1	teaspoon anchovy paste (optional)
2	small bulbs fennel, cored and thinly sliced
1	large onion, sliced
6	small potatoes, such as Yukon Gold, peeled, halved and thinly sliced
1	14-ounce can plum tomatoes, chopped and juice reserved
¼	cup water
1	teaspoon salt, divided
¼	teaspoon freshly ground pepper
3	tablespoons fine dry breadcrumbs (*see Note, page 212*)
2	teaspoons fennel seeds, crushed
1	teaspoon freshly grated lemon zest
1½	pounds striped bass, Pacific halibut *or* Pacific cod (*see Note*), skinned and cut into 6 portions

1. Preheat oven to 450°F.
2. Mince 2 garlic cloves and place in a small bowl. Whisk in 1½ tablespoons oil and anchovy paste, if using. Combine fennel and onion in a 9-by-13-inch (or similar-size 3-quart) baking dish; add the garlic mixture and toss to coat.
3. Roast the fennel mixture, uncovered, stirring occasionally, until softened, 20 to 25 minutes.
4. Add potatoes, tomatoes and their juice, water, ¾ teaspoon salt and pepper. Cover tightly with foil and bake until the potatoes are tender, 35 to 40 minutes more.
5. Meanwhile, mince the remaining garlic clove and place in a small bowl. Add breadcrumbs, fennel seeds, lemon zest, the remaining ½ tablespoon oil and ¼ teaspoon salt; season with pepper. Mix with your fingers until blended.
6. When the potatoes are tender, place fish on top of the vegetables and sprinkle the breadcrumb mixture over all. Roast, uncovered, until the fish is opaque in the center and the breadcrumbs are browned, 10 to 15 minutes. Serve immediately.

NOTE: Look for U.S. wild-caught or farmed **striped bass** or U.S. wild-caught **Pacific halibut** or **cod** for this recipe. All are considered sustainable seafood choices according to Monterey Bay Aquarium Seafood Watch (*seafoodwatch.org*).

SERVE WITH:

Steamed green beans tossed with olive oil and a squeeze of lemon

Chicken Florentine Roll-Ups

ACTIVE TIME: 30 minutes
TOTAL: 1 hour 5 minutes
TO MAKE AHEAD: Prepare through Step 3 and refrigerate for up to 1 day.

MAKES: 8 servings

H✖W   H❤H

PER SERVING: 212 calories; 9 g fat (3 g sat, 2 g mono); 73 mg cholesterol; 5 g carbohydrate; 0 g added sugars; 26 g protein; 2 g fiber; 402 mg sodium; 424 mg potassium.
NUTRITION BONUS: Vitamin A (89% daily value), Magnesium (16% dv).

SERVE WITH:

Whole-grain pasta tossed with marinara sauce and steamed broccoli

Perfect for entertaining, these chicken cutlets are stuffed with spinach, sun-dried tomatoes, walnuts and just enough cream cheese to hold the filling together. Chicken cutlets are available at most supermarkets, but if you can't find them, make your own from boneless, skinless chicken breasts (see Notes). Make a double batch and freeze half the roll-ups individually wrapped in plastic, then just defrost and bake as you like. Serve topped with fresh diced tomatoes or marinara sauce and a sprinkling of fresh chopped basil.

1	**10-ounce package frozen chopped spinach, thawed and squeezed dry**
½	**cup reduced-fat cream cheese (Neufchâtel), at room temperature, or part-skim ricotta**
⅓	**cup thinly sliced soft sun-dried tomatoes (*see Notes*)**
¼	**cup finely chopped toasted walnuts (*see Note, page 212*)**
¾	**teaspoon salt, divided**
¾	**teaspoon freshly ground pepper, divided**
⅛	**teaspoon garlic powder**
8	**4-ounce chicken cutlets (about 2 pounds total; *see Notes*)**
½	**cup dry white wine**

1. Preheat oven to 375°F. Coat a 9-by-13-inch (or similar-size 3-quart) baking dish with cooking spray.
2. Mash spinach, cream cheese (or ricotta), sun-dried tomatoes, walnuts, ¼ teaspoon each salt and pepper and garlic powder with a fork in a medium bowl until well combined.
3. Place chicken cutlets on a work surface. Sprinkle both sides with the remaining ½ teaspoon each salt and pepper. Place about 2 tablespoons of the spinach mixture in the center of each cutlet. Roll up the chicken around the filling and secure each roll-up with 2 toothpicks; place in the prepared pan. Pour wine around the roll-ups. Cover the pan with foil.
4. Bake until an instant-read thermometer inserted into the thickest roll registers 165°F, 30 to 40 minutes. Slice with a serrated knife and serve.

NOTES:

Look for **soft sun-dried tomatoes** (*not* packed in oil) in the produce section of most supermarkets. If you can only find dry (and hard) sun-dried tomatoes, soak them in boiling water for about 20 minutes before using.

If you can't find **chicken cutlets** for this recipe, you can start with regular boneless, skinless chicken breasts and pound them until they are thin. Start with four 10- to 12-ounce chicken breasts, remove each tender and cut each breast in half into 2 roughly equal portions for eight 4-ounce portions. Place the chicken between pieces of plastic wrap. Pound with a rolling pin, meat mallet or heavy skillet until flattened to an even thickness, about ½ inch.

Oven-Barbecued Asian Chicken

This barbecued chicken is truly finger-licking good! You can make this with 2 bone-in chicken breasts (about 12 ounces each) instead of thighs and drumstick, if you prefer. Remove the skin and cut each chicken breast in half on the diagonal to get 4 portions about equal in weight. (Two will be smaller but thicker, the other two larger but thinner.)

ACTIVE TIME: 20 minutes

TOTAL: 1 hour 20 minutes

TO MAKE AHEAD: Prepare through Step 2; cover and refrigerate for up to 1 day. Let stand at room temperature while the oven preheats.

MAKES: 4 servings

PER SERVING: 361 calories; 16 g fat (4 g sat, 6 g mono); 144 mg cholesterol; 11 g carbohydrate; 4 g added sugars; 42 g protein; 1 g fiber; 547 mg sodium; 473 mg potassium.

NUTRITION BONUS: Zinc (29% daily value), Iron (16% dv).

1	bunch scallions
¼	cup hoisin sauce (*see Note, page 212*)
1	tablespoon reduced-sodium soy sauce
1	tablespoon minced fresh ginger
1	tablespoon minced garlic
1	teaspoon Asian hot sauce, such as Sriracha, or to taste
¼	teaspoon Chinese five-spice powder (*see Note, page 212*)
4	bone-in chicken thighs (1 ¼-1 ½ pounds total), skin removed and trimmed
4	chicken drumsticks (1-1 ¼ pounds total), skin removed (*see Note*), trimmed
1 ½	teaspoons toasted sesame seeds (*see Note, page 213*)

1. Preheat oven to 350°F. Coat a 9-by-13-inch (or similar-size 3-quart) baking dish with cooking spray.
2. Thinly slice ¼ cup scallion greens; set aside. Mince the whites. Whisk the scallion whites, hoisin sauce, soy sauce, ginger, garlic, hot sauce and five-spice powder in a large bowl. Add chicken and toss to coat. Arrange the chicken in an even layer in the prepared baking dish, meatier-side down. Pour any remaining sauce from the bowl over the chicken.
3. Bake, turning once halfway through so the meatier side is up, until an instant-read thermometer inserted into the thickest part without touching bone registers 165°F, about 1 hour. Transfer the chicken to a serving platter and top with any remaining sauce from the baking dish. Sprinkle with sesame seeds and the reserved scallion greens.

NOTE: **To remove the skin and thin layer of fat from chicken drumsticks**, tightly grip the skin from the meaty end of the drumstick with a paper towel and pull it down toward the end with the exposed bone until it comes off completely.

SERVE WITH:

. Sautéed zucchini with garlic and scallions and a side of brown rice

Arugula & Chicken Sausage Bread Pudding

ACTIVE TIME: 30 minutes

TOTAL: 1³/₄ hours

TO MAKE AHEAD: Prepare through Step 3; refrigerate overnight. Let stand at room temperature while the oven preheats. Bake as directed in Step 4.

MAKES: 6 servings

H✕W

PER SERVING: 271 calories; 11 g fat (4 g sat, 3 g mono); 157 mg cholesterol; 22 g carbohydrate; 2 g added sugars; 21 g protein; 4 g fiber; 665 mg sodium; 376 mg potassium.

NUTRITION BONUS: Folate (25% daily value), Calcium (23% dv), Vitamin A (18% dv), Magnesium (15% dv).

SERVE WITH:

Sautéed green beans and red peppers, seasoned with sea salt, freshly ground black pepper and a splash of rice-wine vinegar

Sure, you can have bread puddings for dessert, but savory versions make a hearty entree that you won't soon forget. Here we combine whole-grain bread and a lightened egg custard with peppery arugula, artichoke hearts, fontina cheese and chicken sausage, which comes in a multitude of varieties these days. The flavor of sausage will define the dish, so choose carefully. We tried and liked sweet Italian, apple and Chardonnay, and sun-dried tomato and spinach sausage in this recipe.

4	large eggs
4	large egg whites
1	cup nonfat milk
¹/₂	cup sliced fresh basil
2	tablespoons Dijon mustard
¹/₄	teaspoon salt
¹/₄	teaspoon freshly ground pepper
5	cups chopped arugula, wilted (*see Note*)
4	cups whole-grain bread, crusts removed if desired, cut into 1-inch cubes (about 8 ounces, 4-6 slices)
1	cup diced cooked chicken sausage (5 ounces)
³/₄	cup chopped artichoke hearts, frozen (thawed) *or* canned
³/₄	cup shredded fontina cheese

1. Preheat oven to 375°F. Coat an 11-by-7-inch (or similar-size 2-quart) baking dish with cooking spray.
2. Whisk eggs, egg whites and milk in a medium bowl. Add basil, mustard, salt and pepper and whisk to combine.
3. Toss arugula, bread, sausage and artichoke hearts in a large bowl. Add the egg mixture and toss well to coat. Transfer to the prepared baking dish and push down to compact. Cover with foil.
4. Bake until the custard has set, 40 to 45 minutes. Uncover, sprinkle with cheese and continue baking until the pudding is puffed and golden on top, 15 to 20 minutes more. Transfer to a wire rack and cool for 15 to 20 minutes before serving.

NOTE: **To wilt greens,** rinse thoroughly in cool water. Place in to a large microwave-safe bowl. Cover with plastic wrap and punch several holes in it. Microwave on High until wilted, 2 to 3 minutes. Squeeze out any excess moisture from the greens before adding them to the recipe.

Ham & Cheese Strata

A strata does very well if you assemble it ahead of time and then just bake it when you're ready. Or it's also good reheated if you want to bring it to a potluck. Here we've made a typically rich ham-and-cheese version healthier by losing a few egg yolks, using nonfat milk and swapping in nutritious, fiber-rich, whole-grain bread instead of white. Gruyère cheese has a delicious, nutty aroma and flavor, which means that with the relatively small amount in this recipe you still get a big impact.

4	large eggs
4	large egg whites
1	cup nonfat milk
2	tablespoons Dijon mustard
1	teaspoon minced fresh rosemary
¼	teaspoon freshly ground pepper
5	cups chopped spinach, wilted (*see Note*)
4	cups whole-grain bread, crusts removed if desired, cut into 1-inch cubes (about ½ pound, 4-6 slices)
1	cup diced ham steak (5 ounces)
½	cup chopped jarred roasted red peppers
¾	cup shredded Gruyère *or* Swiss cheese

1. Preheat oven to 375°F. Coat a 7-by-11-inch (or similar-size 2-quart) baking dish with cooking spray.
2. Whisk eggs, egg whites and milk in a medium bowl. Add mustard, rosemary and pepper; whisk to combine. Toss spinach, bread, ham and roasted red peppers in a large bowl. Add the egg mixture and toss well to coat. Transfer to the prepared baking dish and push down to compact. Cover with foil.
3. Bake until the custard has set, 40 to 45 minutes. Uncover, sprinkle with cheese and continue baking until the pudding is puffed and golden on top, 15 to 20 minutes more. Transfer to a wire rack and cool for 15 to 20 minutes before serving.

NOTE: **To wilt spinach,** rinse thoroughly with cool water. Transfer to a large microwave-safe bowl. Cover with plastic wrap and punch several holes in it. Microwave on High until wilted, 2 to 3 minutes. Squeeze out excess moisture before adding the spinach to the recipe.

ACTIVE TIME: 30 minutes

TOTAL: 1¾ hours

TO MAKE AHEAD: Prepare through Step 2; refrigerate overnight. Let stand at room temperature while the oven preheats. Bake as directed in Step 3.

MAKES: 6 servings

H✖W

PER SERVING: 286 calories; 10 g fat (4 g sat, 3 g mono); 150 mg cholesterol; 23 g carbohydrate; 2 g added sugars; 23 g protein; 4 g fiber; 809 mg sodium; 507 mg potassium.

NUTRITION BONUS: Vitamin A (74% daily value), Vitamin C (30% dv), Calcium & Folate (29% dv), Magnesium (19% dv), Iron & Zinc (16% dv).

SERVE WITH:

A simple salad of tomato wedges, sliced basil, red onion and a drizzle of olive oil and white-wine vinegar

Moroccan Bulgur & Pork Casserole

Fragrant with North African spices, this bulgur pilaf is ready to go in the oven in just 25 minutes. Vary the dish by substituting shrimp, Pacific cod fillets or chunks of boneless, skinless chicken thighs for the pork.

1	teaspoon salt
½	teaspoon ground cumin
½	teaspoon ground coriander
½	teaspoon ground ginger
¼	teaspoon chili powder
¼	teaspoon freshly ground pepper
⅛	teaspoon ground turmeric
⅛	teaspoon ground cinnamon
	Pinch of ground cloves
1	pound boneless pork loin chops *or* pork tenderloin, trimmed and cut into 1-inch cubes
1	cup water
	Zest of 1 lemon
¼	cup lemon juice
¾	cup bulgur (see Note)
1	15-ounce can chickpeas, rinsed
1	medium onion, finely chopped
½	cup raisins
½	cup chopped roasted red peppers, rinsed
¼	cup chopped fresh mint for garnish

1. Preheat oven to 375°F. Coat a 9-by-13-inch (or similar-size 3-quart) baking dish with cooking spray.
2. Combine salt, cumin, coriander, ginger, chili powder, pepper, turmeric, cinnamon and cloves in a medium bowl. Transfer 1 teaspoon of the mixture to another medium bowl, add pork and toss. Set aside.
3. Add water, lemon zest and juice to the remaining spice mixture; whisk to combine. Stir in bulgur, chickpeas, onion, raisins and red peppers. Transfer to the prepared baking dish and spread evenly. Cover with foil.
4. Bake for 15 minutes. Remove from the oven, carefully uncover and nestle the spiced pork into the bulgur mixture. Cover with foil again and continue to bake until most of the liquid is absorbed and the pork is just cooked through, 25 to 30 minutes more. Let stand, covered, for 5 minutes before serving. Serve sprinkled with mint, if desired.

NOTE: **Bulgur** is made by parboiling, drying and coarsely grinding or cracking wheat berries. Don't confuse bulgur with cracked wheat, which is just that—cracked wheat. Since the parboiling step is skipped, cracked wheat needs to cook longer. Look for bulgur in the natural-foods section of large supermarkets, near other grains.

ACTIVE TIME: 25 minutes
TOTAL: 1¼ hours

MAKES: 4 servings

H✂W   H⬆F   H❤H
PER SERVING: 403 calories; 8 g fat (2 g sat, 2 g mono); 66 mg cholesterol; 57 g carbohydrate; 0 g added sugars; 30 g protein; 11 g fiber; 964 mg sodium; 596 mg potassium.
NUTRITION BONUS: Vitamin C (22% daily value), Magnesium (19% dv), Potassium (17% dv), Zinc (16% dv).

SERVE WITH:

Mesclun green salad with grated carrots, slivered almonds, scallions and a light vinaigrette

Irish Lamb Stew

SLOW COOKER

Choose a slow cooker with an adjustable timer that lets you set the time manually and automatically switches to "warm" when the cook time is up. The switch-to-warm feature keeps your food a safe temperature, so you don't need to be there when it finishes. Slow cookers come in a range of sizes—for a good all-purpose size, choose a 5-to-6-quart one, which will work for all the recipes in this book. (*For more tips for slow-cooker success, see page 209.*)

Barley Risotto with Fennel

ACTIVE TIME: 30 minutes

SLOW-COOKER TIME: 2¾-3¾ hours on High or Low

TOTAL: 3¼ to 4¼ hours

TO PREP AHEAD: Prepare fennel bulb, carrot, shallot and garlic. Crush fennel seeds (Step 1) and add to vegetables. Combine broth, 1 cup water and wine. Refrigerate in separate covered containers for up to 1 day. Heat the cold liquid mixture to a simmer before adding to the slow cooker.

MAKES: 6 servings, generous 1 cup each

H✖W   H⬆F   H❤H

PER SERVING: 235 calories; 5 g fat (2 g sat, 1 g mono); 6 mg cholesterol; 36 g carbohydrate; 0 g added sugars; 9 g protein; 8 g fiber; 750 mg sodium; 467 mg potassium.

NUTRITION BONUS: Vitamin A (35% daily value), Vitamin C (18% dv).

SERVE WITH:

A salad made with a blend of sturdy, assertive greens, including escarole, radicchio and romaine

Here is a convenient alternative to a traditional stovetop risotto. The gentle, uniform heat of a slow cooker allows you to cook a creamy risotto without the usual frequent stirring. This one uses healthy, fiber-rich whole grains—either barley or brown rice—seasoned with Parmesan cheese, lemon zest and oil-cured olives.

2	teaspoons fennel seeds
1	large *or* 2 small bulbs fennel, cored and finely diced, plus 2 tablespoons chopped fronds
1	cup pearl barley *or* short-grain brown rice
1	small carrot, finely chopped
1	large shallot, finely chopped
2	cloves garlic, minced
4	cups reduced-sodium chicken broth *or* "no-chicken" broth
1-1½	cups water, divided
⅓	cup dry white wine
2	cups frozen French-cut green beans, thawed
½	cup grated Parmesan cheese
⅓	cup pitted oil-cured black olives, coarsely chopped
1	tablespoon freshly grated lemon zest
	Freshly ground pepper to taste

1. Coat a 4-quart or larger slow cooker with cooking spray. Crush fennel seeds with the bottom of a saucepan. Combine the fennel seeds, diced fennel, barley (or rice), carrot, shallot and garlic in the slow cooker. Add broth, 1 cup water and wine, and stir to combine.

2. Put the lid on and cook until the barley (or rice) is tender but pleasantly chewy and the risotto is thick and creamy, 2¾ to 3¾ hours on High or Low.

3. Stir in green beans; cover and continue cooking until heated through, about 15 minutes. Turn off the slow cooker and stir Parmesan, olives, lemon zest and pepper into the risotto. If it seems dry, heat the remaining ½ cup water and stir it in. Serve sprinkled with the chopped fennel fronds.

Squash, Chickpea & Red Lentil Stew

The slow-cooked North African-style vegetarian stew is loaded with protein-rich lentils and chickpeas along with plenty of vegetables. The lime juice and fresh cilantro, which are added at the end, give a bright finish to the dish.

3/4	cup dried chickpeas
2 1/2	pounds kabocha (*see Note*) *or* butternut squash, peeled, seeded and cut into 1-inch cubes
2	large carrots, peeled and cut into 1/2-inch pieces
1	large onion, chopped
1	cup red lentils
4	cups vegetable broth
2	tablespoons tomato paste
1	tablespoon minced fresh ginger
1 1/2	teaspoons ground cumin
1	teaspoon salt
1/4	teaspoon saffron (*see Note, page 213*)
1/4	teaspoon freshly ground pepper
1/4	cup lime juice
1/2	cup chopped roasted unsalted peanuts
1/4	cup packed fresh cilantro leaves, chopped

1. Soak chickpeas in enough cold water to cover them by 2 inches for 6 hours or overnight. (*Or use the quick-soak method: see Note, page 212.*) Drain when ready to use.
2. Combine the soaked chickpeas, squash, carrots, onion, lentils, broth, tomato paste, ginger, cumin, salt, saffron and pepper in a 6-quart slow cooker.
3. Put the lid on and cook on Low until the chickpeas are tender and the lentils have begun to break down, 5 to 6 1/2 hours.
4. Stir in lime juice. Serve sprinkled with peanuts and cilantro.

NOTE: **Kabocha** is a squash with a green-streaked rind and tender, sweet orange flesh. An average kabocha weighs two to three pounds.

ACTIVE TIME: 30 minutes

SLOW-COOKER TIME: 5-6 1/2 hours on Low

TOTAL: 8 hours (including the 1-hour quick-soak for chickpeas)

TO PREP AHEAD: Soak chickpeas. Prepare squash, carrots, onion and ginger; cover and refrigerate together in one container for up to 1 day.

TO MAKE AHEAD: Cover and refrigerate for up to 3 days or freeze for up to 1 month.

MAKES: 8 servings

H✖W   H↑F   H♥H

PER SERVING: 288 calories; 7 g fat (1 g sat, 3 g mono); 0 mg cholesterol; 47 g carbohydrate; 1 g added sugars; 14 g protein; 13 g fiber; 578 mg sodium; 873 mg potassium.

NUTRITION BONUS: Vitamin A (487% daily value), Vitamin C (42% dv), Folate (28% dv), Potassium (25% dv), Iron (22% dv), Magnesium (19% dv).

SERVE WITH:

Cooked bulgur with sautéed garlic, shallots and toasted pine nuts

Southwestern Three-Bean & Barley Soup

A good hit of chili powder gives this bean-and-barley soup a zesty flavor. Make it vegetarian by using vegetable broth.

4 cups (32-ounce carton) reduced-sodium chicken broth, "no-chicken" broth *or* vegetable broth
2 cups water
1 large onion, diced
1 large stalk celery, diced
1 large carrot, diced
1/2 cup pearl barley
1/3 cup dried black beans
1/3 cup dried great northern beans
1/3 cup dried kidney beans
1 tablespoon extra-virgin olive oil
1 tablespoon chili powder
1 teaspoon ground cumin
1/2 teaspoon dried oregano
3/4 teaspoon salt

1. Combine broth, water, onion, celery and carrot in a 5- to 6-quart slow cooker. Add barley, black beans, great northern beans, kidney beans, oil, chili powder, cumin and oregano.
2. Put the lid on and cook until the beans are tender, about 4 hours on High or 7 to 8 hours on Low. Season with salt.

ACTIVE TIME: 30 minutes
SLOW-COOKER TIME: 4 hours on High or 7 to 8 hours on Low
TOTAL: 4 1/2 to 8 1/2 hours
TO PREP AHEAD: Prepare onion, celery and carrot; cover and refrigerate together in one container for up to 1 day. Measure out barley and beans; combine in one container.
TO MAKE AHEAD: Cover and refrigerate for up to 3 days.

MAKES: 6 servings, about 1 1/3 cups each

H✖W   H↑F   H♥H
PER SERVING: 205 calories; 3 g fat (0 g sat, 2 g mono); 0 mg cholesterol; 35 g carbohydrate; 0 g added sugars; 11 g protein; 10 g fiber; 714 mg sodium; 602 mg potassium.
NUTRITION BONUS: Vitamin A (49% daily value), Folate (29% dv), Magnesium & Potassium (17% dv), Iron (16% dv).

SERVE WITH:

Toasted sourdough bread with melted pepper Jack cheese

Barbecue Pulled Chicken

ACTIVE TIME: 25 minutes

SLOW-COOKER TIME: 5 hours

TOTAL: 5 1/2 hours

TO PREP AHEAD: Combine sauce ingredients (in Step 1) in a bowl. Trim chicken thighs. Chop onion and mince garlic. Refrigerate in separate covered containers for up to 1 day. Heat the cold sauce to a simmer before adding to the slow cooker.

TO MAKE AHEAD: Cover and refrigerate for up to 3 days or freeze for up to 1 month.

MAKES: 8 servings

H✕W   H♥H

PER SERVING: 210 calories; 9 g fat (2 g sat, 3 g mono); 74 mg cholesterol; 10 g carbohydrate; 4 g added sugars; 21 g protein; 1 g fiber; 312 mg sodium; 390 mg potassium.

NUTRITION BONUS: Vitamin C (17% daily value), Vitamin A & Zinc (15% dv).

SERVE WITH:

Shredded napa cabbage tossed with reduced-fat mayonnaise, cider vinegar, celery seed and honey to taste

While not technically barbecued, these chicken thighs are slow-cooked in a tangy and hot tomato-based sauce that give the meat all the right flavors. It makes a great sandwich, but you can also serve it on top of mashed potatoes or even whole-grain spaghetti.

- **1 8-ounce can reduced-sodium tomato sauce**
- **1 4-ounce can chopped green chiles, drained**
- **3 tablespoons cider vinegar**
- **2 tablespoons honey**
- **1 tablespoon sweet *or* smoked paprika**
- **1 tablespoon tomato paste**
- **1 tablespoon Worcestershire sauce**
- **2 teaspoons dry mustard**
- **1 teaspoon ground chipotle chile (*see Note*)**
- **1/2 teaspoon salt**
- **2 1/2 pounds boneless, skinless chicken thighs, trimmed**
- **1 small onion, finely chopped**
- **1 clove garlic, minced**

1. Stir tomato sauce, chiles, vinegar, honey, paprika, tomato paste, Worcestershire sauce, mustard, ground chipotle and salt in a 6-quart slow cooker until smooth. Add chicken, onion and garlic; stir to combine.
2. Put the lid on and cook on Low until the chicken can be pulled apart, about 5 hours.
3. Transfer the chicken to a clean cutting board and shred with a fork. Return the chicken to the sauce, stir well and serve.

NOTE: Chipotle peppers are dried, smoked jalapeño peppers. **Ground chipotle chile** pepper can be found in the spice section of most supermarkets or online at *penzeys.com*.

Chicken & Sweet Potato Stew

Here's a dinnertime warmer with a hint of spring's sweetness, designed for that day when you'd rather be outside raking the leaves from the garden, getting it ready for what's ahead, than slaving over the stove.

6	bone-in chicken thighs, skin removed, trimmed
2	pounds sweet potatoes, peeled and cut into spears
1/2	pound white button mushrooms, thinly sliced
6	large shallots, peeled and halved
4	cloves garlic, peeled
1	cup dry white wine
2	teaspoons chopped fresh rosemary *or* 1/2 teaspoon dried rosemary, crushed
1	teaspoon salt
1/2	teaspoon freshly ground pepper
1 1/2	tablespoons white-wine vinegar

1. Place chicken, sweet potatoes, mushrooms, shallots, garlic, wine, rosemary, salt and pepper in a 6-quart slow cooker; stir to combine.
2. Put the lid on and cook on low until the potatoes are tender, about 5 hours. Before serving, remove bones from the chicken, if desired, and stir in vinegar.

ACTIVE TIME: 20 minutes
SLOW-COOKER TIME: 5 hours
TOTAL: 5 hours 20 minutes
TO PREP AHEAD: Prepare sweet potatoes, mushrooms, shallot and garlic; cover and refrigerate together in one container for up to 1 day.
TO MAKE AHEAD: Cover and refrigerate for up to 3 days or freeze for up to 1 month.

MAKES: 6 servings

H✖W   H⬆F   H♥H

PER SERVING: 301 calories; 6 g fat (2 g sat, 2 g mono); 50 mg cholesterol; 38 g carbohydrate; 0 g added sugars; 18 g protein; 5 g fiber; 521 mg sodium; 895 mg potassium.
NUTRITION BONUS: Vitamin A (436% daily value), Potassium (26% dv), Magnesium & Zinc (15% dv).

SERVE WITH:

Warm, crusty whole-grain bread and a mixed green salad

Norm Plate

Slow is back—at least for those of us who appreciate the deep flavor that comes only from long cooking times.

—Jerry Anne Di Vecchio

Plug Into Nostalgia

Rediscover the convenience of the slow cooker for healthy dishes with deep, rich flavors

How surely old ideas recycle themselves. In small-town Kansas where I grew up, my family had a "modern" gas stove in the kitchen, but my grandparents and other relatives out on the prairie were still cooking on wood-fueled ranges. Glowing in winter for warmth as well as cooking, these hulky stoves always had something slowly stewing on their smooth black surfaces.

When the electric Crock-Pot appeared in 1971, convenience-minded cooks found that it could nicely perform similar slow-simmering services—albeit with none of the charm of a wood stove. Contemporary versions have revived the old craze with more ample cooking containers and the ability to distribute heat more evenly around the sides of the covered dish. With them, a home cook can produce a surprising variety of dishes that require no attention for hours.

For the health-conscious cook, slow cookers help to tenderize and extract the best from lean meats and poultry. Whole grains and legumes cook up plump and delicious without tending, and vegetables enrich both nutrition and taste. Slow is back—at least for those of us who appreciate the deep flavor that comes only from long cooking times. 🔲

Jerry Anne Di Vecchio is a San Francisco–based writer, retired from 42 years as a food and wine editor of Sunset *magazine. When she was working full-time, slow cooking was vital; now it's a joy.*

Greek Chicken & Vegetable Ragout

This easy braise calls for chicken thighs, which stay so moist and succulent in the slow cooker you'll never want to cook them any other way. The dish is finished with a drizzle of avgolémono, a versatile Greek sauce made with egg, lemon and fresh dill.

1   **pound carrots, cut into 1 ¼-inch pieces, *or* 3 cups baby carrots**
1   **pound (3-4 medium) yellow-fleshed potatoes, such as Yukon Gold, peeled and cut lengthwise into 1 ¼-inch-wide wedges**
2   **pounds boneless, skinless chicken thighs, trimmed**
1   **14-ounce can reduced-sodium chicken broth**
⅓   **cup dry white wine**
4   **cloves garlic, minced**
¼   **teaspoon salt**
1   **15-ounce can artichoke hearts, rinsed and quartered if large**
1   **large egg**
2   **large egg yolks**
⅓   **cup lemon juice**
⅓   **cup chopped fresh dill**
    Freshly ground pepper to taste

1. Spread carrots and potatoes over the bottom and up the sides of a 4-quart or larger slow cooker. Arrange chicken on top of the vegetables. Combine broth, wine, garlic and salt in a medium bowl; pour over the chicken and vegetables.
2. Put the lid on and cook until the chicken is cooked through and vegetables are tender, 2½ to 3 hours on High or 4 to 4½ hours on Low.
3. Add artichoke hearts to the slow cooker, cover and cook on High for 5 minutes. Meanwhile, whisk egg, egg yolks and lemon juice in a medium bowl.
4. Transfer the chicken and vegetables to a serving bowl using a slotted spoon. Cover and keep warm. Ladle about ½ cup of the cooking liquid into the egg mixture. Whisk until smooth. Whisk the egg mixture into the remaining cooking liquid in the slow cooker. Cover and cook, whisking 2 or 3 times, until the sauce is slightly thickened and reaches 160°F on an instant-read thermometer, 15 to 20 minutes. Stir in dill and pepper. Pour the sauce over the chicken and vegetables and serve.

ACTIVE TIME: 40 minutes
SLOW-COOKER TIME: 2½-3 hours on High or 4-4½ hours on Low
TOTAL: 3 hours 10 minutes to 5 hours 10 minutes
TO PREP AHEAD: Peel and cut carrots. Peel and cut potatoes; cover with water. Trim chicken thighs. Combine broth, wine and minced garlic. Refrigerate in separate covered containers for up to 1 day. Heat the cold liquid to a simmer before adding to the slow cooker.
TO MAKE AHEAD: Cover and refrigerate for up to 2 days. Freezing is not recommended.

MAKES: 6 servings, about 1⅓ cups each

H✖W   H↑F   H♥H

PER SERVING: 357 calories; 13 g fat (4 g sat, 5 g mono); 179 mg cholesterol; 28 g carbohydrate; 0 g added sugars; 30 g protein; 5 g fiber; 761 mg sodium; 802 mg potassium.
NUTRITION BONUS: Vitamin A (260% daily value), Vitamin C (37% dv), Potassium (23% dv), Zinc (20% dv).

SERVE WITH:

Rice studded with toasted slivered almonds

Slow-Cooker Braised Pork with Salsa

ACTIVE TIME: 30 minutes
SLOW-COOKER TIME: 6-7 hours
TOTAL: 6 1/2-7 1/2 hours
TO PREP AHEAD: Trim pork and cut into chunks. Cover and refrigerate for up to 1 day.
TO MAKE AHEAD: Cover and refrigerate for up to 2 days or freeze for up to 3 months. Reheat on the stovetop, in a microwave or in the oven.

MAKES: 8 servings, about 1 cup each

PER SERVING: 276 calories; 15 g fat (6 g sat, 7 g mono); 104 mg cholesterol; 6 g carbohydrate; 0 g added sugars; 27 g protein; 1 g fiber; 211 mg sodium; 413 mg potassium.
NUTRITION BONUS: Zinc (35% daily value).

SERVE WITH:

Cooked quinoa blended with diced red and green bell peppers and sliced scallions

Pork shoulder, also called butt, is super-flavorful, but not the leanest cut. We keep the dish from being overly greasy by trimming as much visible fat as possible before cooking.

- **3 pounds boneless pork shoulder *or* butt**
- **1 1/2 cups prepared tomatillo salsa (*see Note*)**
- **3 plum tomatoes, halved and thinly sliced**
- **1 medium onion, thinly sliced**
- **1 teaspoon cumin seeds *or* ground cumin**
- **1/2 cup chopped fresh cilantro, divided**
- **1/2 cup reduced-fat sour cream**

1. Trim and discard pork surface fat. Cut meat apart following layers of fat around muscles; trim and discard fat. Cut the pork into 2-inch chunks and rinse with cold water. Place in a 5- or 6-quart slow cooker. Turn heat to High.
2. Combine salsa, tomatoes, onion and cumin in a bowl. Pour over the meat. Put the lid on and cook until the meat is pull-apart tender, 6 to 7 hours.
3. With a slotted spoon, transfer the pork to a large bowl. Skim any fat from the surface of the sauce. Stir in 1/4 cup cilantro and return the pork to the sauce.
4. To serve, ladle into bowls and garnish each serving with a dollop of sour cream and a sprinkling of the remaining 1/4 cup cilantro.

NOTE: **Tomatillo salsa** (sometimes labeled salsa verde or green salsa) is a blend of green chiles, onions and tomatillos. Look for it near other prepared salsa in most supermarkets.

Chinese Pork & Vegetable Hot Pot

There is more to Chinese cooking than speedy stir-fries. Richly flavored red braises, cooked in clay pots, make warming winter meals that can be adapted to a slow cooker. Typically, seasonings of anise, cinnamon and ginger distinguish these dishes. Pork shoulder becomes meltingly tender during the slow braise.

2	cups baby carrots
2	medium white turnips (8 ounces total), peeled and cut into 3/4-inch-wide wedges
2¼	pounds boneless pork shoulder *or* butt, trimmed and cut into 1½-inch chunks
1	bunch scallions, sliced, white and green parts separated
1	14-ounce can reduced-sodium chicken broth
½	cup water
¼	cup reduced-sodium soy sauce
3	tablespoons medium *or* dry sherry (*see Note, page 213*)
4	teaspoons brown sugar
2	tablespoons minced fresh ginger
1	tablespoon rice vinegar
2-4	teaspoons Chinese chile-garlic sauce
4	cloves garlic, minced
1	star anise pod (*see Note*) *or* 1 teaspoon aniseed
1	cinnamon stick
4	teaspoons cornstarch mixed with 2 tablespoons water
2	tablespoons sesame seeds, toasted (*see Note, page 213*)

1. Place carrots and turnips in the bottom and up the sides of a 4-quart or larger slow cooker. Top with pork and scallion whites. Combine broth, water, soy sauce, sherry, brown sugar, ginger, vinegar, chile-garlic sauce to taste and garlic in a medium bowl. Pour over the pork and vegetables. Nestle star anise pod (or aniseed) and cinnamon stick into the stew.
2. Put the lid on and cook until the pork and vegetables are tender, 3 to 3½ hours on High or 5½ to 6 hours on Low.
3. Discard the star anise pod and cinnamon stick. Skim or blot any visible fat from the surface of the stew. Add the cornstarch mixture, cover and cook on High, stirring 2 or 3 times, until slightly thickened, 10 to 15 minutes. Serve sprinkled with scallion greens and sesame seeds.

NOTE: **Star anise** (named for its star-shaped pods) lends a distinctive licorice-like flavor to numerous Asian dishes. The pods come from a small evergreen tree that is native to China. Look for star anise in the bulk spice sections of natural-foods stores, in Asian markets or online at *penzeys.com*.

ACTIVE TIME: 40 minutes

SLOW-COOKER TIME: 3-3½ hours on High or 5½-6 hours on Low

TOTAL: 3 hours 40 minutes to 6 hours 40 minutes

TO PREP AHEAD: Trim and cube pork. Prepare turnips and scallions. Combine measured liquids and seasonings. Cover and refrigerate separately for up to 1 day. Heat the cold liquid to a simmer before adding to the slow cooker.

TO MAKE AHEAD: Cover and refrigerate for up to 2 days or freeze for up to 4 months.

MAKES: 6 servings, 1 generous cup each

H✖W

PER SERVING: 338 calories; 18 g fat (6 g sat, 8 g mono); 92 mg cholesterol; 15 g carbohydrate; 3 g added sugars; 27 g protein; 2 g fiber; 621 mg sodium; 506 mg potassium.

NUTRITION BONUS: Vitamin A (114% daily value), Zinc (40% dv), Vitamin C (23% dv), Iron (19% dv).

SERVE WITH:

Noodles or brown rice and stir-fried napa cabbage

Middle Eastern Lamb Stew

ACTIVE TIME: 40 minutes

SLOW-COOKER TIME: 3-3 1/2 hours
on High or 5 1/2-6 hours on Low

TOTAL: 3 hours 40 minutes to
6 hours 40 minutes

TO PREP AHEAD: Trim and cube lamb;
coat with spice mixture. Chop
onions. Combine tomatoes, broth
and garlic. Refrigerate in separate
covered containers for up to 1 day.

TO MAKE AHEAD: Prepare the stew,
omitting the spinach, cover and
refrigerate for up to 2 days or
freeze for up to 4 months. Add
spinach after the stew is reheated.

MAKES: 8 servings, about 1 cup each

H✕W

PER SERVING: 275 calories; 14 g fat
(5 g sat, 6 g mono); 61 mg
cholesterol; 17 g carbohydrate;
0 g added sugars; 20 g protein;
4 g fiber; 451 mg sodium;
586 mg potassium.

NUTRITION BONUS: Vitamin A
(37% daily value), Zinc (26% dv),
Vitamin C (23% dv), Iron (22% dv),
Folate (19% dv), Potassium
(17% dv).

SERVE WITH:

Classic tabbouleh salad of
bulgur, chopped tomatoes and
a generous amount of chopped
parsley, all tossed in a lemon
and extra-virgin olive oil dressing

An assertive blend of ground cumin, coriander and cayenne pepper gives this brothy stew its characteristic Middle Eastern flavor profile. The seasoned lamb shoulder tenderizes beautifully when leisurely slow-cooked with onions and tomatoes and is then finished with fresh baby spinach and fiber-rich chickpeas.

1 1/2   **pounds boneless lamb stew meat (shoulder cut)** *or* **boneless leg of lamb**
        or **2 1/2 pounds lamb shoulder chops, deboned, trimmed and cut into**
        1-inch chunks
1   **tablespoon extra-virgin olive oil** *or* **canola oil**
4   **teaspoons ground cumin**
1   **tablespoon ground coriander**
1/4   **teaspoon cayenne pepper**
1/4   **teaspoon salt**
        Freshly ground pepper to taste
1   **large** *or* **2 medium onions, chopped**
1   **28-ounce can diced tomatoes**
3/4   **cup reduced-sodium chicken broth**
4   **cloves garlic, minced**
1   **15-** *or* **19-ounce can chickpeas, rinsed**
6   **ounces baby spinach**

1. Place lamb in a 4-quart or larger slow cooker. Mix oil, cumin, coriander, cayenne, salt and pepper in a small bowl. Coat the lamb with the spice paste and toss to coat well. Top with onion, tomatoes, broth and garlic.

2. Put the lid on and cook until the lamb is very tender, 3 to 3 1/2 hours on High or 5 1/2 to 6 hours on Low.

3. Skim or blot any visible fat from the surface of the stew. Mash 1/2 cup chickpeas with a fork in a small bowl. Stir the mashed and whole chickpeas into the stew, along with spinach. Cover and cook on High until the spinach is wilted, about 5 minutes.

Irish Lamb Stew

ACTIVE TIME: 30 minutes

SLOW-COOKER TIME: 8 hours

TOTAL: 8 1/2 hours

TO PREP AHEAD: Trim and cube lamb. Peel and cut potatoes; cover with water. Prepare leeks, carrots and celery. Cover and refrigerate in separate containers for up to 1 day. (Save preparing potatoes until just before adding to the slow cooker.)

TO MAKE AHEAD: Cover and refrigerate for up to 2 days or freeze for up to 1 month.

MAKES: 8 servings, generous 1 cup each

H✕W   H♥H

PER SERVING: 261 calories; 7 g fat (2 g sat, 3 g mono); 64 mg cholesterol; 26 g carbohydrate; 0 g added sugars; 23 g protein; 3 g fiber; 504 mg sodium; 793 mg potassium.

NUTRITION BONUS: Vitamin A (104% daily value), Vitamin C (25% dv), Potassium (23% dv), Zinc (21% dv), Folate (15% dv).

SERVE WITH:

Sautéed kale and hearty bread

Stew, even in a slow cooker, can be a time-consuming affair if everything is browned at the beginning. Here, in the traditional Irish fashion, everything is just tossed in the pot and stewed together, so the prep time is kept to a minimum, but all the fabulous flavors of the lamb, potatoes, leeks and carrots shine nonetheless. (Photograph: page 128.)

2	pounds boneless leg of lamb, trimmed and cut into 1-inch pieces
1 3/4	pounds white potatoes, peeled and cut into 1-inch pieces
3	large leeks, white part only, halved, washed (*see Note*) and thinly sliced
3	large carrots, peeled and cut into 1-inch pieces
3	stalks celery, thinly sliced
1	14-ounce can reduced-sodium chicken broth
2	teaspoons chopped fresh thyme
1	teaspoon salt
1	teaspoon freshly ground pepper
1/4	cup packed fresh parsley leaves, chopped

1. Combine lamb, potatoes, leeks, carrots, celery, broth, thyme, salt and pepper in a 6-quart slow cooker; stir to combine.
2. Put the lid on and cook on Low until the lamb is fork-tender, about 8 hours. Stir in parsley before serving.

NOTE: **To clean leeks,** trim and discard green tops and white roots. Split leeks lengthwise and place in plenty of water. Swish the leeks in the water to release any sand or soil. Drain. Repeat until no grit remains.

Fragrant Shredded Beef Stew

Flank steak is known for its outstanding flavor, but also its grainy and sometimes tough texture. For this stew, however, its long grains are an advantage: after slow cooking, the meat shreds apart easily into tasty strips.

1 ½   **cups reduced-sodium chicken broth**
¼   **cup sherry vinegar**
2   **stalks celery, thinly sliced**
1   **large onion, chopped**
1   **large red bell pepper, chopped**
3   **cloves garlic, minced**
1   **tablespoon ground cumin**
1   **teaspoon salt**
½   **teaspoon freshly ground pepper**
3   **pounds flank steak, trimmed, each steak cut into thirds**
½   **cup packed fresh cilantro leaves, chopped**
½   **cup chopped pickled jalapeños**
10   **corn tortillas, heated (see Note)**

1. Combine broth, vinegar, celery, onion, bell pepper, garlic, cumin, salt and pepper in a 6-quart slow cooker. Add steak, submerging it by tucking the vegetables under, over and between the pieces.
2. Put the lid on and cook on Low until the meat is fork-tender, about 8 hours.
3. Transfer the meat to a cutting board; let stand for 10 minutes. Shred the meat with 2 forks and return it to the slow cooker. Stir in cilantro. Garnish with jalapeños and serve warm tortillas on the side.

NOTE: **To heat corn tortillas,** wrap in foil and bake at 300°F until steaming, about 10 minutes.

ACTIVE TIME: 25 minutes
SLOW-COOKER TIME: 8 hours
TOTAL: 8 ½ hours
TO PREP AHEAD: Prepare celery, onion, bell pepper and garlic. Cut flank steak. Cover and refrigerate in separate containers for up to 1 day.
TO MAKE AHEAD: Cover and refrigerate for up to 3 days or freeze for up to 1 month.

MAKES: 10 servings

H✗W   H♥H
PER SERVING: 224 calories; 8 g fat (3 g sat, 3 g mono); 60 mg cholesterol; 15 g carbohydrate; 0 g added sugars; 23 g protein; 3 g fiber; 416 mg sodium; 415 mg potassium.
NUTRITION BONUS: Vitamin C (152% daily value), Zinc (27% dv), Vitamin A (16% dv).

SERVE WITH:

Black-eyed peas (canned, rinsed) sautéed with garlic and onions and stirred into brown rice

Hungarian Beef Goulash

This hearty goulash is a streamlined, slow-cooker version of the traditional Hungarian recipe. Instead of the time-consuming process of browning the beef, the chunks are coated in a spice crust to give a rich mahogany hue.

2	pounds beef stew meat (such as chuck), trimmed and cubed
2	teaspoons caraway seeds
1 1/2-2	tablespoons sweet *or* hot paprika (*or* a mixture of the two), preferably Hungarian (*see Note*)
1/4	teaspoon salt
	Freshly ground pepper to taste
1	large *or* 2 medium onions, chopped
1	small red bell pepper, chopped
1	14-ounce can diced tomatoes
1	14-ounce can reduced-sodium beef broth
1	teaspoon Worcestershire sauce
3	cloves garlic, minced
2	bay leaves
1	tablespoon cornstarch mixed with 2 tablespoons water
2	tablespoons chopped fresh parsley

1. Place beef in a 4-quart or larger slow cooker. Crush caraway seeds with the bottom of a saucepan. Transfer to a small bowl and stir in paprika, salt and pepper. Sprinkle the beef with the spice mixture and toss to coat well. Top with onion and bell pepper.
2. Combine tomatoes, broth, Worcestershire sauce and garlic in a medium bowl. Pour over the beef and vegetables. Place bay leaves on top.
3. Put the lid on and cook until the beef is very tender, 4 to 4 1/2 hours on High or 7 to 7 1/2 hours on Low.
4. Discard the bay leaves; skim or blot any visible fat from the surface of the stew. Add the cornstarch mixture to the stew and cook on High, stirring 2 or 3 times, until slightly thickened, 10 to 15 minutes. Serve sprinkled with parsley.

NOTE: **Paprika** specifically labeled as "Hungarian" is worth seeking out for this dish because it delivers a fuller, richer flavor than regular or Spanish paprika. Find it at specialty-foods stores or online at *HungarianDeli.com* and *penzeys.com*.

ACTIVE TIME: 30 minutes

SLOW-COOKER TIME: 4-4 1/2 hours on High or 7-7 1/2 hours on Low

TOTAL: 4 1/2 to 8 hours

TO PREP AHEAD: Trim beef and coat with spice mixture. Prepare onions and peppers. Combine tomatoes, broth, Worcestershire sauce and garlic. Refrigerate in separate covered containers for up to 1 day. Heat the liquid to a simmer before adding to the slow cooker.

TO MAKE AHEAD: Cover and refrigerate for up to 2 days or freeze for up to 4 months.

MAKES: 8 servings, about 1 cup each

H✖W   H❤H

PER SERVING: 177 calories; 5 g fat (2 g sat, 2 g mono); 71 mg cholesterol; 7 g carbohydrate; 0 g added sugars; 25 g protein; 1 g fiber; 340 mg sodium; 288 mg potassium.

NUTRITION BONUS: Vitamin C & Zinc (38% daily value), Vitamin A (27% dv).

SERVE WITH:

Whole-wheat egg noodles or spaetzle

White Fish Stew (Bianco)

DUTCH OVEN

A 5- to 6-quart Dutch oven is a good all-purpose size that will work for many recipes, from cooking pasta to braising beef. We use both stainless-steel and enamel-coated cast-iron pots and find that the heavier and sturdier the material, the better it conducts heat and keeps foods from scorching. Check to make sure the lid is tight-fitting to keep moisture in.

Jamaican Curried Shrimp & Mango Soup

Sweet, tangy and spicy are the keynotes of this Jamaican-inspired soup, brimming with fresh shrimp and ripe mangoes. Standard store-bought curry powder works fine with this recipe, but if you can get your hands on Jamaican-style curry powder, which has a hint of allspice, the taste will be all the more authentic.

1	tablespoon extra-virgin olive oil
1	large onion, chopped
2	stalks celery, sliced
4	cloves garlic, chopped
1	serrano chile, minced (optional)
2	tablespoons curry powder
1	teaspoon dried thyme
2	cups seafood broth *or* stock *or* clam juice
1	14-ounce can "lite" coconut milk
3	ripe mangoes, diced (*see Note*)
1¼	pounds raw shrimp, peeled and deveined (21-25 per pound; *see Note, page 213*)
1	bunch scallions, sliced
¼	teaspoon salt

1. Heat oil in a Dutch oven over medium heat. Add onion and celery and cook, stirring occasionally, until beginning to brown, 3 to 5 minutes. Add garlic, chile (if using), curry powder and thyme; stir constantly for 30 seconds. Add broth (or stock or clam juice), coconut milk and mangoes. Bring to a simmer over medium-high heat. Reduce heat to maintain a simmer and cook, stirring occasionally, for 5 minutes.
2. Puree 3 cups of the soup in a blender. (Use caution when pureeing hot liquids.) Return the puree to the pot and bring to a simmer. Add shrimp and cook until pink and firm, about 3 minutes. Stir in scallions and salt.

NOTE: **To peel and dice a mango,** slice both ends off to reveal the long, slender seed. Set the fruit upright and remove the skin with a sharp knife. With the seed perpendicular to you, slice the fruit from both sides of the seed, yielding two large pieces. Turn the seed parallel to you and slice the two smaller pieces of fruit from each side. Dice into desired size.

ACTIVE TIME: 40 minutes
TOTAL: 40 minutes

MAKES: 4 servings, about 2 cups each

H✖W   H↑F   H♥H

PER SERVING: 388 calories; 13 g fat (6 g sat, 3 g mono); 143 mg cholesterol; 51 g carbohydrate; 0 g added sugars; 22 g protein; 7 g fiber; 1,078 mg sodium; 804 mg potassium.
NUTRITION BONUS: Vitamin C (168% daily value), Vitamin A (66% dv), Folate (41% dv), Potassium (23% dv), Magnesium (17% dv)

SERVE WITH:

Brown rice blended with a sauté of garlic, baby lima beans, diced sweet potato and some minced Scotch bonnet pepper if you want to add some Caribbean-style heat

Green Vegetable Minestrone

Minestrone is sort of a catch-all Italian term for soup, but it's always a welcome meal, especially when it's fortified, as it is here, with plenty of vegetables and protein-packed chickpeas. If you want a little more bite in the veggie blend, consider substituting mildly bitter escarole for the chard.

 3 tablespoons extra-virgin olive oil, divided
 2 small leeks, white and light green parts only, quartered, washed and sliced
 2 small stalks celery, diced
 1 medium onion, chopped
 1½ teaspoons salt, divided
 2 small zucchini, quartered lengthwise and sliced
 1 medium potato, peeled and diced
 2 cloves garlic, minced
 8 cups water
 1 cup whole-wheat short pasta, such as elbows, bowties *or* shells
 8 cups chopped green chard leaves
 1 15-ounce can chickpeas, rinsed
 1 cup frozen peas
 Freshly ground pepper to taste
 ½ cup freshly grated Parmesan cheese
 ¼ cup chopped fresh parsley *or* basil

1. Heat 1 tablespoon oil in a Dutch oven, over medium heat. Add leeks, celery, onion and ½ teaspoon salt and cook, stirring, until softened, 7 to 10 minutes. Add zucchini, potato and garlic and cook, stirring, about 1 minute more. Add water and the remaining 1 teaspoon salt. Bring to a boil. Reduce heat to low and simmer, partially covered, until the vegetables are tender, 12 to 15 minutes.
2. Add pasta and chard; cook, uncovered, for 5 minutes. Add chickpeas and peas and simmer until the pasta is just tender, 3 to 4 minutes more. Season with pepper. Ladle the soup into bowls and drizzle with the remaining 2 tablespoons oil. Top with Parmesan and parsley (or basil). Serve immediately.

ACTIVE TIME: 45 minutes
TOTAL: 1 hour 10 minutes
TO MAKE AHEAD: Prepare through Step 1, cover and refrigerate for up to 2 days. Reheat before continuing.

MAKES: 8 servings, about 1½ cups each

H✖W H⬆F H❤H
PER SERVING: 217 calories; 8 g fat (2 g sat, 5 g mono); 4 mg cholesterol; 31 g carbohydrate; 0 g added sugars; 8 g protein; 5 g fiber; 686 mg sodium; 502 mg potassium.
NUTRITION BONUS: Vitamin A (58% daily value), Vitamin C (38% dv), Magnesium (19% dv), Folate (17% dv), Iron (15% dv).

SERVE WITH:

Toasted whole-wheat pita bread brushed with extra-virgin olive oil and rubbed with the cut side of a garlic clove

Smoky Black Bean Soup

ACTIVE TIME: 30 minutes

TOTAL: 2 hours (not including bean-soaking time)

TO MAKE AHEAD: Prepare through Step 3, cover and refrigerate for up to 3 days; thin with a little water if necessary after reheating.

MAKES: 6 servings, 1⅓ cups each

H✖W   H⬆F   H♥H

PER SERVING: 298 calories; 8 g fat (2 g sat, 4 g mono); 6 mg cholesterol; 43 g carbohydrate; 0 g added sugars; 15 g protein; 15 g fiber; 423 mg sodium; 769 mg potassium.

NUTRITION BONUS: Folate (64% daily value), Vitamin C (50% dv), Magnesium (31% dv), Potassium (22% dv), Iron (21% dv), Vitamin A (16% dv).

SERVE WITH:

Mixed green salad or a grilled cheese sandwich with pickled jalapeños

This will probably be the most hauntingly delicious black bean soup you've ever tasted. The coffee adds a slightly toasty, woodsy background note. The optional ham hock adds smoky, salty ham flavor.

1 **pound dried black beans (2 cups)**
2 **tablespoons extra-virgin olive oil**
2 **medium onions, finely chopped, ⅓ cup reserved for garnish**
1 **medium red bell pepper, finely chopped**
2 **large stalks celery, chopped**
1 **jalapeño pepper, seeded and finely chopped**
3 **large cloves garlic, minced**
1 **tablespoon ground cumin**
4 **cups water**
2 **cups brewed coffee**
1 **ham hock (optional)**
1 **bay leaf**
1 **teaspoon salt, plus more if needed**
6 **tablespoons reduced-fat sour cream *or* plain Greek yogurt for garnish**
   Chopped fresh cilantro for garnish

1. Pick over beans; rinse well. Place in a large bowl with cold water to cover by 2 inches. Let soak for at least 6 hours or overnight. (*Or use the quick-soak method: see Note, page 212.*) Drain.
2. Heat oil in a Dutch oven over medium-high heat. Add onions (all but ⅓ cup), bell pepper, celery, jalapeño and garlic and cook, stirring frequently, until the vegetables are beginning to brown, 5 to 8 minutes. Add cumin and cook, stirring, 1 minute more. Add the beans, water, coffee, ham hock (if using) and bay leaf; cover and bring to a boil, stirring occasionally. Skim off any foam that rises to the top, reduce the heat, cover and simmer until the beans are very tender, 1¼ to 1½ hours. If using, remove the ham hock and set it aside to cool; remove the bay leaf. Stir in salt.
3. Puree about half of the soup in a blender or food processor until fairly smooth. (Use caution when pureeing hot liquids.) Return the pureed soup to the pot and heat through. If desired, cut meat off the ham hock, trim away any fat and chop the meat into small pieces; stir back into the soup.
4. Serve the soup garnished with the reserved chopped onion, a dollop of sour cream (or yogurt) and cilantro, if desired.

Meatless *Harira* (Moroccan Ramadan Soup)

ACTIVE TIME: 1 hour 20 minutes
TOTAL: 3 hours (not including bean-soaking time)

MAKES: 8 servings, about 1 cup each

H✂W   H⬆F   H❤H

PER SERVING: 246 calories; 6 g fat (1 g sat, 3 g mono); 23 mg cholesterol; 39 g carbohydrate; 0 g added sugars; 13 g protein; 12 g fiber; 329 mg sodium; 817 mg potassium.
NUTRITION BONUS: Folate (56% daily value), Vitamin A (27% dv), Iron (25% dv), Potassium (23% dv), Magnesium (21% dv).

SERVE WITH:

Crusty, olive-studded bread or slices of seeded baguette spread with prepared olive tapenade

This is a vegetarian take on a traditional Moroccan soup that usually contains lamb and sometimes chicken, but here is fortified by three types of protein-rich legumes instead: chickpeas, great northern beans and lentils. Turmeric, cinnamon, saffron and ginger give the soup a heady perfume that is well balanced by the brightness and acidity of tomatoes and cilantro.

1/2	cup dried chickpeas, washed and picked over
1/2	cup dried white beans, such as great northern, washed and picked over
2	tablespoons extra-virgin olive oil *or* canola oil
2	medium yellow onions, chopped
3/4	cup chopped celery, including leaves
1/2	cup finely chopped fresh parsley
2	tablespoons finely chopped fresh cilantro, plus more for garnish
1	teaspoon ground turmeric
1	teaspoon ground cinnamon, plus more for garnish
1	teaspoon freshly ground pepper, plus more to taste
1/2	teaspoon saffron (*see Note, page 213*)
1/4	teaspoon ground ginger
2	pounds tomatoes, peeled, seeded (*see Note, page 213*) and chopped, *or* two 28-ounce cans, well drained and chopped
3/4	cup lentils, picked over and rinsed
10	cups water
1	teaspoon salt
1/2	cup whole-wheat spaghetti (small broken pieces)
1	large egg, beaten
	Juice of 1 large lemon (5 tablespoons), plus 8 lemon slices for garnish

1. Pick over chickpeas and white beans; rinse well. Place in a large bowl with cold water to cover by 2 inches. Let soak for at least 6 hours or overnight. (*Or use the quick-soak method: see Note, page 212.*) Drain.

2. Heat oil in a Dutch oven over medium-low heat. Add onions and cook, stirring, until tender and beginning to color, 5 to 7 minutes. Add celery, parsley, cilantro, turmeric, cinnamon, 1 teaspoon pepper, saffron and ginger, and cook, stirring, for 2 to 3 minutes more. Add tomatoes, cover, and continue to cook, stirring occasionally, until the celery is almost tender, 10 to 15 minutes more.

3. Add the chickpeas and beans to the pot, along with lentils and water. Bring to a boil. Reduce heat and simmer, partially covered, until the beans are thoroughly tender, 1½ to 2¼ hours. Mash some of the beans against the side of the pot with a wooden spoon to thicken the broth slightly. Season with salt and pepper.

4. About 10 minutes before serving, remove ½ cup soup from the pot and set aside to cool. Stir spaghetti into the pot. Mix together egg and lemon juice. When the spaghetti is cooked, remove from the heat. Gradually add the egg mixture to the cooled ½ cup soup and quickly stir into the pot. Serve at once, garnished with lemon slices, a light sprinkling of cinnamon and cilantro.

Vietnamese-Style Beef & Noodle Broth

One of the most enjoyable things about eating pho—a traditional Vietnamese soup—is all the fresh herbs and condiments that get served along with it. Our simplified version calls for garnishes of crunchy mung bean sprouts and chopped fresh basil, but don't let that stop you from going to town and topping it with sprigs of fresh cilantro, a squirt of Asian chile sauce, such as sriracha, and a squeeze of lime juice as well.

2	teaspoons canola oil
1	pound flank steak, very thinly sliced against the grain (*see Note*)
4	cups chopped bok choy (1 small head, about 1 pound)
4	cups reduced-sodium chicken broth
1	cup water
4	ounces wide rice noodles
2	teaspoons reduced-sodium soy sauce
1½	cups mung bean sprouts
4	tablespoons chopped fresh basil, or to taste

1. Heat oil in a Dutch oven or soup pot over high heat. Add beef and cook, stirring often, until just cooked, about 2 minutes. Transfer to a plate using tongs, leaving the juices in the pot.
2. Add bok choy to the pot and cook, stirring, until wilted, about 2 minutes. Add broth and water, cover and bring to a boil. Add noodles and soy sauce; simmer until the noodles are soft, about 4 minutes. Return the beef to the pot and cook until heated through, 1 to 2 minutes more. Ladle into bowls and sprinkle with bean sprouts and basil. Serve hot.

NOTE: If you have a little extra time before dinner, put the **flank steak** in the freezer for about 20 minutes to help make it easier to slice thinly.

ACTIVE TIME: 15 minutes
TOTAL: 30 minutes

MAKES: 6 servings, 1 ⅓ cups each

H✕W   H♥H

PER SERVING: 214 calories; 6 g fat (2 g sat, 3 g mono); 47 mg cholesterol; 19 g carbohydrate; 0 g added sugars; 21 g protein; 1 g fiber; 523 mg sodium; 616 mg potassium.
NUTRITION BONUS: Vitamin A (41% daily value), Vitamin C (27% dv), Zinc (23% dv), Potassium (18% dv).

SERVE WITH:

A salad of shredded napa cabbage and carrots tossed with a dressing made with equal parts peanut oil, lime juice, rice vinegar and a splash each of soy sauce and fish sauce

Creamy Hungarian Mushroom Soup

ACTIVE TIME: 45 minutes
TOTAL: 45 minutes

TO MAKE AHEAD: Cover and refrigerate for up to 2 days; reheat over low.

MAKES: 6 servings, about 1½ cups each

H✕W H♥H

PER SERVING: 233 calories; 6 g fat (2 g sat, 3 g mono); 12 mg cholesterol; 37 g carbohydrate; 0 g added sugars; 10 g protein; 4 g fiber; 703 mg sodium; 975 mg potassium.

NUTRITION BONUS: Vitamin A (29% daily value), Potassium (28% dv), Vitamin C (20% dv), Calcium (16% dv).

SERVE WITH:

Mesclun green salad tossed with red-wine vinaigrette

Mushroom-soup lovers, this soup is for you! Russet potatoes make it hearty, and dill and paprika add plenty of flavor. We skip the generous amount of full-fat sour cream and butter typically used in creamy mushroom soups.

1	tablespoon extra-virgin olive oil
1½	pounds mushrooms, thinly sliced
1	medium onion, diced
3	tablespoons all-purpose flour
2	tablespoons paprika, preferably Hungarian (*see Note*)
2	tablespoons dried dill
4	cups mushroom broth *or* reduced-sodium beef broth
2	cups low-fat milk
1½	pounds russet potatoes, peeled and cut into ½-inch pieces
½	cup reduced-fat sour cream
¾	teaspoon salt

1. Heat oil in a Dutch oven over medium-high heat. Add mushrooms and onion and cook, stirring occasionally, until most of the liquid evaporates, 10 to 15 minutes.
2. Reduce heat to medium and cook, stirring frequently, until the mushrooms are very soft, about 3 minutes more. Add flour, paprika and dill and cook, stirring, for 15 seconds. Add broth, milk and potatoes; cover and bring to a simmer. Reduce heat to maintain a lively simmer and cook, uncovered, until the potatoes are tender, about 5 minutes. Remove from the heat and stir in sour cream and salt.

NOTE: Paprika labeled "Hungarian" is worth seeking out for this soup because it delivers a fuller, richer flavor than regular paprika. Find it at well-stocked supermarkets, specialty-foods stores or online at *penzeys.com*.

Swedish Cabbage Soup with Meatballs

A gently sweetened chicken broth teases out the more delicate side of typically robust cabbage in this simple soup that's made undeniably satisfying by the addition of bite-size turkey meatballs.

1	tablespoon extra-virgin olive oil
1	head green cabbage, cored and cut into 1-inch cubes (12 cups)
2	tablespoons dark corn syrup
8	ounces 93%-lean ground turkey
1/4	teaspoon freshly ground pepper, plus more to taste
8	cups reduced-sodium chicken broth
2	bay leaves

1. Heat oil in a large Dutch oven over medium heat. Add cabbage and cook, stirring, until it starts to release some of its liquid, 2 to 3 minutes. Reduce heat to low and add syrup. Simmer, uncovered, until the cabbage is tender and most of the liquid has evaporated, about 15 minutes.
2. Meanwhile, combine turkey and ¼ teaspoon pepper in a small bowl. With wet hands, shape the mixture into meatballs the size of marbles. Set them aside in the refrigerator.
3. Add broth and bay leaves to the cooked cabbage. Bring to a boil; reduce heat to low and simmer, uncovered, for 10 minutes.
4. Drop the meatballs into the soup and simmer until they are no longer pink inside, 5 to 10 minutes. Remove the bay leaves. Season the soup with a generous grinding of pepper before serving.

ACTIVE TIME: 25 minutes
TOTAL: 45 minutes

MAKES: 6 servings, 1½ cups each

H✕W   H♥H

PER SERVING: 150 calories; 5 g fat (1 g sat, 3 g mono); 26 mg cholesterol; 15 g carbohydrate; 4 g added sugars; 14 g protein; 4 g fiber; 797 mg sodium; 604 mg potassium.
NUTRITION BONUS: Vitamin C (88% daily value), Folate (18% dv), Potassium (17% dv).

SERVE WITH:

Toasted pumpernickel topped with a melted slice of Gruyère or Swiss cheese

Stovetop Fideos

ACTIVE TIME: 45 minutes
TOTAL: 45 minutes

MAKES: 4 servings, about 1½ cups each

H⬆F   H♥H

PER SERVING: 443 calories; 17 g fat (4 g sat, 8 g mono); 13 mg cholesterol; 64 g carbohydrate; 0 g added sugars; 16 g protein; 12 g fiber; 672 mg sodium; 547 mg potassium.
NUTRITION BONUS: Vitamin C (39% daily value), Vitamin A (33% dv), Magnesium (30% dv), Folate (23% dv), Calcium (19% dv), Iron (18% dv), Potassium (16% dv).

SERVE WITH:

Crisp romaine, red onion and avocado salad tossed with vinaigrette

Fideos, a toasted pasta dish served in both Mexico and Spain, always begins with toasting vermicelli-style pasta and varies quite a bit from there. Some versions morph into vegetable-noodle soup, some versions are less brothy and more like a pasta main course. Our vegetarian, summer-vegetable-packed version features green beans, corn and tomatoes. Omit the cheese to make it vegan.

3   tablespoons extra-virgin olive oil, divided
8   ounces whole-wheat angel hair pasta, broken into 2-inch pieces (about 3 cups)
2   cups 1-inch green bean pieces
1   medium onion, diced
4   cloves garlic, minced
2   medium tomatoes, diced
1   cup corn kernels, fresh *or* frozen (thawed)
½   teaspoon dried oregano
2   cups "no-chicken" broth (*see Notes*) *or* vegetable broth
½   teaspoon salt
½   cup finely shredded Cotija (*see Notes*) *or* Asiago cheese
2   scallions, sliced
    Lime wedges

1. Heat 2 tablespoons oil in a Dutch oven over medium heat. Add pasta pieces and cook, stirring, until toasted and browned in spots, 2 to 3 minutes. Transfer to a bowl.
2. Add the remaining 1 tablespoon oil to the pot and heat over medium heat. Add green beans, onion and garlic and cook, stirring, until the beans are beginning to soften, 3 to 5 minutes. Add tomatoes, corn and oregano and cook, stirring, until the tomatoes are just beginning to break down, 1 to 2 minutes. Stir in broth, salt and the toasted pasta; bring to a boil over high heat.
3. Reduce heat to medium-low, cover and cook, stirring once or twice, until the pasta is tender and most of the broth is absorbed, about 10 minutes. Serve topped with cheese and scallions, with lime wedges on the side.

NOTES:

Chicken-flavored broth, a vegetarian broth despite its name, is preferable to vegetable broth in some recipes for its hearty, rich flavor. Sometimes called "no-chicken" broth, it can be found with the soups in the natural-foods section of most supermarkets.

Cotija cheese, also called *queso añejo* or *queso añejado*, is an aged Mexican cheese similar in texture and flavor to Asiago or Parmesan. Find it near other specialty cheeses or in Mexican grocery stores.

Fusilli with Garden-Fresh Tomato "Sauce"

ACTIVE TIME: 35 minutes
TOTAL: 35 minutes
TO MAKE AHEAD: Prepare sauce (Step 2), cover and let stand at room temperature for up to 1½ hours.

MAKES: 6 servings, 1⅔ cups each

H↑F

PER SERVING: 391 calories; 18 g fat (5 g sat, 11 g mono); 17 mg cholesterol; 49 g carbohydrate; 0 g added sugars; 12 g protein; 6 g fiber; 503 mg sodium; 347 mg potassium.
NUTRITION BONUS: Vitamin C (43% daily value), Vitamin A (22% dv), Magnesium (16% dv).

SERVE WITH:

Fresh spinach salad topped with mushrooms and chopped hard-boiled egg

A heavy tomato-based pasta dish wouldn't be a top choice for a warm summer night, but this fresh, uncooked tomato sauce is cool and bursting with seasonal flavor. The easy-to-prepare topping can be served right away, but it tastes even better if you let the flavors meld for an hour or so.

3	cups diced seeded ripe tomatoes
½	cup finely diced green bell pepper
2	scallions, white and pale green parts only, thinly sliced
1	clove garlic, minced
¼	cup extra-virgin olive oil
1	cup crumbled feta cheese
½	cup Kalamata olives, pitted and coarsely chopped
2	tablespoons chopped flat-leaf parsley
2	tablespoons chopped fresh basil
2	tablespoons balsamic vinegar
1	tablespoon red-wine vinegar
1	tablespoon lemon juice
⅛	teaspoon salt
	Freshly ground pepper to taste
12	ounces whole-wheat fusilli *or* other whole-wheat pasta

1. Put a Dutch oven of water on to boil.
2. Combine tomatoes, bell pepper, scallions, garlic and oil in a large bowl; toss to mix well. Add feta, olives, parsley, basil, balsamic vinegar, wine vinegar and lemon juice; toss again. Season with salt and pepper.
3. Shortly before serving, cook pasta according to package directions. Drain and add to the sauce; toss to coat well.

Spicy Peanut Noodles

Peanut sauces can be complex or simple to make. This one is made with just a few easy-to-find ingredients, but has fabulous, nuanced flavor. For a variation, add a teaspoon of minced fresh ginger.

12	ounces whole-wheat pasta
½	cup natural creamy peanut butter
¾	cup boiling water
4	tablespoons reduced-sodium soy sauce
3	tablespoons rice vinegar
4	sliced scallions
1	clove garlic, minced
½	teaspoon sugar
	Cayenne pepper to taste
	Sliced cucumber for garnish

1. Bring a Dutch oven of water to a boil. Cook pasta until just tender, according to package directions.
2. Meanwhile, whisk peanut butter with ¾ cup boiling water in a bowl until smooth. Stir in soy sauce, vinegar, scallions, garlic, sugar and cayenne.
3. Toss the sauce with the hot pasta. Garnish with cucumber. Serve hot or at room temperature.

ACTIVE TIME: 25 minutes
TOTAL: 25 minutes

MAKES: 6 servings, about 1 cup each

H✕W   H↑F   H♥H
PER SERVING: 342 calories; 12 g fat (1 g sat, 0 g mono); 0 mg cholesterol; 49 g carbohydrate; 0 g added sugars; 14 g protein; 9 g fiber; 443 mg sodium; 172 mg potassium.
NUTRITION BONUS: Magnesium (22% daily value), Iron (15% dv).

SERVE WITH:

Sliced cucumbers tossed with sesame seeds, rice vinegar, toasted sesame oil and a squeeze of lime juice

Spinach Pasta with Pesto, Potatoes & Green Beans

ACTIVE TIME: 30 minutes
TOTAL: 30 minutes
TO MAKE AHEAD: Prepare pesto (Step 1), cover and refrigerate for up to 3 days or freeze for up to 2 months.

MAKES: 4 servings, 1⅓ cups each

H↑F

PER SERVING: 465 calories; 17 g fat (4 g sat, 8 g mono); 75 mg cholesterol; 62 g carbohydrate; 0 g added sugars; 17 g protein; 6 g fiber; 498 mg sodium; 535 mg potassium.
NUTRITION BONUS: Magnesium & Vitamin A (25% daily value), Calcium (23% dv), Iron (22% dv), Vitamin C (18% dv), Zinc (16% dv), Potassium (15% dv).

SERVE WITH:

A salad of cherry tomato halves and bocconcini (small balls of mozzarella) drizzled with extra-virgin olive oil and balsamic vinegar

The beauty of this delicious pasta dish lies in its simplicity: The potatoes, green beans and pasta are all cooked in the same pot of lightly salted water. If you want to make it even easier, use store-bought pesto and skip making your own in Step 1.

PESTO

1	**cup loosely packed fresh basil leaves**
3	**tablespoons pine nuts**
1	**clove garlic, peeled**
½	**teaspoon salt**
1	**tablespoon freshly grated Pecorino Romano *or* Parmesan cheese**
2	**tablespoons extra-virgin olive oil**

PASTA

1	**medium potato, peeled and cut into ¾-inch pieces**
2	**cups 1-inch pieces trimmed green beans (about 8 ounces)**
12	**ounces fresh spinach linguine**
¼	**cup freshly grated Pecorino Romano cheese**

1. **To prepare pesto:** Place basil, pine nuts, garlic and salt in a food processor and pulse until a fairly smooth paste forms. Transfer to a small bowl. Stir in 1 tablespoon cheese, then stir in oil.
2. **To prepare pasta:** Bring 4 quarts water to a boil in a Dutch oven. Add potatoes and cook for 3 minutes. Add green beans and pasta and simmer until the pasta is just tender, 1 to 4 minutes.
3. Reserving about ½ cup of the cooking water, drain the pasta, green beans and potatoes in a colander. Divide the mixture evenly among 4 shallow bowls, top each with one-fourth of the pesto and 1 to 2 tablespoons of the hot cooking water, and toss well. Sprinkle with cheese and serve.

Southern Pasta Salad with Black-Eyed Peas

Lapsang Souchong tea or black coffee along with tidbits of smoked turkey give this hearty pasta, vegetable and bean mélange a wonderful, complex flavor. The dish makes a great, 30-minute weeknight meal or the perfect take-along for a potluck or picnic.

8 ounces whole-wheat small elbows *or* other small pasta shape
8 ounces white *or* green chard, cut crosswise into thin strips
8 ounces smoked turkey, chopped
2 15-ounce cans black-eyed peas, rinsed
1 cup oil-packed sun-dried tomatoes, drained and sliced
1/2 cup chopped sweet onion, such as Vidalia

DRESSING

1/4 cup brewed coffee *or* tea, such as Lapsang Souchong
2 tablespoons extra-virgin olive oil
2 tablespoons lime juice
2 tablespoons cider vinegar
1 1/2 teaspoons molasses
1 teaspoon Worcestershire sauce
1 1/2 teaspoons chili powder
1/2 teaspoon ground cumin
   Freshly ground pepper to taste

1. Bring a Dutch oven of water to a boil. Cook pasta until just tender, about 5 minutes; add chard during the last minute of cooking. Drain in a colander and rinse under cold water until cool. Press to remove excess water and transfer to a large bowl. Add turkey, black-eyed peas, sun-dried tomatoes and onion.
2. **To prepare dressing:** Whisk coffee (or tea), oil, lime juice, vinegar, molasses, Worcestershire sauce, chili powder, cumin and pepper in a small bowl.
3. Add the dressing to the pasta and chard; toss until well combined.

ACTIVE TIME: 20 minutes
TOTAL: 20 minutes

MAKES: 6 servings, about 1 1/3 cups each

H✖W   H↑F   H♥H
PER SERVING: 355 calories; 9 g fat (2 g sat, 6 g mono); 16 mg cholesterol; 53 g carbohydrate; 1 g added sugars; 19 g protein; 9 g fiber; 690 mg sodium; 919 mg potassium.
NUTRITION BONUS: Vitamin A (51% daily value), Vitamin C (50% dv), Magnesium (37% dv), Potassium (26% dv), Iron (24% dv), Folate (22% dv), Zinc (16% dv).

SERVE WITH:

Halved romaine lettuce hearts topped with crumbled blue cheese and a small drizzle of your favorite creamy dressing

Vermicelli Puttanesca

ACTIVE TIME: 30 minutes
TOTAL: 30 minutes

MAKES: 6 servings

H↑F   H♥H

PER SERVING: 380 calories; 10 g fat
(2 g sat, 6 g mono); 5 mg
cholesterol; 64 g carbohydrate;
0 g added sugars; 15 g protein;
11 g fiber; 370 mg sodium;
493 mg potassium.

NUTRITION BONUS: Vitamin C (35%
daily value), Magnesium (32% dv),
Vitamin A (25% dv), Iron (20% dv),
Folate (17% dv), Zinc (15% dv).

SERVE WITH:

Spinach or broccoli rabe
sautéed with minced garlic

*A triple play of olives, capers and anchovies are the all-stars of this no-cook tomato sauce.
To give the dish an additional kick, consider adding a few pinches of crushed red pepper.*

  4   large ripe tomatoes, coarsely chopped, *or* one 28-ounce can plum tomatoes,
         drained and coarsely chopped (3 1/2 cups)
  1/4 cup chopped flat-leaf parsley
 16   large black Greek olives, pitted and chopped
  3   tablespoons capers, rinsed and finely chopped
  4   anchovy fillets, finely chopped
  2   tablespoons extra-virgin olive oil
  3   large cloves garlic, finely chopped
  1/2 teaspoon freshly ground pepper
  1   pound whole-wheat vermicelli *or* spaghettini
  1/4 cup freshly grated Pecorino Romano *or* Parmesan cheese

1. Put a Dutch oven of water on to boil.
2. Combine tomatoes, parsley, olives, capers, anchovies, oil, garlic and pepper in a large
   pasta-serving bowl.
3. Cook pasta until just tender, 8 to 10 minutes or according to package directions.
4. Drain the pasta and add it to the bowl with the sauce. Toss well to combine. Sprinkle
   with cheese and serve immediately.

One-Pot Wonders

A heavy Dutch oven is the workhorse of the kitchen and will deliver a lifetime of mouthwatering, nourishing meals

For as long as I can remember, our kitchen in Barcelona where I grew up had a heavy pot simmering away on the stove. In winter, it usually contained a stew. Spring brought with it the aroma of asparagus or sorrel soup. Summer was the time for apricot, cherry or strawberry purees to spread on morning toast. And in the fall the unmistakable aroma of beans stewed with the last of summer's tomatoes and peppers suffused the air.

My mother and my grandmother made almost everything in old-fashioned heavy enameled cast-iron pots, known as Dutch ovens. These pots, in various flame colors, were lined up against the kitchen walls according to size, ranging from the largest, which resembled a small tub, down to the smallest one, just roomy enough to melt some butter or hard-boil a couple of eggs. The pots were well worn from years of use over a high flame or in the fireplace. But they still worked perfectly—they conducted the heat evenly and they were nearly indestructible. Together with a few cast-iron skillets, a couple of copper saucepans and some earthenware casseroles, they covered all the cooking needs of our family.

Ours was not an unusual kitchen for that time and place. It was in keeping with a tradition of slow cooking that began when hunters put tough cuts of moose, wild boar or hare in makeshift vessels and cooked them for hours over wood fires, breaking down the tough fibers until the meat became tender and flavorful. By the 1600s, heavy cast-iron pots were being manufactured in the Netherlands and braising had become a more sophisticated method of cooking. European cooks were simmering tough cuts of meat and then adding garden vegetables and the spices and herbs of their regional cuisines to achieve distinctive flavors and textures. By the nineteenth century, dishes like the French Daube or Coq au Vin, the Italian Osso Buco, the Spanish Cocido Madrileño and all-American New England Baked Beans were becoming classics.

Today in New York City, my kitchen is tight on space. But I do have Dutch ovens in several sizes that I use all the time. I pull out my 6-quart pot again and again, be it for a batch of soup, some poached fruit or a quick tomato sauce. It's the perfect size to make a hearty braise for six or eight people and it works flawlessly every time. Like all Dutch ovens, mine have tight-fitting lids that retain moisture. Plus they're coated with enamel, so I can cook with acidic ingredients, such as tomatoes and wine, without affecting the flavor. Best of all, cast iron conducts and retains heat exceptionally well, so foods cook evenly both on top of the stove and in the oven and stay hot on the dining table.

When I look at some of the pots that I inherited and lugged overseas from Barcelona, I feel nostalgic. They have been part of my life for such a long time. I wonder if it's time for a change now that they come in so many gorgeous colors. But why change? My pots, even after decades of use, are still going strong. 🍲

Perla Meyers is an award-winning food writer whose classic cookbooks include Spur of the Moment Cook *(Morrow Cookbooks, 1999) and* Perla Meyers' Art of Seasonal Cooking *(Simon & Schuster, 1991).*

When I look at some of the pots that I inherited and lugged overseas from Barcelona, I feel nostalgic. They have been part of my life for such a long time. I wonder if it's time for a change now that they come in so many gorgeous colors. But why change? My pots, even after decades of use, are still going strong.

—Perla Meyers

Creamy Garlic Pasta with Shrimp & Vegetables

This fast shrimp-and-vegetable pasta is coated in a tart, garlicky yogurt sauce that gives it a decidedly Middle Eastern feel. The dish is loaded with enough goodies to be substantial, but light enough to make a perfect supper for a hot summer night.

6	ounces whole-wheat spaghetti
12	ounces peeled and deveined raw shrimp (*see Note, page 213*), cut into 1-inch pieces
1	bunch asparagus, trimmed and thinly sliced
1	large red bell pepper, thinly sliced
1	cup fresh *or* frozen peas
3	cloves garlic, chopped
1¼	teaspoons kosher salt
1½	cups nonfat *or* low-fat plain yogurt
¼	cup chopped flat-leaf parsley
3	tablespoons lemon juice
1	tablespoon extra-virgin olive oil
½	teaspoon freshly ground pepper
¼	cup toasted pine nuts (*see Note*; optional)

1. Bring a Dutch oven of water to a boil. Add spaghetti and cook 2 minutes less than package directions. Add shrimp, asparagus, bell pepper and peas and cook until the pasta is tender and the shrimp are cooked, 2 to 4 minutes more. Drain well.
2. Mash garlic and salt in a large bowl until a paste forms. Whisk in yogurt, parsley, lemon juice, oil and pepper. Add the pasta mixture and toss to coat. Serve sprinkled with pine nuts (if using).

NOTE: **To toast pine nuts**, place in a small dry skillet and cook over medium-low heat, stirring, until fragrant, 2 to 4 minutes.

ACTIVE TIME: 30 minutes
TOTAL: 30 minutes

MAKES: 4 servings, about 2 cups each

H✕W   H▲F   H♥H

PER SERVING: 361 calories; 6 g fat (1 g sat, 3 g mono); 109 mg cholesterol; 53 g carbohydrate; 0 g added sugars; 28 g protein; 10 g fiber; 949 mg sodium; 827 mg potassium.
NUTRITION BONUS: Vitamin C (125% daily value), Vitamin A (71% dv), Folate (64% dv), Magnesium (32% dv), Calcium (29% dv), Zinc (25% dv), Potassium (24% dv), Iron (21% dv).

SERVE WITH:

Grilled slices of eggplant

Braised Winter Vegetable Pasta

ACTIVE TIME: 25 minutes
TOTAL: 40 minutes

MAKES: 4 servings, about 2 cups each

H▲F   H♥H

PER SERVING: 468 calories; 9 g fat
(1 g sat, 6 g mono); 0 mg
cholesterol; 76 g carbohydrate;
0 g added sugars; 16 g protein;
13 g fiber; 655 mg sodium;
863 mg potassium.
NUTRITION BONUS: Vitamin A (172%
daily value), Vitamin C (78% dv),
Magnesium (32% dv), Iron &
Potassium (25% dv), Folate
(18% dv).

SERVE WITH:

Arugula salad with roasted baby
beets or jarred pickled beets

Pasta and an array of hearty vegetables are braised all together in a savory white wine and broth blend with delicious results. If lima beans aren't your thing, consider adding frozen shelled edamame instead.

2 tablespoons extra-virgin olive oil
1 small onion, diced
4 cloves garlic, minced
1 tablespoon finely chopped fresh sage *or* 1 teaspoon dried rubbed
4 cups vegetable broth
1 cup dry white wine
8 ounces whole-wheat medium pasta shells *or* other small pasta
2 cups bite-size cauliflower florets
2 cups bite-size butternut squash cubes
¼ teaspoon salt
   Freshly ground pepper to taste
1 10-ounce bag frozen lima beans, thawed

1. Heat oil in a Dutch oven over medium heat. Add onion, garlic and sage and cook, stirring, until softened, 3 to 4 minutes.
2. Add broth and wine; bring to a boil over medium-high heat. Add pasta, cauliflower, squash, salt and pepper and cook, stirring occasionally, until the pasta is not quite tender, about 10 minutes. Stir in lima beans and cook, stirring occasionally, until the lima beans and pasta are tender and most of the liquid is absorbed, about 5 minutes more.

Sauté of Cauliflower & Mustard Greens with Peanuts

Assertive vegetables like mustard greens are commonly found in Chinese cooking, so they work particularly well when, as done in this dish, they are sautéed with cauliflower florets and tossed in a tangy peanut sauce.

2   tablespoons natural peanut butter
3   tablespoons water
1   tablespoon rice-wine vinegar
2   teaspoons reduced-sodium soy sauce
2   teaspoons extra-virgin olive oil
3   cloves garlic, finely chopped
3   cups cauliflower florets
1/2 cup vegetable broth *or* water
8   cups firmly packed, coarsely chopped mustard greens, stems included
     (1-pound bunch)
     Freshly ground pepper to taste
2   tablespoons chopped peanuts

1. Whisk peanut butter, water, vinegar and soy sauce in a small bowl.
2. Heat oil in a Dutch oven over medium heat until very hot. Add garlic and cook, stirring, until golden, about 30 seconds. Add cauliflower and broth (or water) and bring to a boil. Cover and simmer until the cauliflower is almost tender, about 5 minutes. Add greens and simmer, covered, until the greens are tender, 5 minutes more. (Do not overcook the greens or they will lose their vibrant color.) Stir in the peanut sauce and cook, uncovered, for 2 minutes. Season with pepper. Serve garnished with peanuts.

ACTIVE TIME: 20 minutes
TOTAL: 20 minutes

MAKES: 2 servings

PER SERVING: 316 calories; 18 g fat (2 g sat, 6 g mono); 0 mg cholesterol; 29 g carbohydrate; 0 g added sugars; 16 g protein; 13 g fiber; 549 mg sodium; 1,363 mg potassium.
NUTRITION BONUS: Vitamin A (475% daily value), Vitamin C (392% dv), Folate (131% dv), Potassium (39% dv), Calcium & Magnesium (29% dv), Iron (26% dv).

SERVE WITH:

Buckwheat soba noodles

Sweet Potato & Black Bean Chili

ACTIVE TIME: 25 minutes
TOTAL: 40 minutes
TO MAKE AHEAD: Cover and refrigerate for up to 3 days or freeze for up to 3 months.

MAKES: 4 servings, about 2 cups each

H✖W H⬆F H❤H

PER SERVING: 318 calories; 8 g fat (1 g sat, 5 g mono); 0 mg cholesterol; 54 g carbohydrate; 0 g added sugars; 12 g protein; 15 g fiber; 547 mg sodium; 1,040 mg potassium.
NUTRITION BONUS: Vitamin A (242% daily value), Iron & Vitamin C (32% dv), Potassium (30% dv), Folate (29% dv), Calcium (16% dv).

SERVE WITH:

Slices of grilled store-bought polenta with shredded extra-sharp Cheddar cheese on top

Ground chipotle chile gives the perfect smoky heat to diced sweet potato and convenient canned black beans in this easy-to-make vegetarian chili. Make a double batch and eat it for lunch the next day or freeze the extras for a heat-and-serve dinner another night.

1	tablespoon plus 2 teaspoons extra-virgin olive oil
1	medium-large sweet potato, peeled and diced
1	large onion, diced
4	cloves garlic, minced
2	tablespoons chili powder
4	teaspoons ground cumin
1/2	teaspoon ground chipotle chile (*see Note*)
1/4	teaspoon salt
2 1/2	cups water
2	15-ounce cans black beans, rinsed
1	14-ounce can diced tomatoes
4	teaspoons lime juice
1/2	cup chopped fresh cilantro

1. Heat oil in a Dutch oven over medium-high heat. Add sweet potato and onion and cook, stirring often, until the onion is beginning to soften, about 4 minutes. Add garlic, chili powder, cumin, chipotle and salt and cook, stirring constantly, for 30 seconds. Add water and bring to a simmer. Cover, reduce heat to maintain a gentle simmer and cook until the sweet potato is tender, 10 to 12 minutes.
2. Add beans, tomatoes and lime juice; increase heat to high and return to a simmer, stirring often. Reduce heat and simmer until slightly reduced, about 5 minutes. Remove from heat and stir in cilantro.

NOTE: Chipotle peppers are dried, smoked jalapeño peppers. **Ground chipotle chile** pepper can be found in the spice section of most supermarkets or online at *penzeys.com*.

One-Pot Vegetable Stew from Ikaria (*Soufiko*)

ACTIVE TIME: 30 minutes
TOTAL: 1 1/2 hours
TO MAKE AHEAD: Cover and refrigerate for up to 4 days.

MAKES: 6 servings, about 1 1/3 cups each

H✕W   H⬆F

PER SERVING: 307 calories; 26 g fat (4 g sat, 19 g mono); 0 mg cholesterol; 18 g carbohydrate; 0 g added sugars; 4 g protein; 6 g fiber; 309 mg sodium; 774 mg potassium.
NUTRITION BONUS: Vitamin C (65% daily value), Potassium (22% dv), Folate (18% dv), Vitamin A (16% dv).

SERVE WITH:

Warm pita bread and hummus drizzled with olive oil

This olive-oil-rich stew, "soufiko," is a traditional medley from the Greek island of Ikaria. It is loaded with summer vegetables—eggplant, zucchini and tomatoes—so cook it when those are in season. If the weather's really hot, let it cool a bit before you serve it as it still tastes great at room temperature.

4   long, thin eggplants (about 1 pound total), such as Japanese eggplant, cut into 3/8-inch-thick rounds
1   teaspoon salt, divided
2/3 cup extra-virgin olive oil, preferably Greek
1   pound onions (2-3 medium), slivered
4   medium zucchini (about 1 1/2 pounds total), cut into 1/4 -inch-thick rounds
2   cloves garlic, minced
2   large, firm, ripe tomatoes, seeded and diced
    Freshly ground pepper to taste

1. Layer eggplant slices in a colander, lightly salting each layer (use 1/2 teaspoon salt). Place a weight on top of the eggplant and let drain for 30 minutes. Rinse well and pat dry.
2. Heat oil in a Dutch oven over medium-low heat. Add onions and cook until softened, about 5 minutes. Add the eggplant, zucchini and garlic. Sprinkle tomatoes evenly over the top. Season with the remaining 1/2 teaspoon salt and pepper.
3. Cover the pot and reduce heat to low. Cook until all the vegetables are very soft and have melded together, 45 minutes to 1 hour. Serve warm or at room temperature.

Tofu Curry

A blend of fresh garlic and ginger, plus turmeric, fennel seeds, oregano, red pepper, coriander and cumin, gives this tofu-and-vegetable curry big, bold, spicy flavor. Fragrant coconut milk and tangy nonfat yogurt definitely tame the spice, but luckily don't put out the fire completely.

ACTIVE TIME: 1 hour
TOTAL: 1¼ hours

MAKES: 4 servings, 2 cups each

H❊W   H↑F   H♥H
PER SERVING: 263 calories; 10 g fat (2 g sat, 4 g mono); 0 mg cholesterol; 32 g carbohydrate; 0 g added sugars; 17 g protein; 10 g fiber; 360 mg sodium; 1,075 mg potassium.
NUTRITION BONUS: Vitamin C (102% daily value), Vitamin A (34% dv), Folate (38% dv), Calcium (32% dv), Potassium (31% dv), Magnesium (26% dv), Iron (23% dv), Zinc (17% dv).

1	14- to 16-ounce package firm tofu, drained and cut into 1-inch-thick slabs
1	tablespoon canola oil
4	teaspoons minced garlic
4	teaspoons minced fresh ginger
½-1	teaspoon crushed red pepper, or to taste
1	teaspoon ground turmeric
1	teaspoon fennel seeds
1	teaspoon dried oregano
1	teaspoon ground coriander
¼	teaspoon ground cumin
1½	cups coarsely chopped onions (2 medium)
4	medium tomatoes, diced, *or* one 28-ounce can diced tomatoes, drained
¼	cup "lite" coconut milk
3½	cups cauliflower florets
2	cups peas, fresh *or* frozen (*not* thawed)
¼	cup nonfat plain yogurt, plus more for serving if desired
½	teaspoon salt
1	tablespoon chopped fresh cilantro for garnish

SERVE WITH:

Brown basmati rice

1. Press tofu (*see Note*). Cut into ½-inch cubes. Set aside.
2. Heat oil in a Dutch oven over medium heat. Add garlic, ginger, crushed red pepper, turmeric, fennel, oregano, coriander and cumin and cook, stirring, until fragrant, 20 seconds. Reduce heat to medium-low, add onions and cook, stirring, until softened, 4 to 5 minutes.
3. Stir in tomatoes and coconut milk; cook, stirring, until most of the liquid has evaporated, 5 to 7 minutes. Add cauliflower and the reserved tofu, cover and cook until the cauliflower is almost tender, 12 to 15 minutes.
4. Add peas, cover and cook, stirring once, until the peas are tender, about 3 minutes. Remove from the heat, stir in ¼ cup yogurt and salt. Garnish with cilantro and/or more yogurt, if desired.

NOTE: **To press tofu,** cut it to the thickness specified in the recipe. Wrap in a kitchen towel and place a heavy weight (such as a skillet) on top. Let stand at room temperature for 30 minutes. Remove weight, unwrap and cut as specified in the recipe.

Oyster Stew

ACTIVE TIME: 45 minutes
TOTAL: 45 minutes

TO MAKE AHEAD: Prepare through Step 3 and refrigerate for up to 1 day. Finish with Step 4 just before serving.

MAKES: 6 servings, about 1 1/3 cups each

H✂W   H♥H

PER SERVING: 222 calories; 8 g fat (3 g sat, 3 g mono); 38 mg cholesterol; 26 g carbohydrate; 0 g added sugars; 9 g protein; 3 g fiber; 435 mg sodium; 736 mg potassium.
NUTRITION BONUS: Zinc (193% daily value), Iron (31% dv), Vitamin C (27% dv), Potassium (21% dv), Magnesium (16% dv), Folate (15% dv).

SERVE WITH:

Salad of Boston lettuce topped with grape tomatoes, red onion and a buttermilk dressing

One of the wonderful things about an oyster stew is that it can be part of a celebratory Thanksgiving or Christmas meal or just as easily be a humble, comforting supper. If oysters aren't available, try this one-pot soup with clams or even mussels. To top it with Caviar Toasts (as shown): Dollop toasted slices of baguette with 1 teaspoon sour cream, 1/2 teaspoon caviar and a sprinkle of herbs. Place each toast atop a steaming bowl of stew.

3	slices bacon
2	teaspoons canola oil
2	cups diced onion
1	cup diced celery
1/4	teaspoon salt
1/4	teaspoon freshly ground pepper
1/2	cup dry white wine
2	8-ounce bottles clam juice (*see Notes*)
1 1/2	cups water, divided
1	pound baby *or* new potatoes, cut into bite-size chunks
3	tablespoons all-purpose flour
1	pound shucked oysters (*see Notes*), drained and chopped into bite-size pieces
1/2	cup light cream
2	tablespoons chopped fresh herbs, such as dill and chives

1. Cook bacon in a Dutch oven over medium heat, turning often, until crispy, 5 to 7 minutes. Drain on a paper towel. When cool, chop the bacon and set aside.
2. Wipe out the pot; add oil and heat over medium heat. Add onion, celery, salt and pepper and cook, stirring often, until the vegetables start to soften and brown slightly, about 2 minutes. Pour in wine, increase heat to medium-high and cook, scraping up any browned bits, until the wine is evaporated, 1 to 3 minutes. Add clam juice, 1 cup water and potatoes; cover and bring to a simmer. Reduce heat to medium-low and simmer, stirring occasionally, until the vegetables are tender, 10 to 15 minutes.
3. Whisk the remaining 1/2 cup water with flour until smooth and stir into the stew. Return to a simmer over medium-high heat, stirring constantly. Cook, stirring, until thickened, about 1 minute.
4. Stir in oysters, cream and herbs; return to a simmer and immediately remove from the heat. Let stand for 5 minutes to finish cooking the oysters. Serve sprinkled with the reserved bacon.

NOTES:
Bottled clam juice can be very high in sodium. We like Bar Harbor brand, which has 120 mg sodium per 2-ounce serving. Look for it in the canned-fish section or the supermarket seafood department.

Look for **shucked oysters** by the pound at the seafood counter or packed in plastic containers in the seafood department of most supermarkets. If your oysters are prepacked, be sure to look at the drained weight on the label—we needed to buy three 8-ounce containers to get 1 pound of drained shucked oysters.

Thai Bouillabaisse

The classic French seafood soup gets a Southeast Asian makeover with the flavors of lemongrass, lime, chile peppers and fresh ginger. The chiles give the soup heat, which a typical bouillabaisse wouldn't have, but fresh cilantro and diced avocado as garnishes (also not typical) help to cool things down. Be sure to simmer, not boil, the soup or the seafood will be overcooked.

ACTIVE TIME: 40 minutes
TOTAL: 1 hour

MAKES: 8 servings,
about 1¼ cups each

H✕W   H♥H
PER SERVING: 266 calories; 11 g fat
(1 g sat, 6 g mono); 92 mg
cholesterol; 14 g carbohydrate;
0 g added sugars; 28 g protein;
2 g fiber; 823 mg sodium;
765 mg potassium.
NUTRITION BONUS: Potassium (22%
daily value), Vitamin C (20% dv),
Folate (19% dv), Iron (15% dv).

- 3 tablespoons canola oil
- 1 cup diced shallots (5-6 large)
- 4 large cloves garlic, minced
- 2 tablespoons minced fresh ginger
- 1 5-inch piece lemongrass (*see Note*), cut into ¾-inch pieces, *or* zest of 1 lime
- 1-2 small chile peppers, such as serranos *or* jalapeños, seeded and thinly sliced
- 3 tablespoons all-purpose flour
- 4 cups reduced-sodium chicken broth
- 4 cups fish *or* seafood stock *or* bottled clam juice
- 12 ounces Pacific cod *or* halibut, cut into 2-inch pieces
- 12 ounces raw shrimp, peeled, deveined (*see Note, page 213*) and cut into 1-inch pieces
- 8 ounces dry sea scallops (*see Note, page 213*), cut in half crosswise
- 16 mussels, cleaned (*see Note, page 212*)
- 10 large shiitake mushrooms caps, cut into 1-inch pieces
- Juice of 1 large lime
- 1 ripe avocado, peeled and diced
- ¼ cup fresh cilantro leaves

SERVE WITH:

Crusty whole-grain baguette
to soak up the broth

1. Heat oil in a Dutch oven over medium heat. Add shallots, garlic, ginger, lemongrass (or lime zest) and chile pepper to taste; cook, stirring, until very soft, 3 to 4 minutes. Add flour; stir well to combine. Add chicken broth and fish or seafood stock (or clam juice). Bring to a simmer; reduce heat and gently simmer for 15 minutes.
2. Carefully submerge fish, shrimp, scallops, mussels and mushrooms in the broth. Return to a gentle simmer and cook until just cooked through, 3 to 4 minutes. Remove the pot from the heat and stir in lime juice. Serve garnished with avocado and cilantro.

NOTE: Look for **lemongrass**—a woody, scallion-shaped herb with an aromatic lemon flavor—in the produce department of well-stocked supermarkets. To use, trim off the root end and grassy top. Peel off the woody outer leaves. Thinly slice the softer inner stalk, then finely chop.

White Fish Stew (*Bianco*)

ACTIVE TIME: 30 minutes
TOTAL: 1½ hours

MAKES: 6 servings

H✂W   H♥H
PER SERVING: 203 calories; 3 g fat
(0 g sat, 2 g mono); 45 mg
cholesterol; 26 g carbohydrate;
0 g added sugars; 18 g protein;
4 g fiber; 512 mg sodium;
863 mg potassium.
NUTRITION BONUS: Vitamin C (57%
daily value), Potassium (25% dv).

SERVE WITH:

Crusty sourdough bread
and a salad of fresh tomatoes,
cucumber, Kalamata olives
and feta cheese drizzled with
red-wine vinegar and olive oil

A whole head of garlic, minced, gives this simple Greek fisherman's stew gutsy flavor, but don't worry—it mellows out considerably while cooking. The recipe calls for Pacific cod, but any sturdy white fish, such as halibut or haddock, will do. (Photograph: page 148.)

1	tablespoon extra-virgin olive oil
1	medium onion, chopped
1	head garlic, cloves separated, peeled and minced
½	teaspoon dried oregano
½	teaspoon salt
	Pinch of freshly ground pepper
2½	cups water
4	medium red potatoes, cut into 1-inch chunks
1½	pounds Pacific cod (*see Note*), cut into 6 portions
1	lemon

1. Heat oil in a 4½-quart Dutch oven over medium heat. Add onion, garlic, oregano, salt and pepper. Cook until the onion is tender, 2 to 3 minutes. Add water and bring to a boil. Reduce heat to low, cover and simmer for 30 minutes.
2. Add potatoes and simmer, covered, for 15 minutes. Remove the potatoes with a slotted spoon to a bowl. Place fish in the sauce. (The fish should be at least halfway covered with liquid; if necessary, add more water.) Return the potatoes to the pot, cover and simmer until the fish is opaque and the potatoes are tender, 25 to 30 minutes more. Squeeze lemon juice over the stew just before serving.

NOTE: U.S.-caught **Pacific cod**, a.k.a. Alaska cod, is considered a good choice for the environment because it is sustainably fished and has a larger, more stable population.

Mussels alla Marinara

Convenient and nutrition-packed canned tomatoes make for an easy, homemade marinara to cook mussels in. Try this recipe with cherrystone clams as well.

2 teaspoons extra-virgin olive oil
2 carrots, peeled and cut diagonally into ¹/₂-inch slices
1 onion, cut in eighths
4 cloves garlic, sliced
²/₃ cup dry white wine
1 28-ounce can no-salt *or* low-sodium diced tomatoes
¹/₄ teaspoon salt, or to taste
¹/₄ teaspoon freshly ground pepper
2 pounds mussels, cleaned (*see Note*)

Heat oil in a Dutch oven over medium heat. Add carrots, onion and garlic and cook, stirring, until softened, 3 to 4 minutes. Add wine, tomatoes, salt and pepper and bring to a boil over high heat. Add mussels, cover and cook until they have opened, 3 to 4 minutes. (Discard any that do not open.)

NOTE: **To clean mussels:** Discard mussels with broken shells or whose shell remains open after you tap it. Hold mussels under running water and use a stiff brush to remove any barnacles; pull off any black fibrous "beards." (Some mussels may not have a beard.) Mussels should be "debearded" no more than 30 minutes before cooking.

ACTIVE TIME: 30 minutes
TOTAL: 30 minutes

MAKES: 2 servings

H↑F   H♥H

PER SERVING: 377 calories; 9 g fat (2 g sat, 5 g mono); 48 mg cholesterol; 37 g carbohydrate; 0 g added sugars; 25 g protein; 7 g fiber; 693 mg sodium; 1,333 mg potassium.
NUTRITION BONUS: Vitamin A (218% daily value), Vitamin C (97% dv), Iron (57% dv), Potassium (38% dv), Folate (30%), Magnesium (25% dv), Zinc (22% dv), Calcium (20%).

SERVE WITH:

Crusty whole-grain Italian bread and a watercress salad

North Country Braised Chicken

ACTIVE TIME: 30 minutes
TOTAL: 45 minutes

MAKES: 8 servings

H✖W   H⬆F   H❤H
PER SERVING: 266 calories; 5 g fat
(1 g sat, 2 g mono); 63 mg
cholesterol; 31 g carbohydrate;
0 g added sugars; 26 g protein;
6 g fiber; 290 mg sodium;
690 mg potassium.
NUTRITION BONUS: Vitamin C (55%
daily value), Potassium (20% dv).

SERVE WITH:

Mesclun green salad with slices
of orange, toasted walnuts and
a champagne-vinegar dressing

This quick chicken braise is the perfect opportunity to reacquaint yourself with the humble rutabaga. Here, its earthy flavors are brought to life when simmered with apple cider, pears, onions and chicken broth. A splash of tart lemon juice rounds out the dish.

- ¼ cup all-purpose flour
- 8 5-ounce *or* four 8-to-10-ounce boneless, skinless chicken breasts (*see Note*), trimmed
- 3 teaspoons canola oil, divided
- ½ teaspoon salt, divided
- ½ teaspoon freshly ground pepper, divided
- 2 medium onions, coarsely chopped
- 1 cup apple cider
- 1 large rutabaga, peeled and cut into ¼-by-2-inch julienne (about 8 cups)
- 1 cup reduced-sodium chicken broth
- 4 firm ripe pears, such as Anjou, Bosc *or* Comice
- ¼ cup lemon juice
- 1 tablespoon chopped fresh thyme *or* 1 teaspoon dried

1. Place flour on a plate and dredge chicken breasts to coat well on all sides, shaking off excess. (Reserve unused flour.)
2. Heat 1 teaspoon oil in a large Dutch oven over medium-high heat. Add half the chicken and cook until golden, about 3 minutes per side. Remove to a plate and season with ⅛ teaspoon each salt and pepper. Add 1 teaspoon oil to the pot and brown the remaining chicken. Remove to the plate and season with ⅛ teaspoon each salt and pepper. Set the chicken aside.
3. Reduce heat to medium-low. Add the remaining 1 teaspoon oil and onions. Stir until golden brown, about 5 minutes. Add the reserved flour and stir 1 minute more. Gradually add apple cider and stir until thickened, about 2 minutes. Add rutabaga and broth. Bring to a simmer. Reduce heat to low, cover and simmer until the rutabaga is tender, 15 to 20 minutes.
4. Meanwhile, peel pears and cut into ½-inch dice. Transfer to a bowl and stir in lemon juice and thyme. Add to the cooked rutabaga and season with the remaining ¼ teaspoon each salt and pepper. Lay the reserved chicken on top and cover the pot. Cook until the chicken is no longer pink in the center and the pears are tender, 5 to 6 minutes more.

NOTE: It can be difficult to find an individual **chicken breast** small enough for one portion. Removing the thin strip of meat from the underside of a 5-ounce breast—the chicken tender—removes about 1 ounce of meat and yields a perfect 4-ounce portion. Wrap and freeze the tenders and when you have gathered enough, use them in a stir-fry or for oven-baked chicken fingers. If you can only find chicken breasts closer to 8-9 ounces each, you'll only need 4 breasts for 8 servings—cut each one in half before cooking.

Hunter's Chicken Stew

Meaty chicken thighs are perfect for this classic cacciatore because they stay moist even when they're cooked for a long time. Our version is fortified with plenty of onions, mushrooms and tomatoes and gets a wonderful, woodlands flavor from bay leaf and chopped fresh rosemary.

2	teaspoons plus 2 tablespoons extra-virgin olive oil, divided
3	medium onions, finely chopped
2	cloves garlic, minced
1/2	cup all-purpose flour
12	bone-in chicken thighs (about 4 pounds), skin removed, trimmed
1	teaspoon salt, divided
1/4	teaspoon freshly ground pepper, plus more to taste
1	cup dry white wine *or* vermouth
1 1/2	pounds button mushrooms, halved *or* quartered, depending on size
4	plum tomatoes, chopped
1	cup reduced-sodium chicken broth
2	bay leaves
2	teaspoons chopped fresh rosemary *or* 3/4 teaspoon dried
1	tablespoon thinly sliced fresh basil

1. Heat 2 teaspoons oil in a large Dutch oven over medium-low heat. Add onions and cook, stirring occasionally, for 5 minutes. Add garlic and cook, stirring, until the onions are very soft and translucent, 2 to 4 minutes more. Using a slotted spoon, transfer the onions to a bowl; set aside. Remove the pot from the heat.

2. Place flour in a shallow dish. Sprinkle chicken with 1/2 teaspoon salt and pepper. Dredge the chicken in the flour. Gently shake off any excess.

3. Cook the chicken in 2 batches in the Dutch oven, using 1 tablespoon oil for each batch. Cook over medium-high heat, turning once, until browned on both sides, 2 to 4 minutes per side. Transfer the chicken to a plate.

4. Pour wine (or vermouth) into the pot and cook, stirring and scraping up any browned bits with a wooden spoon, for 1 minute. Stir in mushrooms, tomatoes, broth, bay leaves and rosemary. Return the reserved onions to the pot. Add the chicken and any accumulated juices, making sure each piece is partially submerged. Bring to a simmer, then reduce heat to medium-low. Partially cover the pot and cook, gently stirring once or twice, until the chicken is very tender, about 1 hour.

5. Remove the chicken to a plate and tent with foil to keep warm. Bring the liquid in the pot to a boil over medium-high heat and cook until thickened, 10 to 15 minutes. Skim or blot any visible fat from the surface. Season with the remaining 1/2 teaspoon salt and pepper to taste. Return the chicken to the pot. Gently stir in basil.

ACTIVE TIME: 1 hour

TOTAL: 2 1/2 hours

TO MAKE AHEAD: Prepare through Step 5, but don't add basil. Cover and refrigerate for up to 1 day. To serve, reheat stew and stir in basil.

MAKES: 8 servings

H ♥ H

PER SERVING: 345 calories; 16 g fat (4 g sat, 8 g mono); 100 mg cholesterol; 13 g carbohydrate; 0 g added sugars; 31 g protein; 1 g fiber; 454 mg sodium; 746 mg potassium.
NUTRITION BONUS: Zinc (24% daily value), Potassium (21% dv), Vitamin C (15% dv).

SERVE WITH:

Creamy polenta cooked with bold-flavored Pecorino Romano cheese

Chicken Tagine with Green Olives

ACTIVE TIME: 30 minutes

TOTAL: 1¼ hours

MAKES: 6 servings

PER SERVING: 392 calories; 21 g fat (4 g sat, 11 g mono); 113 mg cholesterol; 15 g carbohydrate; 0 g added sugars; 34 g protein; 3 g fiber; 847 mg sodium; 632 mg potassium.

NUTRITION BONUS: Zinc (23% daily value), Potassium & Vitamin C (18% dv), Iron (16% dv).

SERVE WITH:

Whole-wheat couscous or brown rice flecked with golden raisins, pistachios and toasted sliced almonds

Tagine is both the name of the cooking vessel and the one-pot meal of choice in Morocco. The chimney-like top of the pot promotes condensation, which helps in achieving flavorful braises and slow-cooked dishes, but a Dutch oven or covered heavy skillet works as well. Here, bone-in chicken thighs are stewed with the classic Moroccan flavor duo of lemon and green olives.

- **12   bone-in chicken thighs (3½-4 pounds), skin removed, trimmed**
  Coarsely ground pepper to taste
- **2   tablespoons extra-virgin olive oil, divided**
- **1   large onion, thinly sliced**
- **3   cloves garlic, finely chopped**
- **1   tablespoon finely chopped fresh ginger**
- **2   teaspoons finely chopped fresh red *or* green chile pepper**
- **4   cups reduced-sodium chicken broth**
- **2   medium potatoes, preferably Yukon Gold, peeled and diced**
- **½   cup large green olives, pitted and coarsely chopped**
- **2   tablespoons lemon juice**
- **1   tablespoon chopped fresh thyme *or* 1 teaspoon dried**
- **1   tablespoon ground cumin**
- **1   tablespoon ground cinnamon**
- **1   teaspoon ground turmeric**
- **1   teaspoon paprika**
- **½   cup chopped fresh cilantro**

1. Preheat oven to 375°F.
2. Pat chicken dry and season with pepper. Heat 1 tablespoon oil in a Dutch oven or large ovenproof skillet over medium-high heat until hot but not smoking. Add the chicken thighs (in batches if necessary) and cook, moving them around every couple of minutes, until browned on all sides, 5 to 7 minutes. Remove from the pot and set aside. Pour off fat.
3. Reduce heat to medium and add the remaining 1 tablespoon oil to the pot. Add onion and cook, stirring frequently, until beginning to brown, 5 to 7 minutes. Add garlic, ginger and chiles and cook for 2 minutes more. Add broth, potatoes, olives, lemon juice, thyme, cumin, cinnamon, turmeric, paprika and the reserved chicken. Bring to a simmer.
4. Cover the pot and transfer it to the oven. Bake until the chicken thighs are tender, 45 minutes. Stir in cilantro. Season with pepper and serve.

Marsala Chicken Stew

ACTIVE TIME: 1 hour
TOTAL: 1 hour

MAKES: 4 servings, about 1¼ cups each

H❯⟨W   H♥H

PER SERVING: 320 calories; 10 g fat (2 g sat, 6 g mono); 63 mg cholesterol; 21 g carbohydrate; 0 g added sugars; 29 g protein; 3 g fiber; 421 mg sodium; 790 mg potassium.
NUTRITION BONUS: Potassium (23% daily value), Vitamin C (15% dv).

SERVE WITH:

Potatoes mashed with buttermilk and chives
Steamed green beans

Marsala wine turns plain old chicken breasts into a rich, complex stew. Of course, plenty of mushrooms and onions add substance and layers of earthy flavor to the mix.

- **2 tablespoons extra-virgin olive oil, divided**
- **1 pound boneless, skinless chicken breasts, trimmed and cut into 1-inch pieces**
- **¼ teaspoon salt, divided**
- **¼ teaspoon freshly ground pepper, divided, plus more to taste**
- **1 pound mushrooms, sliced**
- **3 medium onions, chopped**
- **3 tablespoons all-purpose flour**
- **2 cloves garlic, finely chopped**
- **½ cup Marsala (*see Note*)**
- **1½ cups reduced-sodium chicken broth**
- **1 tablespoon balsamic vinegar**

1. Heat 1½ teaspoons oil in a Dutch oven over medium-high heat. Reduce heat to medium. Add half the chicken and season with ⅛ teaspoon each salt and pepper. Cook, stirring occasionally, until the chicken is browned on all sides and no longer pink in the center, 5 to 8 minutes. Transfer to a plate and repeat with another 1½ teaspoons oil, the remaining chicken and ⅛ teaspoon each salt and pepper. Set aside.

2. Add another 1½ teaspoons oil to the pot. Add mushrooms and cook, stirring, until they begin to soften and give off liquid, 3 to 5 minutes. Add the remaining 1½ teaspoons oil and onions. Cook, stirring and reducing heat as necessary to keep them from burning, until the onions soften and start to turn golden, 10 to 15 minutes.

3. Add flour and garlic to the pot and cook, stirring, for 1 minute. Pour in Marsala and cook, stirring, for 1 minute more. Add broth and bring to a simmer. Reduce the heat to low, cover and cook, stirring often, until thickened, about 5 minutes. Add vinegar and the reserved chicken, along with any juice. Return to a simmer. Season with additional pepper, if desired.

NOTE: **Marsala**, a fortified wine from Sicily, is a flavorful addition to many sauces. Don't use the "cooking Marsala" sold in many supermarkets—it can be surprisingly high in sodium. Instead, purchase Marsala that's sold with other fortified wines in your wine or liquor store. An opened bottle can be stored in a cool, dry place for months.

Arroz con Pollo

Arroz con pollo, or chicken cooked with rice, is a staple dish in Spanish, Latin American and Caribbean home-cooking repertoires, but it's often a slow-cooked dish. In our version, we use quick-cooking brown rice and some prepared tomato sauce to help you get this comforting dinner on the table in just 40 minutes.

2½ pounds bone-in chicken thighs *and/or* drumsticks (about 8 pieces),
       skin removed, trimmed
½   teaspoon salt, divided
2   tablespoons canola oil
1   large onion, chopped
4   cloves garlic, minced
½   cup tomato sauce
1¼ cups reduced-sodium chicken broth
1   cup instant brown rice
1   cup frozen mixed vegetables, thawed

1. Sprinkle chicken with ¼ teaspoon salt. Heat oil in a Dutch oven over medium-high heat. Reduce heat to medium and add half the chicken pieces, skinned-side down. Cook until browned on one side, 4 to 8 minutes. Transfer to a plate. Repeat with the remaining chicken; transfer to the plate.
2. Add onion, garlic and tomato sauce to the pot and cook, stirring, for 1 minute. Add broth and the remaining ¼ teaspoon salt; bring to a boil. Stir in rice, return the chicken to the pot, cover and simmer until an instant-read thermometer inserted into the thickest part of the chicken registers 165°F, 8 minutes. Stir in vegetables, cover and cook until heated through, about 2 minutes. Serve the chicken over the rice.

ACTIVE TIME: 40 minutes
TOTAL: 40 minutes

MAKES: 4 servings, 2 pieces of chicken & ¾ cup rice each

PER SERVING: 378 calories; 16 g fat (3 g sat, 7 g mono); 87 mg cholesterol; 27 g carbohydrate; 0 g added sugars; 31 g protein; 3 g fiber; 735 mg sodium; 506 mg potassium.
NUTRITION BONUS: Vitamin A (70% daily value), Zinc (24% dv), Magnesium & Vitamin C (17% dv).

SERVE WITH:

Canned butter beans quickly heated with roasted red peppers, a few pinches of hot or sweet smoked paprika and a pinch of garlic powder

Orange-Tomato Couscous with Chicken

ACTIVE TIME: 45 minutes
TOTAL: 45 minutes

MAKES: 6 servings, about 1 chicken thigh & 1 cup couscous each

H✂W   H⬆F   H♥H

PER SERVING: 417 calories; 14 g fat (3 g sat, 7 g mono); 74 mg cholesterol; 44 g carbohydrate; 0 g added sugars; 29 g protein; 8 g fiber; 458 mg sodium; 509 mg potassium.
NUTRITION BONUS: Vitamin C (37% daily value), Iron (20% dv), Zinc (18% dv).

SERVE WITH:

Steamed green beans
or broccoli

This cinnamon- and cumin-spiked couscous with chicken takes its inspiration from Morocco. It's made mostly with pantry staples—all you have to pick up is some chicken thighs, a bunch of cilantro and an orange. The orange slices become tender after cooking— you can eat them skin and all. For a variation, substitute cubed, boneless leg of lamb for the chicken.

6   boneless, skinless chicken thighs (about 1 1/2 pounds), trimmed
1 1/4 teaspoons ground cinnamon, divided
1 1/4 teaspoons ground cumin, divided
1/4 teaspoon salt
1/4 teaspoon freshly ground pepper
2   tablespoons extra-virgin olive oil, divided
1   medium onion, thinly sliced
1   orange, scrubbed, halved and cut into 1/4-inch slices
1   14-ounce can diced tomatoes, with juice
1   15-ounce can chickpeas, rinsed
1   cup reduced-sodium chicken broth
4   tablespoons chopped fresh cilantro, divided
1   cup whole-wheat couscous

1. Pat chicken thighs dry with a paper towel. Season with 1/4 teaspoon each cinnamon and cumin, salt and pepper.
2. Heat 1 tablespoon oil in a Dutch oven over medium heat. Add the chicken thighs and cook until browned, 3 to 4 minutes per side. Transfer to a plate.
3. Add the remaining 1 tablespoon oil and onion to the pot. Cook, stirring occasionally, until the onion is softened, about 2 minutes. Add the remaining 1 teaspoon each cinnamon and cumin and cook, stirring constantly, for 30 seconds. Add orange slices, tomatoes and their juice, chickpeas, broth and 2 tablespoons cilantro; bring to a simmer, stirring with a wooden spoon to scrape up any browned bits. Return the chicken and any collected juice to the pot; cover and cook over medium-low heat until the chicken is cooked through, 5 to 10 minutes. Transfer the chicken to a clean plate.
4. Bring the cooking liquid back to a boil; stir in couscous and place the chicken thighs on top of the mixture. Remove from heat, cover and let stand for 5 minutes before serving. Garnish with the remaining 2 tablespoons cilantro.

Chile & Beer Braised Brisket

ACTIVE TIME: 30 minutes
TOTAL: 3 1/2 hours
TO MAKE AHEAD: Cover and refrigerate for up to 3 days or freeze for up to 3 months.

MAKES: 8 servings, about 3/4 cup each

H✕W   H↑F   H♥H

PER SERVING: 282 calories; 9 g fat (2 g sat, 4 g mono); 78 mg cholesterol; 19 g carbohydrate; 0 g added sugars; 30 g protein; 6 g fiber; 528 mg sodium; 664 mg potassium.
NUTRITION BONUS: Vitamin A (65% daily value), Zinc (45% dv), Iron (26% dv), Potassium (19% dv), Vitamin C (18% dv).

SERVE WITH:

Warm corn tortillas and cabbage slaw with cilantro and fresh lime

A nice long braise with Mexican beer and chiles coaxes the tenderness out of brisket in this cowboy-style chili. The addition of pinto beans brings texture, plenty of nutrients and a healthy dose of fiber to this dish.

6   dried New Mexico, Anaheim *or* ancho chiles, stemmed and seeded
1   14-ounce can diced tomatoes, preferably fire-roasted
1   large onion, coarsely chopped
4   cloves garlic, coarsely chopped
1   tablespoon plus 1 teaspoon chili powder
2   teaspoons ground cumin
1   teaspoon salt
1   cup Mexican lager, such as Corona *or* Dos Equis
1   tablespoon canola oil
2   pounds trimmed flat, first-cut brisket (*see Note*)
1   15-ounce can pinto beans, rinsed

1. Tear chiles into 1-inch pieces and place in a large bowl. Cover with hot water and let sit until softened, at least 20 minutes. Drain.
2. Preheat oven to 350°F.
3. Place tomatoes and their juice, onion, garlic, chili powder, cumin, salt and the drained chile pieces in a food processor. Process until smooth. Transfer to a large bowl and stir in beer.
4. Heat oil in a large Dutch oven over medium heat. Add brisket and brown on all sides, about 6 minutes total. Pour the chile sauce over the meat and bring to a simmer.
5. Cover the pot, transfer to the oven and bake for 2 hours. Stir in beans and continue baking until the meat is fall-apart tender, 45 minutes to 1 hour more.
6. Transfer the meat to a cutting board and pull apart into long shreds using two forks. Stir the shredded meat back into the sauce.

NOTE: **"Flat, first-cut brisket"** is a far better choice for healthy eating than the fattier point cut. If the briskets at your store aren't labeled as such, ask the butcher to help you select the right cut. You'll need 2 pounds of brisket after it's been trimmed of fat.

Braised Brisket & Roots

ACTIVE TIME: 1 1/4 hours

TOTAL: 3 to 5 1/2 hours

MAKES: 8 servings: 3 ounces meat, 1 cup vegetables, 1/4 cup sauce each

H✂W   H⬆F   H❤H

PER SERVING: 274 calories; 6 g fat (2 g sat, 3 g mono); 76 mg cholesterol; 19 g carbohydrate; 27 g protein; 5 g fiber; 439 mg sodium; 872 mg potassium. **NUTRITION BONUS:** Vitamin A (105% daily value), Zinc (45% dv), Vitamin C (35% dv), Potassium (25% dv), Folate & Iron (16% dv).

SERVE WITH:

Steamed cauliflower and broccoli drizzled with truffle-infused olive oil

While a barbecued brisket served with corn on the cob is perfect for backyard entertaining, this braised brisket has a decidedly wintery feel. A root vegetable trio of carrots, parsnips and rutabaga imparts sweet and earthy flavors to the brisket.

1	tablespoon canola oil
2	pounds flat, first-cut brisket (*see Note, page 212*), trimmed
3	medium onions, sliced
6	allspice berries *or* pinch of ground allspice
2	teaspoons chopped fresh thyme *or* 3/4 teaspoon dried
1	teaspoon sweet paprika
1/2	teaspoon salt
1/2	teaspoon freshly ground pepper
2	bay leaves
1	cup dry vermouth *or* dry white wine
3	cups reduced-sodium beef broth
4	medium carrots, peeled
3	medium parsnips, peeled and cored (*see Note, page 212*)
1	medium rutabaga (about 12 ounces), peeled (*see Note, page 213*)
1	teaspoon Dijon mustard
2	teaspoons arrowroot *or* 1 tablespoon cornstarch
1-2	tablespoons water

1. Preheat oven to 325°F. Heat oil in a Dutch oven over medium-high heat. Add brisket and cook until browned, 3 to 5 minutes per side. Transfer to a large plate and set aside.
2. Add onions to the pot; cook, stirring frequently, until softened, about 2 minutes. Stir in allspice, thyme, paprika, salt, pepper and bay leaves, then pour in vermouth (or wine). Bring to a boil. Cook for 3 minutes.
3. Stir in broth and return the brisket to the pot along with any accumulated juices. Bring to a simmer. Cover, place in the oven and bake for 1 1/2 hours. Meanwhile, cut carrots, parsnips and rutabaga into 2-by-1/2-inch sticks.
4. Transfer the brisket to a plate. Discard the bay leaves and allspice berries (if using). Stir mustard into the sauce. Add the carrots, parsnips and rutabaga. Return the brisket to the pot; cover and bake for 1 hour more.
5. Test the vegetables and brisket for tenderness by piercing with the tip of a sharp knife. As they get done, transfer to a cutting board or platter, cover with foil and set aside. If necessary, continue to cook, testing for doneness every 20 minutes. Total cooking time for the brisket may range from 2 1/2 to 5 hours, depending on the particular piece of meat.
6. Skim fat from the sauce. Bring the sauce to a boil over high heat. Cook for 5 minutes, stirring occasionally, to reduce and intensify flavors. Dissolve arrowroot in 1 tablespoon water (or cornstarch in 2 tablespoons water); add to the sauce and cook, stirring constantly, just until thickened, about 10 seconds.
7. Slice the brisket thinly against the grain and arrange slices on a serving platter. Using a slotted spoon, mound the vegetables around the brisket. Spoon half the sauce over the meat and vegetables; pass the remaining sauce separately.

Red Curry Bison Short Ribs with Baby Bok Choy

Short ribs, which start out very tough but become tender when cooked slowly over low heat, are notoriously fatty. Bison short ribs, on the other hand, are quite lean and therefore can be enjoyed as part of a healthy diet. Here, Thai red curry paste, garlic, ginger, cilantro and fish sauce flavor a coconut braising broth that is the foundation of a truly unique and satisfying dish. If you have time, prepare this dish through Step 2 a day ahead—the flavor of the sauce and tenderness of the meat get even better overnight. (Photograph: front cover.)

ACTIVE TIME: 45 minutes
TOTAL: 3 hours
TO MAKE AHEAD: Prepare through Step 2; let cool, cover and refrigerate for up to 1 day. Skim fat from the top, reheat and finish with Step 3.

MAKES: 6 servings

H✕W   H❤H

PER SERVING: 208 calories; 4 g fat (1 g sat, 2 g mono); 77 mg cholesterol; 12 g carbohydrate; 0 g added sugars; 31 g protein; 3 g fiber; 862 mg sodium; 833 mg potassium.
NUTRITION BONUS: Vitamin C (78% daily value), Vitamin A (76% dv), Zinc (26% dv), Iron & Potassium (24% dv), Folate (20% dv).

½	**cup water**
½	**cup coarsely chopped cilantro stems, plus ½ cup chopped cilantro leaves, divided**
6	**scallions, coarsely chopped**
3	**cloves garlic, peeled**
3	**⅛ inch thick slices peeled fresh ginger**
1½-2	**teaspoons red curry paste (*see Note, page 213*), or more to taste**
2	**teaspoons canola oil**
3	**pounds bone-in bison *or* beef short ribs *or* 2 pounds boneless (*see Note*), trimmed**
2	**cups thinly sliced red onion**
1½	**cups reduced-sodium chicken broth**
3	**tablespoons fish sauce (*see Note, page 212*)**
2	**tablespoons lime juice, or more to taste**
3	**ripe tomatoes, seeded and diced**
1	**cup "lite" coconut milk (optional)**
6	**baby bok choy, cut in half, *or* 3 regular bok choy, cut into quarters**
	Freshly ground pepper to taste

SERVE WITH:

Brown rice noodles

1. Place water, cilantro stems, scallions, garlic, ginger and curry paste to taste in a blender or food processor. Blend or process to form a loose paste. Add more water if the mixture is too dense to blend.
2. Heat oil in a Dutch oven over medium heat. Add ribs and brown on all sides, 6 to 8 minutes total. Stir in the curry mixture, onion, broth, fish sauce and 2 tablespoons lime juice. Bring to a simmer. Cover, reduce heat to maintain a simmer, and cook, turning the ribs every 30 minutes, until the meat is very tender when pierced with a fork, 2 to 2½ hours.
3. Transfer the ribs to a plate; cover and keep warm. Add tomatoes and coconut milk (if using) to the broth; bring to a simmer. Add bok choy; cover and cook until the bok choy bases can be pierced with a fork, 10 to 20 minutes, depending on the size. Season with pepper and more lime juice, if desired. Serve the ribs and bok choy topped with cilantro leaves.

NOTE: Bison short ribs can be found at specialty meat markets and online. For bone-in short ribs, both English-style (a single bone with a chunk of meat attached) and flanken-style (thinner cut with 3 to 4 ribs per strip) will work for this recipe. Remove any silver skin—the tough, silvery-looking membrane lining the meat-side of the ribs—before cooking. If you can't find bison short ribs, bone-in or boneless **beef short ribs** are a good alternative.

Lamb, Fig & Olive Stew

⏱ **ACTIVE TIME:** 45 minutes
TOTAL: 45 minutes

MAKES: 4 servings,
about 1½ cups each

H✂W   H♥H

PER SERVING: 317 calories; 10 g fat
(2 g sat, 5 g mono); 77 mg
cholesterol; 25 g carbohydrate;
0 g added sugars; 27 g protein;
3 g fiber; 709 mg sodium;
816 mg potassium.
NUTRITION BONUS: Zinc (32% daily
value), Vitamin C (30% dv),
Potassium (23% dv), Iron (18% dv),
Vitamin A (17% dv), Magnesium
(15% dv).

SERVE WITH:

Steamed whole artichokes

Making a lamb stew can easily be an all-day affair, but we've significantly shortened the process by using convenient ground lamb instead of chunks of meat. The dish features the classic Provençal flavor combination of green olives, dried figs and red wine finished with a fresh burst of parsley and grated lemon zest.

1	**pound lean ground lamb (*see Notes*)**
2	**teaspoons extra-virgin olive oil**
¼	**cup plus 2 teaspoons minced garlic, divided**
1½	**teaspoons herbes de Provence (*see Notes*)**
½	**cup dry red wine**
2	**14-ounce cans reduced-sodium beef broth (3½ cups)**
2	**tablespoons cornstarch**
4	**plum tomatoes, diced**
½	**cup chopped dried figs**
¼	**cup finely chopped pitted green olives**
¼	**teaspoon freshly ground pepper**
¼	**cup chopped fresh parsley**
2	**teaspoons freshly grated lemon zest**

1. Heat a Dutch oven over medium heat. Add lamb and cook, breaking up with a wooden spoon, until browned, 4 to 6 minutes. Transfer to a sieve set over a bowl to drain; discard the fat.
2. Wipe out the pot; add oil and heat over medium-high heat. Add ¼ cup garlic and herbes de Provence and cook, stirring constantly, until fragrant, about 30 seconds. Add wine and cook, scraping up any browned bits, until slightly reduced, 1 to 2 minutes.
3. Combine broth and cornstarch in a small bowl. Add to the pot, increase the heat to high and bring to a simmer, stirring constantly. Add tomatoes, figs, olives and pepper; return to a simmer, stirring often. Reduce heat to maintain a simmer and cook, stirring occasionally, for 5 minutes. Add the reserved lamb and cook, stirring occasionally, until heated through, about 2 minutes.
4. Combine the remaining 2 teaspoons garlic, parsley and lemon zest in a small bowl. Serve the stew topped with the parsley mixture.

NOTES:
It's not always easy to find **lean lamb**, but it's easy to grind your own. Choose a lean cut, such as leg or loin, trim any excess fat and cut into ¾-inch pieces. Pulse in a food processor until uniformly ground, being careful not to overprocess. Or ask your butcher to grind a lean cut for you.

Herbes de Provence is a blend of aromatic herbs including thyme, rosemary, oregano, marjoram and sometimes lavender and/or aniseed. To make your own, mix equal amounts dried thyme, rosemary, oregano, marjoram and savory in a small jar. If desired, add a pinch of dried lavender and crushed aniseed.

Lamb Osso Buco

ACTIVE TIME: 40 minutes
TOTAL: 2 hours 10 minutes
TO MAKE AHEAD: Cover and refrigerate for up to 2 days or freeze for up to 6 months. Thaw, if necessary, and heat on the stovetop or in a 350°F oven for about 30 minutes. Sprinkle with parsley just before serving.

MAKES: 6 servings

H✂W   H♥H

PER SERVING: 226 calories; 6 g fat (2 g sat, 3 g mono); 63 mg cholesterol; 11 g carbohydrate; 0 g added sugars; 20 g protein; 2 g fiber; 777 mg sodium; 531 mg potassium.
NUTRITION BONUS: Vitamin A (76% daily value), Zinc (37% dv), Potassium & Vitamin C (15% dv).

SERVE WITH:

Short-grain brown rice cooked with chopped yellow onion and a pinch of saffron, plus some baby sweet peas stirred in at the end

Flavor-packed lamb shanks stand in for the traditional veal in our version of the classic Milanese dish osso buco. If you like, add a bright flavor accent by grating a bit of orange zest over the top of the shanks before serving.

2	tablespoons all-purpose flour
1	teaspoon salt
1/2	teaspoon freshly ground pepper
3	pounds lamb shanks, trimmed and cut into 1 1/2-inch-thick pieces
1	tablespoon extra-virgin olive oil, divided
1	onion, diced
2	carrots, diced
1	stalk celery, diced
2	cloves garlic, finely chopped
1 1/2	cups tomato sauce
1 1/2	cups dry white wine *or* vermouth
1	tablespoon chopped fresh basil *or* 1 teaspoon dried
1 1/2	teaspoons chopped fresh thyme *or* 1/2 teaspoon dried
1	bay leaf
1	tablespoon chopped fresh parsley

1. Preheat oven to 350°F.
2. Combine flour, salt and pepper in a shallow dish. Roll lamb pieces in the flour mixture and shake off excess.
3. Heat 1 1/2 teaspoons oil in a Dutch oven over medium-high heat. In two batches, brown the lamb on all sides, about 8 to 10 minutes per batch, using the remaining 1 1/2 teaspoons oil for the second batch. Transfer the lamb to a bowl.
4. Reduce heat to medium, add onion, carrots and celery to the pot and cook, stirring, until softened, 3 to 5 minutes. Add garlic and cook until aromatic, about 30 seconds. Stir in tomato sauce, wine (or vermouth), basil, thyme and bay leaf. Return the lamb to the pot and bring to a simmer.
5. Cover the pot and transfer it to the oven. Bake until the lamb is tender, turning the meat once halfway through, about 1 1/2 hours. Discard the bay leaf. Sprinkle with parsley and serve.

Red-Cooked Lamb with Sweet Potatoes

You don't see it on enough menus at Chinese restaurants in America, but in China lamb is prized and used in many dishes, especially during the wintertime. In this recipe, it is "red cooked," which describes the hue of the meat after it is braised in soy sauce. Diced sweet potato and wilted spinach bring a sweet and colorful contrast to the salty, spicy lamb.

2	teaspoons canola oil
8	scallions, trimmed, cut into 1-inch pieces and smashed lightly
8	cloves garlic, peeled, lightly crushed and sliced
8	slices fresh ginger, about the size of a quarter, smashed lightly with the flat side of a knife
2	cinnamon sticks
1½	teaspoons Asian chile sauce, such as Sriracha (*see Notes*)
1	teaspoon aniseed
⅓	cup reduced-sodium soy sauce
3	tablespoons Shao Hsing rice wine *or* sake (*see Notes*)
1	tablespoon sugar
5	cups water
2½	pounds boneless leg of lamb, trimmed and cut into 1½-inch cubes
2	pounds sweet potatoes *or* yams (3-4 medium), peeled and cut into 1½-inch cubes
8	ounces spinach, trimmed

1. Heat a Dutch oven over high heat. Add oil and heat until hot. Add scallions, garlic, ginger, cinnamon sticks, chile sauce and aniseed; stir-fry until fragrant, about 15 seconds. Add soy sauce, rice wine (or sake) and sugar. Pour in water and bring to a boil. Add lamb and return to a boil. Reduce the heat to low, partially cover, and simmer until the lamb is just tender, about 1 hour.
2. Add sweet potatoes (or yams) and continue to cook, partially covered, until they are tender, about 20 minutes. Discard the ginger slices and cinnamon sticks.
3. Lightly mix in spinach, leaving some on top. Cover and cook until the spinach is wilted, about 1½ minutes. Serve.

NOTES:
Sriracha, a Thai chile sauce, can be found in the Asian section of many large supermarkets and at Asian markets.

Shao Hsing (or Shaoxing) is a seasoned Chinese rice wine. It is available at most Asian specialty markets and in the Asian section of some larger supermarkets. If unavailable, dry sherry is a good substitute. For this recipe, **sake** (Japanese rice wine) could also be used as a substitute. Chinese rice vinegar should not be used as a substitute.

ACTIVE TIME: 55 minutes
TOTAL: 2¼ hours

MAKES: 8 servings, about 1½ cups each

H✕W   H♥H
PER SERVING: 306 calories; 8 g fat (2 g sat, 3 g mono); 84 mg cholesterol; 27 g carbohydrate; 2 g added sugars; 30 g protein; 4 g fiber; 509 mg sodium; 868 mg potassium.
NUTRITION BONUS: Vitamin A (413% daily value), Vitamin C (43% dv), Zinc (36% dv), Folate (26% dv), Iron & Potassium (25% dv), Magnesium (22% dv).

SERVE WITH:
Sautéed baby bok choy with scallions and a sprinkle of sea salt

RESOURCES

Besides having a great recipe, there's a lot more that goes into getting dinner on the table each night. Think of this section as your dinner support team, full of tips, notes and guides to help make cooking easier. You'll find charts to show how to roast or steam vegetables, easy ways to season them, how to cook whole grains, how to season a cast-iron skillet and even how to stock a healthy pantry. Plus the index is the best place to look up recipes; it not only includes recipes organized by ingredients (chicken or fish, for example), it also includes special indexes to show you all the recipes that take less than 30 minutes or those that are gluten-free.

Vegetable-Roasting Guide

Roasting vegetables is a quick, easy way to give them tons of rich flavor with barely any work. Here's how:

TO ROAST VEGETABLES: Preheat oven to 450°F. Prepare the vegetable of your choice (*see instructions below*). Toss with 4 teaspoons extra-virgin olive oil (or canola oil), ½ teaspoon salt and ¼ teaspoon pepper—or with the seasoning combination of your choice (*see opposite*). Spread the vegetables on a rimmed baking sheet and roast, stirring once or twice, until tender. Follow roasting times below.

	VEGETABLE	AMOUNT FOR 4 SERVINGS	ROASTING TIME	ANALYSIS PER SERVING
	Beets & Turnips	1½ pounds, greens removed, ends trimmed, peeled, cut into 1-inch pieces or wedges	20-25 minutes	**beets:** 116 calories; 16 g carbohydrate; 5 g fiber **turnips:** 90 calories; 11 g carbohydrate; 3 g fiber
	Broccoli & Cauliflower	1 pound, cut into 1-inch florets	15-20 minutes	**broccoli:** 74 calories; 6 g carbohydrate; 3 g fiber **cauliflower:** 71 calories; 6 g carbohydrate; 3 g fiber
	Brussels Sprouts	1 pound, outer leaves removed, stem trimmed; larger ones quartered, smaller ones halved	15-20 minutes	91 calories; 10 g carbohydrate; 4 g fiber
	Butternut Squash	2 pounds, peeled, seeded, cut into 1-inch pieces	25-35 minutes	120 calories; 20 g carbohydrate; 6 g fiber
	Cabbage, Savoy	1½ pounds (1 small head), cored, cut into 1-inch squares	15-20 minutes	83 calories; 9 g carbohydrate; 5 g fiber
	Carrots & Parsnips	1½ pounds, peeled or scrubbed, woody core removed from parsnips; cut into ¼-inch slices	20-25 minutes	**carrots:** 105 calories; 15 g carbohydrate; 4 g fiber **parsnips:** 138 calories; 23 g carbohydrate; 5 g fiber
	Fennel	2 large bulbs, stalks and fronds trimmed from the bulb, the bulb cored and cut into 1-inch wedges	25-30 minutes	79 calories; 9 g carbohydrate; 4 g fiber
	Green Beans	1 pound, stem ends trimmed	15-20 minutes	78 calories; 8 g carbohydrate; 4 g fiber
	Sweet Potatoes	1½ pounds, scrubbed (peeled if desired), cut into 1-inch pieces or wedges	20-25 minutes	196 calories; 35 g carbohydrate; 6 g fiber

10 ways to season roasted vegetables

Toss prepared vegetables (*see chart, opposite*) with any of these easy flavor combinations.

1 **CARDAMOM-BUTTER:**
BEFORE ROASTING: Toss the vegetables with 3 teaspoons melted **butter**, 1 teaspoon **canola oil**, ¾ teaspoon ground **cardamom** and ½ teaspoon **salt**.

2 **CHILE-GARLIC & SOY:**
BEFORE ROASTING: Toss the vegetables with 4 teaspoons extra-virgin **olive oil** (or canola oil), 1 tablespoon each **chile-garlic sauce** *(see Note, page 212)* and reduced-sodium **soy sauce** and ⅛ teaspoon ground **white pepper**.

3 **CHILI-LIME:**
BEFORE ROASTING: Toss the vegetables with 4 teaspoons **canola oil**, ¾ teaspoon each **chili powder** and ground **cumin** and ½ teaspoon salt. AFTER ROASTING: Toss with 2 tablespoons chopped fresh **cilantro** and **lime juice** to taste.

4 **GARLIC-THYME:**
BEFORE ROASTING: Toss the vegetables with 2 tablespoons extra-virgin **olive oil**, 1 tablespoon chopped fresh **thyme** (or 1 teaspoon dried), ¼ teaspoon each **salt** and freshly ground **pepper**. About 5 minutes before the vegetables are done, stir in ¼ cup thinly sliced **garlic** and continue roasting. AFTER ROASTING: Toss with 2 tablespoons chopped **fennel fronds** if desired.

5 **GINGER-SESAME:**
BEFORE ROASTING: Toss the vegetables with 2 tablespoons each **toasted sesame oil** and reduced-sodium **soy sauce**, 1 tablespoon each grated fresh **ginger** and minced **garlic**, 4 teaspoons **rice vinegar** and ½ teaspoon freshly ground **pepper**. AFTER ROASTING: Toss with 1 tablespoon toasted **sesame seeds** *(see Note, page 213)*.

6 **LEMON-HERB:**
BEFORE ROASTING: Toss the vegetables with 4 teaspoons extra-virgin **olive oil** (or canola oil), 2 tablespoons chopped fresh **herbs**, such as marjoram, oregano, tarragon and/or rosemary (or 2 teaspoons dried), 1 teaspoon freshly grated **lemon zest**, ½ teaspoon salt and ¼ teaspoon freshly ground **pepper**. AFTER ROASTING: Toss with 1 tablespoon **lemon juice** if desired.

7 **MAPLE:**
BEFORE ROASTING: Toss the vegetables with 2 tablespoons pure **maple syrup**, 1 tablespoon melted **butter**, 1½ teaspoons **lemon juice**, ½ teaspoon **salt** and freshly ground **pepper** to taste.

8 **MEDITERRANEAN:**
BEFORE ROASTING: Toss the vegetables with 4 teaspoons extra-virgin **olive oil**, 2 minced **garlic** cloves and ¼ teaspoon **salt**. AFTER ROASTING: Toss with ½ teaspoon freshly grated **lemon zest**, 1 tablespoon **lemon juice**, 10 pitted sliced **black olives**, 1 teaspoon dried **oregano** and 2 teaspoons rinsed **capers** (optional).

9 **MOROCCAN:**
BEFORE ROASTING: Toss the vegetables with 2 tablespoons extra-virgin **olive oil**, 2 minced **garlic** cloves, 1 teaspoon each **paprika** (preferably sweet Hungarian) and ground **cumin** and ½ teaspoon **salt**.

10 **SPICY ORANGE:**
BEFORE ROASTING: Toss the vegetables with 4 teaspoons extra-virgin **olive oil**, the **zest of 1 orange**, ½ teaspoon **salt** and ¼-½ teaspoon **crushed red pepper**.

Vegetable-Steaming Guide

Steamed vegetables can't be beat for simplicity or health. Serve them plain with a drizzle of olive oil and a little salt and pepper or season them with one of our flavor combinations (*opposite*).

TO STEAM VEGETABLES: Bring an inch of water to a steady boil in a large saucepan over high heat. Prepare the vegetable of your choice and place in a steamer basket in the saucepan. Cover and steam until just tender. See the chart below for prep instructions and timing.

VEGETABLE	AMOUNT FOR 4 SERVINGS	STEAMING TIME	ANALYSIS PER SERVING
Asparagus	1½ pounds (1-2 bunches), trimmed	4 minutes	37 calories; 7 g carbohydrate; 3 g fiber
Beets	1½ pounds, greens removed, ends trimmed, peeled, cut into 1-inch pieces or wedges	10-15 minutes	75 calories; 17 g carbohydrate; 3 g fiber
Broccoli & Cauliflower	1 pound broccoli, 1½-2 pounds cauliflower (about 1 head), cut into 1-inch florets	5-6 minutes	**broccoli:** 32 calories; 6 g carbohydrate; 3 g fiber **cauliflower:** 39 calories; 7 g carbohydrate; 4 g fiber
Brussels Sprouts	1 pound, stems trimmed	6-8 minutes	41 calories; 8 g carbohydrate; 3 g fiber
Carrots	1½ pounds, cut into ⅛-inch-thick rounds	4 minutes	60 calories; 14 g carbohydrate; 5 g fiber
Green Beans	1 pound, trimmed	5 minutes	40 calories; 9 g carbohydrate; 4 g fiber
Potatoes (baby), red or Yukon Gold	1½ pounds, scrubbed	10-15 minutes	140 calories; 30 g carbohydrate; 2 g fiber
Snap Peas	1 pound, trimmed	4-5 minutes	53 calories; 9 g carbohydrate; 3 g fiber
Summer Squash	1½ pounds, cut into ¼-inch-thick rounds	4-5 minutes	27 calories; 6 g carbohydrate; 2 g fiber

10 ways to perk up steamed vegetables

Toss or top steamed vegetables (*see chart, opposite*) with any of these easy flavor combinations.

1 **BACON-HORSERADISH:**
Combine 4 strips crisp-cooked **bacon**, finely chopped, ¼ cup reduced-fat **sour cream**, 2 teaspoons prepared **horseradish**, ¼ teaspoon **salt** and ⅛ teaspoon freshly ground **pepper**.

2 **CAPER & PARSLEY:**
Combine ⅓ cup chopped **shallot**, ¼ cup flat-leaf **parsley** leaves, 3 tablespoons rinsed **capers**, 2 tablespoons **white-wine vinegar**, 2 teaspoons extra-virgin **olive oil**, ¼ teaspoon each **salt** and freshly ground **pepper**.

3 **CREAMY GARLIC:**
Whisk ½ cup nonfat plain **yogurt**, 1 tablespoon extra-virgin **olive oil**, 1 tablespoon chopped fresh **parsley** (optional), ½ teaspoon each **garlic powder** and **kosher salt**, and freshly ground **pepper** to taste.

4 **FRESH TOMATO & SHALLOT:**
Combine 2 chopped **tomatoes**, 1 minced **shallot**, 1 tablespoon each extra-virgin **olive oil** and **balsamic vinegar**, and **salt** & freshly ground **pepper** to taste.

5 **LEMON-DILL:**
Whisk 4 teaspoons chopped fresh **dill**, 1 tablespoon each minced **shallot**, extra-virgin **olive oil** and **lemon juice**, 1 teaspoon **whole-grain mustard**, ¼ teaspoon each **salt** and freshly ground **pepper**.

6 **MUSTARD-SCALLION:**
Combine ¼ cup sliced **scallions**, 2 tablespoons **Dijon mustard**, 1 tablespoon **lemon juice**, and **salt** & freshly ground **pepper** to taste.

7 **ORANGE-ALMOND:**
Whisk 1 teaspoon extra-virgin **olive oil**, ½ teaspoon freshly grated **orange zest**, ¼ teaspoon **salt** and freshly ground **pepper** to taste; toss with steamed vegetables and top with ¼ cup toasted **sliced almonds** (*see Tip, page 213*).

8 **SESAME-ORANGE:**
Combine 3 tablespoons **orange juice**, 2 teaspoons **sesame oil**, ¼ teaspoon each **salt** and freshly ground **pepper**. Add 2 teaspoons toasted **sesame seeds** (*see Tip, page 213*).

9 **SPICY ASIAN:**
Combine 3 tablespoons each chopped **red bell pepper**, chopped **red onion** and **rice-wine vinegar** (*or* distilled white vinegar), 1 tablespoon **sesame oil**, 2 teaspoons **light brown sugar**, 1 teaspoon **crushed red pepper** and **salt** to taste.

10 **TARRAGON CREAM:**
Whisk 2 tablespoons each low-fat **mayonnaise** and low-fat plain **yogurt** (*or* nonfat or low-fat buttermilk), 1 tablespoon chopped fresh **tarragon** (*or* 1 teaspoon dried), ¼ teaspoon **salt**, and freshly ground **pepper** to taste.

Grain-Cooking Guide

Start with **1 cup uncooked grain**; serving size is ½ cup cooked. See the chart below for prep instructions and timing. IN A HURRY? Make instant brown rice, quick-cooking barley or quick-cooking wild rice, ready in under 10 minutes (follow package directions).

GRAIN (1 CUP)	LIQUID (WATER/BROTH)	DIRECTIONS	YIELD	ANALYSIS (PER 1/2-CUP SERVING)
Barley (Pearl)	2½ cups	Bring barley and liquid to a boil. Reduce heat to low and simmer, covered, 35-50 minutes.	3-3½ cups	97 calories; 22 g carbohydrate; 3 g fiber
Bulgur (see Note, page 212)	1½ cups	Bring bulgur and liquid to a boil. Reduce heat to low; simmer, covered, until tender and most of the liquid has been absorbed, 10-15 minutes.	2½-3 cups	76 calories; 17 g carbohydrate; 4 g fiber
Couscous (Whole-wheat)	1¾ cups	Bring liquid to a boil; stir in couscous. Remove from heat and let stand, covered, for 5 minutes. Fluff with a fork.	3-3½ cups	70 calories; 15 g carbohydrate; 2 g fiber
Polenta (Cornmeal)	4⅓ cups	Bring cold water and 1 teaspoon salt to a boil. Slowly whisk in cornmeal until smooth. Reduce heat to low, cover and cook, stirring occasionally, until very thick and creamy, 10 to 15 minutes.	4-4⅓ cups	55 calories; 12 g carbohydrate; 1 g fiber
Quinoa (see Note, page 212)	2 cups	Rinse in several changes of cold water. Bring quinoa and liquid to a boil. Reduce heat to low and simmer, covered, until tender and most of the liquid has been absorbed, 15-20 minutes. Fluff with a fork.	3 cups	111 calories; 20 g carbohydrate; 3 g fiber
Rice Brown	2½ cups	Bring rice and liquid to a boil. Reduce heat to low and simmer, covered, until tender and most of the liquid has been absorbed, 40-50 minutes. Let stand for 5 minutes, then fluff with a fork.	3 cups	109 calories; 23 g carbohydrate; 2 g fiber
Wild	At least 4 cups	Cook rice in a large saucepan of lightly salted boiling water until tender, 45-55 minutes. Drain.	2-2½ cups	83 calories; 18 g carbohydrate; 1 g fiber

10 ways to jazz up whole grains

Add any of these flavor combinations to grains after they're cooked (*see chart, opposite*).

1 APRICOT NUT:
STIR INTO COOKED GRAINS: ⅓ cup chopped **dried apricots**, ¼ cup chopped toasted **nuts**, such as walnuts, pecans *or* pistachios, 3 tablespoons **orange juice**, 1 teaspoon extra-virgin **olive oil**, and **salt** & freshly ground **pepper** to taste.

2 LIME-CILANTRO:
STIR INTO COOKED GRAINS: ⅔ cup coarsely chopped fresh **cilantro**, ⅓ cup chopped **scallions**, 2 tablespoons **lime juice**, and **salt** & freshly ground **pepper** to taste.

3 MEDITERRANEAN:
STIR INTO COOKED GRAINS: 1 chopped medium **tomato**, ¼ cup chopped **kalamata olives**, ½ teaspoon **herbes de Provence**, and **salt** & freshly ground **pepper** to taste.

4 MINT & FETA:
STIR INTO COOKED GRAINS: ¾ cup sliced **scallions**, ¼ cup each finely crumbled **feta cheese** and sliced fresh **mint**, and **salt** & freshly ground **pepper** to taste.

5 PARMESAN & BALSAMIC:
STIR INTO COOKED GRAINS: ¼ cup freshly grated **Parmesan cheese**, 1 teaspoon **butter,** 2 teaspoons **balsamic vinegar**, and **salt** & freshly ground **pepper** to taste.

6 PARMESAN-DILL:
STIR INTO COOKED GRAINS: ⅓ cup freshly grated **Parmesan cheese**, 2 tablespoons chopped fresh **dill**, 1 teaspoon freshly grated **lemon zest**, and **salt** & freshly ground **pepper** to taste.

7 PEAS & LEMON:
STIR INTO COOKED GRAINS: 1 cup frozen **peas**; cover and let stand for 5 minutes. Stir in 3 tablespoons chopped fresh **parsley**, 1½ teaspoons extra-virgin **olive oil**, 1 teaspoon freshly grated **lemon zest**, and **salt** & freshly ground **pepper** to taste.

8 SPICY & SWEET SESAME-SOY:
STIR INTO COOKED GRAINS: 3 tablespoons **rice-wine vinegar**, 1 tablespoon reduced-sodium **soy sauce**, 2 teaspoons each **sesame oil** and finely chopped fresh **ginger**, 1 teaspoon each **chile-garlic sauce** and **honey**, and ¼ cup chopped toasted **cashews**.

9 SPINACH:
STIR INTO COOKED GRAINS: 3 cups sliced **baby spinach** (*or* arugula); cover and let stand for 5 minutes. Season with **salt** & freshly ground **pepper** to taste.

10 TOMATO-TARRAGON:
STIR INTO COOKED GRAINS: ¾ cup chopped **tomatoes**, 3 tablespoons minced fresh **tarragon** (*or* parsley *or* thyme), and **salt** & freshly ground **pepper** to taste.

Bulgur

Quinoa

Barley

Know Your Pots

Skillets & Woks

WHAT IS SEASONING?

Seasoned cast-iron skillets and woks have been coated with oil and heated to a high temperature—allowing the oil to deeply penetrate the metal of the pan. A well-seasoned cast-iron skillet or wok is a secret weapon in the kitchen because its surface is naturally "nonstick" and allows you to cook with less oil while preventing foods from sticking to the pan.

HOW TO SEASON A CAST-IRON SKILLET

Most new cast-iron skillets come from the factory preseasoned, so you can skip seasoning them. Just rinse well with hot water and dry thoroughly with a clean towel before use. If you purchase one that is not seasoned or want to reseason an older skillet that looks dull or rusty, here's what to do. Clean the skillet inside and out with hot soapy water and a stiff brush. (For everyday use, cast-iron should not be cleaned with soap; *see how to clean, opposite.*) Dry the pan, then apply a thin layer of canola oil (or other cooking oil) to the inside and outside of the pan. Set oven racks in the upper and lower third of the oven; preheat the oven to 375°F. Place a large baking sheet on the bottom rack to catch any drips of oil. Place the skillet upside-down on the upper rack. Bake for 1 hour. Turn off the oven and let cool completely in the oven. Repeat as necessary to restore the black seasoning on the skillet. (*For another way to season a cast-iron skillet, see page 59.*)

HOW TO SEASON A WOK

Most woks do not come from the factory preseasoned. You will need to season a new wok yourself before using. First scrub it well to remove the factory coating. Use hot water, soap and a scouring pad. (For everyday use, woks should not be cleaned with soap; *see how to clean, opposite.*) Rinse and dry thoroughly. Here are two different methods for seasoning your new wok:

TRADITIONAL WOK-SEASONING METHOD: Heat the wok over high heat until a bead of water vaporizes within 1 to 2 seconds. Add 3 tablespoons peanut or vegetable oil and swirl it in the pan. Add ½ cup sliced unpeeled ginger and one bunch of scallions cut into 2-inch pieces. Reduce the heat to medium and stir-fry the mixture, pressing it into the sides of the wok as you go. Keep stir-frying and pressing the seasonings all over the wok for about 15 minutes. Remove the wok from the heat and let cool. (Discard the scallions and ginger.)

OVEN WOK-SEASONING METHOD: Preheat oven to 425°F. If you have an exhaust fan in your kitchen, turn it on and open a window. If your wok has plastic or wooden handles that can be removed, remove them. If they can't be removed, wrap each handle with a wet, but not dripping-wet, small rag or washcloth (one you don't mind throwing out after the seasoning process). Then, completely wrap the rags (or washcloths) with heavy-duty foil. (This will prevent the handles from burning during the seasoning process.) Using a paper towel that has been folded over several times, spread ½ teaspoon peanut or canola oil over the interior of the wok. Put the wok in the oven for 20 minutes. Remove from the oven and place on a turned-off burner on the stove; let cool for about 10 minutes. Evenly spread another ½ teaspoon oil over the interior of the wok and return to the oven for 20 minutes more. Repeat these steps one more time for a total of 60 minutes in the oven. The wok interior should be several shades darker than when you started. After the last heating, let the wok cool completely, remove the foil and washcloths (the washcloths may still be warm; use caution as you unwrap the foil).

HOW TO CLEAN YOUR SEASONED CAST-IRON SKILLET OR WOK

Never use soap and do not wash in the dishwasher. Soap will damage the seasoning on the pan. Simply clean it with hot water and a nonabrasive tool to release any stuck-on food—a stiff nylon brush is perfect for cast-iron skillets; a soft sponge is usually the best choice for a wok. If you have any pesky, hard-to-release food, fill the pan with an inch or so of water and gently heat on the stovetop to help loosen the food. Rinse the pan thoroughly, place on a burner and heat over low heat until all the water has evaporated. Or wipe completely dry with a kitchen towel before storing.

USING A CAST-IRON SKILLET ON AN ELECTRIC FLAT-TOP STOVE

Although some manufacturers warn that cast-iron can damage the surface of the stove, we've found it can be safely used as long as you avoid dragging the pan across the surface.

HOW TO USE YOUR NONSTICK SKILLET

We like nonstick skillets because you can use less oil and delicate foods, such as fish or eggs, won't stick to the pan or break apart. When you cook with them, use nonstick-safe utensils, such as a heatproof spatula or wooden spoon—metal utensils will damage the nonstick surface. (If you have a nonstick skillet with a scratched or flaking interior, it's best to discard the pan.) Don't heat an empty skillet or cook over high heat, because the nonstick coating may break down at high temperatures and release potentially toxic fumes. For an alternative to conventional nonstick cookware, look for pans marketed under names like "green cookware" or "eco-friendly cookware" that are made with a nonstick coating that won't break down when used over high heat. A cast-iron skillet is a good alternative to nonstick skillets for many recipes.

HOW TO MAKE YOUR SKILLET OVENPROOF

Stainless-steel skillets with metal handles or cast-iron skillets are good ovenproof skillets. If your skillet has a plastic or wood handle, wrap the handle in foil before transferring to the oven to prevent melting or overheating.

Slow-Cooker Savvy

When cooking in a slow cooker, there are a few essential tips to keep in mind:

KNOW YOUR QUARTS: Slow cookers are available in a range of sizes, from 1 quart to 8½ quarts. Use the size cooker recommended in each recipe. A 5- to 6-quart size will work for the recipes in this book.

NOT TOO FULL: For accurate cooking and food safety, don't overfill your slow cooker. Most manufacturers recommend filling them no more than two-thirds full, but it differs among brands, so check your owner's manual.

KEEP A LID ON IT: Opening the slow cooker lets heat escape and slows cooking. Only open it 30 to 45 minutes before the low end of the cooking range to check doneness.

PLAN AHEAD: If you want to turn your slow cooker on first thing in the morning, a little planning goes a long way.
- The night before: Cut and trim any meat, chop any vegetables, measure out dry ingredients and prepare any sauce; refrigerate the components in separate containers. (Do not refrigerate components in the slow-cooker insert; a cold insert takes too long to heat up and affects cooking time and food safety.)
- In the morning: Add ingredients to the cooker according to the recipe; reheat any sauce to a simmer before adding.

KEEP IT WARM: If you won't be home close to the end of the cooking time, make sure you have a slow cooker that can switch to the warm setting when cooking is done.

Key to EatingWell Recipes & Nutritional Analyses

HOW WE TEST RECIPES

Each of our recipes is thoroughly tested in the EATINGWELL Test Kitchen. Our goal is to provide healthy, delicious recipes that really work.

- Recipes are tested on average seven times each.
- Each recipe is tested by multiple testers.
- Both home cooks and culinary school graduates test our recipes.
- We test on both gas and electric stoves.
- We use a variety of ingredients, tools and techniques.
- Testers shop major supermarkets to research availability of ingredients.
- Testers measure active and total time to prepare each recipe.

WHAT THESE TERMS MEAN

ACTIVE TIME includes prep time (the time it takes to chop, dice, puree, mix, combine, etc. before cooking begins). It also includes the time spent tending something on the stovetop, in the oven or on the grill—and getting it to the table. If you can't walk away from it for more than 10 minutes, we consider it active time.

TOTAL includes both active and inactive time and indicates the entire amount of time required for a recipe, start to finish.

is ready to eat in 45 minutes or less.

TO MAKE AHEAD tells when a recipe or part of a recipe can be made in advance and gives storage instructions. If particular EQUIPMENT is needed to prepare a recipe, we tell you that too.

WHAT THESE ICONS MEAN

Icons identify recipes that are most appropriate for certain eating goals. (For more on our nutritional analysis process and our complete guidelines on how we define each icon, visit *eatingwell.com/go/guidelines*.) A recipe marked…

H✕W [**Healthy Weight**] has reduced calories and limited saturated fat:

	CALORIES	SAT FAT
Entree	≤350	≤5g
Combination meal*	≤420	≤7g
Complete meal**	≤500	≤7g

H↑F [**High Fiber**] provides significant total fiber: entrees/combination meals/complete meals have ≥5 grams of fiber per serving. All other recipes have ≥3 grams.

H♥H [**Healthy Heart**] has limited saturated fat (sodium is not considered):

	SAT FAT
Entree	≤3g
Combination meal*	≤5g
Complete meal**	≤7g

*Combination meal: A serving of protein plus a starch *or* vegetable serving.
**Complete meal: A serving of protein plus a starch *and* a vegetable.

HOW WE DO NUTRITIONAL ANALYSIS OF RECIPES

- All recipes are analyzed for nutrition content by a Registered Dietitian.
- We analyze for calories, total fat, saturated (sat) fat, monounsaturated (mono) fat, cholesterol, carbohydrate, added sugars, protein, fiber, sodium and potassium, using The Food Processor® SQL Nutrition Analysis Software from ESHA Research, Salem, Oregon. (Note: Nutrition information is updated regularly, following changes to the USDA database of ingredients. The current analyses appear with the recipes on *eatingwell.com*.)
- When a recipe provides 15 percent or more of the Daily Value (dv) of a nutrient, it is listed as a nutrition bonus. These values are FDA benchmarks for adults eating 2,000 calories a day.
- Recipes are tested and analyzed with iodized table salt unless otherwise indicated.
- We estimate that rinsing with water reduces the sodium in some canned foods, such as beans, by 35 percent. (People on sodium-restricted diets can reduce or eliminate the salt in a recipe.)
- When a recipe gives a measurement range of an ingredient, we analyze the first amount.
- When alternative ingredients are listed, we analyze the first one suggested.
- Garnishes and optional ingredients are not included in analyses.
- Analyses do not include trimmings or marinade that is not absorbed.

The Healthy Pantry

While a good shopping list is the key to a quick and painless trip to the supermarket, a well-stocked pantry is the best way to ensure you'll have everything you need to cook once you get home. Our Healthy Pantry includes many of the items you need to prepare the recipes in this book plus a few other ingredients that will make impromptu meals easier.

OILS, VINEGARS & CONDIMENTS

Oils: extra-virgin olive, canola
Vinegars: balsamic, red-wine, white-wine, rice, cider
Asian condiments: reduced-sodium soy sauce, fish sauce, hoisin sauce, oyster sauce, chile-garlic sauce, toasted sesame oil
Barbecue sauce
Hot sauce
Worcestershire sauce
Mustard: Dijon, whole-grain
Ketchup
Mayonnaise, low-fat

FLAVORINGS

Salt: kosher, iodized table
Black peppercorns
Herbs and spices, assorted dried
Onions
Garlic, fresh
Ginger, fresh
Olives: Kalamata, green
Capers
Anchovies or anchovy paste
Lemons, limes, oranges

DRY GOODS

Pasta, whole-wheat (assorted shapes)
Barley: pearl, quick-cooking
Bulgur
Couscous, whole-wheat
Quinoa
Rice: brown, instant brown, wild
Dried beans and lentils
Flour: all-purpose, whole-wheat, whole-wheat pastry (store opened packages in the refrigerator or freezer)
Rolled oats
Cornmeal
Breadcrumbs: plain dry, coarse whole-wheat
Crackers, whole-grain
Unsweetened cocoa powder
Bittersweet chocolate
Sweeteners: granulated sugar, brown sugar, honey, pure maple syrup

CANNED & BOTTLED GOODS

Broth: reduced-sodium beef, chicken and/or vegetable
Clam juice
"Lite" coconut milk
Tomatoes, tomato paste
Beans: black, cannellini, kidney, pinto, great northern, chickpeas, lentils
Chunk light tuna
Wild Pacific salmon
Wine: red, white or nonalcoholic
Madeira
Sherry, dry

NUTS, SEEDS & FRUITS

(Store opened packages of nuts and seeds in the refrigerator or freezer.)
Nuts: walnuts, pecans, almonds, hazelnuts, peanuts, pine nuts
Natural peanut butter
Seeds: pepitas, sesame seeds, sunflower seeds
Tahini (sesame paste)
Dried fruits: apricots, prunes, cherries, cranberries, dates, figs, raisins

REFRIGERATOR ITEMS

Milk, low-fat or nonfat
Buttermilk or buttermilk powder
Yogurt, plain and/or vanilla, low-fat or nonfat
Sour cream, reduced-fat or nonfat
Parmesan cheese, good-quality
Cheddar cheese, sharp
Eggs (large) or egg substitute, such as Egg Beaters
Orange juice
Tofu, water-packed
Tortillas: corn, whole-wheat

FREEZER BASICS

Fruit: berries, other fruit
Vegetables: peas, spinach, broccoli, corn
Ice cream or frozen yogurt, low-fat or nonfat

Notes from the Test Kitchen

BEANS, QUICK-SOAK METHOD: To soak beans using a quick-soak method, place in a large saucepan with enough cold water to cover them by 2 inches. Bring to a boil. Boil for 2 minutes. Remove from the heat, cover and let stand for 1 hour

BREADCRUMBS, HOW TO MAKE: To make your own fresh breadcrumbs, trim crusts from whole-wheat bread. Tear bread into pieces and process in a food processor until coarse crumbs form. To make fine breadcrumbs, process until very fine. To make dry bread-crumbs, spread coarse or fine breadcrumbs on a baking sheet and bake at 250°F until dry, about 10 to 15 minutes. One slice of bread makes about ½ cup fresh breadcrumbs or about ⅓ cup dry breadcrumbs. For store-bought coarse dry breadcrumbs we like Ian's brand, labeled "Panko breadcrumbs." Find them at well-stocked supermarkets.

BRISKET: "Flat, first-cut brisket" is a far better choice for healthy eating than the fattier point cut. If the briskets at your store aren't labeled as such, ask the butcher to help you select the right cut.

BULGUR: Bulgur is made by parboiling, drying and coarsely grinding or cracking wheat berries. Don't confuse bulgur with cracked wheat, which is simply that—cracked wheat. Since the parboiling step is skipped, cracked wheat must be cooked for up to an hour, whereas bulgur simply needs a quick soak in hot water for most uses. Look for it in the natural-foods section of large super-markets, near other grains.

CHILE-GARLIC SAUCE: A blend of ground chiles, garlic and vinegar, chile-garlic sauce is commonly used to add heat and flavor to Asian soups, sauces and stir-fries. It can be found in the Asian section of large supermarkets (sometimes labeled as chili-garlic sauce or paste) and keeps up to 1 year in the refrigerator.

CHINESE FIVE-SPICE POWDER: A blend of cinnamon, cloves, fennel seed, star anise and Szechuan peppercorns, you can find it in the spice section of the supermarket or with other Asian ingredients.

EGGS, HOW TO HARD-BOIL: Place eggs in a single layer in a saucepan; cover with water. Bring to a simmer over medium-high heat. Reduce heat to low and cook at the barest simmer for 10 min-utes. Remove from heat, pour out hot water and cover the eggs with ice-cold water. Let stand until cool enough to handle before peeling.

FISH SAUCE: Fish sauce is a pungent Southeast Asian condiment made from salted, fermented fish. Find it in the Asian-food sec-tion of well-stocked supermarkets and at Asian specialty mar-kets. We use Thai Kitchen fish sauce, lower in sodium than other brands (1,190 mg per tablespoon), in our recipe testing and nutritional analyses.

HOISIN SAUCE: Hoisin sauce is a dark brown, thick, spicy-sweet sauce made from soybeans and a complex mix of spices. Look for it in the Asian section of your supermarket and in Asian markets.

MUSSELS, HOW TO CLEAN: Discard mussels with broken shells or whose shell remains open after you tap it. Hold mussels under running water and use a stiff brush to remove any barnacles; pull off any black fibrous "beards". (Some mussels may not have a beard.) Mussels should be "debearded" no more than 30 min-utes before cooking.

NUTS, HOW TO TOAST: To toast whole nuts, spread on a baking sheet and bake at 350°F, stirring once, until fragrant, 7 to 9 minutes. To toast chopped, small or sliced nuts, cook in a small dry skillet over medium-low heat, stirring constantly, until fragrant and lightly browned, 2 to 4 minutes.

PARSNIPS, HOW TO PREP: Remove the peel with a vegetable peeler, then quarter the parsnip lengthwise and cut out the fibrous, woody core with a paring knife.

POMEGRANATE MOLASSES: Pomegranate molasses has a bright, tangy flavor. (Don't confuse it with grenadine syrup, which con-tains little or no pomegranate juice.) Find it in Middle Eastern markets and some large supermarkets near the vinegar or molasses. To make your own: Simmer 4 cups pomegranate juice, uncovered, in a medium nonreactive saucepan over medium heat until thick enough to coat the back of a spoon, 45 to 50 minutes. (Do not let the syrup reduce too much or it will darken and become very sticky.) Makes about ½ cup. Refrigerate in an airtight container for up to 3 months.

▲ POMEGRANATES, TO SEED: Fill a large bowl with water. Lightly score the fruit into quarters from crown to stem end, cutting through the skin but not into the interior of the fruit. Hold the fruit under water, break it apart and use your hands to gently separate the plump seeds (arils) from the outer skin and white pith. The seeds will drop to the bottom of the bowl and the pith will float to the surface. Discard the pith. Pour the seeds into a colander. Rinse and pat dry. Seeds can be frozen for up to 3 months.

QUINOA: Quinoa is a delicately flavored, protein-rich grain. Rinsing removes any residue of saponin, quinoa's natural, bitter protec-tive covering. Find it at natural-foods stores and well-stocked supermarkets.

RED CURRY PASTE: Red curry paste is a blend of chile peppers, garlic, lemongrass and galangal (a root with a flavor similar to ginger). Look for it in jars or cans in the Asian section of the supermarket or specialty stores. The heat and salt level can vary widely depending on brand. Be sure to taste as you go.

ROOT VEGETABLES, HOW TO PEEL: For tougher-skinned roots like celery root, rutabaga and turnips, removing the peel with a paring knife can be easier than using a vegetable peeler. Cut off one end of the root to create a flat surface to keep it steady on the cutting board. Follow the contour of the vegetable with your knife. If you use a peeler on the tougher roots, peel around each vegetable at least three times to ensure all the fibrous skin has been removed.

RUTABAGA: see Root Vegetables.

SAFFRON: The dried stigma from the *Crocus sativus* flower, saffron is the world's most expensive spice. Each crocus produces only 3 stigma, requiring over 75,000 flowers for each pound of saffron. It's used sparingly to add golden yellow color and flavor to a wide variety of Middle Eastern, African and European dishes. Find it in the specialty-herb section of large supermarkets and gourmet-food shops and online at *tienda.com*. Wrapped in foil and placed in an airtight container, it will keep in a cool, dry place for several years.

SCALLOPS, DRY: Be sure to buy "dry" sea scallops. "Wet" scallops, which have been treated with sodium tripolyphosphate (STP), are not only mushy and less flavorful, but will not brown properly. Some scallops have a small white muscle on the side; remove it before cooking.

SEEDS, HOW TO TOAST: To toast pumpkin seeds (pepitas), poppy seeds, sunflower seeds or sesame seeds, place in a small dry skillet and cook over medium-low heat, stirring constantly, until fragrant and lightly browned, 2 to 4 minutes.

SHAO HSING: Shao Hsing (or Shaoxing) is a seasoned Chinese rice wine. It is available at most Asian specialty markets and in the Asian section of some larger supermarkets. Chinese rice vinegar should not be used as a substitute. If unavailable, dry sherry is the best substitute. Some recipes also recommend sake, Japanese rice wine, as a substitute.

SHERRY: Sherry is a type of fortified wine originally from southern Spain. Don't use the "cooking sherry" sold in many supermarkets—it can be surprisingly high in sodium. Instead, purchase medium or dry sherry that's sold with other fortified wines in your wine or liquor store.

SHRIMP: Shrimp is usually sold by the number needed to make one pound. For example, "21-25 count" means there will be 21 to 25 shrimp in a pound. Size names, such as "large" or "extra large," are not standardized, so to get the size you want, order by the count per pound. Both wild-caught and farm-raised shrimp can damage the surrounding ecosystems when not managed properly. Fortunately, it is possible to buy shrimp that have been raised or caught with sound environmental practices. Look for fresh or frozen shrimp certified by an independent agency, such as the Marine Stewardship Council. If you can't find certified shrimp, choose wild-caught shrimp from North America—it's more likely to be sustainably caught.

SHRIMP, HOW TO PEEL AND DEVEIN: To peel, grasp the legs and hold onto the tail while you twist off the shell. To devein, use a paring knife to make a slit along the length of the shrimp. Remove the dark digestive tract (or "vein") with the knife tip.

TILAPIA: U.S. farmed tilapia is considered the best choice—it's raised in closed-farming systems that protect nearby ecosystems. Central and South American tilapia is considered a good alternative. Avoid farmed tilapia from China and Taiwan, where the fish farming pollutes the surrounding environment.

TOMATOES, HOW TO PEEL AND SEED: Bring a large pot of water to a boil. Place a large bowl of ice water next to the stove. Using a sharp paring knife, core the tomatoes and score a small X into the flesh on the bottom. Place the tomatoes in the boiling water, in batches, until the skins are slightly loosened, 30 seconds to 2 minutes. Using a slotted spoon, transfer the tomatoes to the ice water and let sit for 1 minute before removing. Place a sieve over a bowl; working over it, peel the tomatoes using a paring knife, and let the skins fall into the sieve. Halve the tomatoes crosswise and scoop out the seeds with a hooked finger, letting the sieve catch the seeds.

Special Indexes

30 Minutes or Less

Recipes marked with * are ready in 20 minutes or less.

Vegetarian

Seafood

Poultry

Meat

Gluten-Free Index

These recipes do not include wheat, rye, barley or oats. But it's important to read the labels of processed foods, such as broths and condiments, to make sure they don't contain hidden sources of gluten. And not all serving suggestions are gluten-free.

Vegetarian

Seafood

Poultry

Meat

BEEF & BISON

LAMB

PORK

Recipe Index

Page numbers in italics indicate photographs.

Recipe Contributors

Our thanks to these fine food writers whose work previously appeared in EATINGWELL *Magazine.*

Bruce Aidells | Whole Roasted Lemon-Herb Chicken on a Bed of Vegetables, 99; Red Curry Bison Short Ribs with Baby Bok Choy, 195

Nancy Baggett | Chicken & White Bean Salad, 20; Broccoli, Ham & Pasta Salad, 23; Thyme, Pork Chop & Pineapple Skillet Supper, 84

Marialisa Calta | Hunter's Chicken Stew, 183

James Chatto | White Fish Stew (*Bianco*), 180

Ruth Cousineau | Molasses-Glazed Pork with Sweet Potatoes, 106; Mediterranean Roasted Fish & Vegetables, 119; Spicy Peanut Noodles, 163

Jerry Anne Di Vecchio | Slow-Cooker Braised Pork with Salsa, 138

Ken Haedrich | Fusilli with Garden-Fresh Tomato "Sauce," 162

Joyce Hendley | Smoky Black Bean Soup, 154

Patsy Jamieson | Skillet-Roasted Strip Steaks with Pebre Sauce & Avocado, 78; Rack of Lamb with a Cilantro-Mustard Seed Crust, 87; Turkish-Style Pizza, 94; Barley Risotto with Fennel, 130; Greek Chicken & Vegetable Ragout, 137; Chinese Pork & Vegetable Hot Pot, 141; Middle Eastern Lamb Stew, 142; Hungarian Beef Goulash, 147; Chile & Beer Braised Brisket, 192

Cheryl & Bill Jamison | Pan-Fried Trout with Red Chile Sauce, 52

Wendy Kalen | Better Than Mom's Meatloaf, 104

Bharti Kirchner | Sauté of Cauliflower & Mustard Greens with Peanuts, 171

Diane Kochilas | One-Pot Vegetable Stew from Ikaria (*Soufiko*), 174

Deborah Madison | Braised Squash with Peppers & Hominy, 48; Zucchini-Ricotta Frittata with Tomato Garnish, 49; Green Vegetable Minestrone, 153

Carolyn Malcoun | Italian White Bean & Polenta Bake, 116; Chicken Florentine Roll-Ups, 120; Oven-Barbecued Asian Chicken, 123; Moroccan Bulgur & Pork Casserole, 127

Perla Meyers | Pan-Roasted Chicken & Gravy, 74; Chicken with Tarragon Cream Sauce, 72; Vegetable Stew with Sausage & Chickpeas, 86; Thai Bouillabaisse, 179

Melissa Pasanen | Lemon-Rosemary Turkey Meatballs, 62; Lemon & Oregano Lamb Chops, 88

G. Franco Romagnoli | Spinach Pasta with Pesto, Potatoes & Green Beans, 164

Jim Romanoff | Pork Chops with Creamy Marsala Sauce, 83

Scott Rosenbaum | Garlic-Roasted Pork, 105

Martha Rose Shulman | Meatless *Harira* (Moroccan Ramadan Soup), 156

Marie Simmons | Crispy Potatoes with Green Beans & Eggs, 50; Halibut Roasted with Red Bell Peppers, Onions & Russet Potatoes, 98; Rosemary & Garlic Crusted Pork Loin with Butternut Squash & Potatoes, 107

Nina Simonds | Spicy Tofu with Shrimp, 31; Chicken with Peppers, 36; Mu Shu Pork, 38; Tofu Curry, 175; Red-Cooked Lamb with Sweet Potatoes, 199

Romney Steele | Roast Chicken with Pomegranate Glaze, 100

Bruce Weinstein & Mark Scarbrough Roast Salmon with Salsa, 96; Bistro Beef Tenderloin, 103; Mint-Pesto Rubbed Leg of Lamb, 110; Squash, Chickpea & Red Lentil Stew, 131; Barbecue Pulled Chicken, 134; Chicken & Sweet Potato Stew, 135; Irish Lamb Stew, 144; Fragrant Shredded Beef Stew, 145; Braised Brisket & Roots, 194

John Willoughby | Chicken Tagine with Green Olives, 184

Grace Young | Farmers' Market Fried Rice, 26; Scallop Scampi with Peppers, 29; Sweet & Sour Pork, 40

Other EATINGWELL Books

EatingWell Fast & Flavorful Meatless Meals
150 Healthy Recipes Everyone Will Love
(The Countryman Press, 2011) ISBN: 978-0-88150-943-4 (hardcover)

The Simple Art of EatingWell
400 Easy Recipes, Tips and Techniques for Delicious, Healthy Meals
(The Countryman Press, 2010) ISBN: 978-0-88150-935-9 (hardcover)

EatingWell on a Budget
140 Delicious, Healthy, Affordable Recipes
(The Countryman Press, 2010) ISBN: 978-0-88150-913-7 (softcover)

EatingWell 500-Calorie Dinners
Easy, Delicious Recipes & Menus
(The Countryman Press, 2010) ISBN: 978-0-88150-846-8 (hardcover)

EatingWell in Season
The Farmers' Market Cookbook
(The Countryman Press, 2009) ISBN: 978-0-88150-856-7 (hardcover)

EatingWell Comfort Foods Made Healthy
The Classic Makeover Cookbook
(The Countryman Press, 2009) ISBN: 978-0-88150-829-1 (hardcover) | ISBN: 978-0-88150-887-1 (softcover, 2009)

EatingWell for a Healthy Heart Cookbook
A Cardiologist's Guide to Adding Years to Your Life
(The Countryman Press, 2008) ISBN: 978-0-88150-724-9 (hardcover)

The EatingWell Diet
7 Steps to a Healthy, Trimmer You: 150+ Delicious, Healthy Recipes with Proven Results
(The Countryman Press, 2007) ISBN: 978-0-88150-722-5 (hardcover) | ISBN: 978-0-88150-822-2 (softcover, 2008)

EatingWell Serves Two
150 Healthy in a Hurry Suppers
(The Countryman Press, 2006) ISBN: 978-0-88150-723-2 (hardcover)

The EatingWell Healthy in a Hurry Cookbook
150 Delicious Recipes for Simple, Everyday Suppers in 45 Minutes or Less
(The Countryman Press, 2006) ISBN: 978-0-88150-687-7 (hardcover)

The EatingWell Diabetes Cookbook
275 Delicious Recipes and 100+ Tips for Simple, Everyday Carbohydrate Control
(The Countryman Press, 2005) ISBN: 978-0-88150-633-4 (hardcover) | ISBN: 978-0-88150-778-2 (softcover, 2007)

The Essential EatingWell Cookbook
Good Carbs, Good Fats, Great Flavors
(The Countryman Press, 2004) ISBN: 978-0-88150-630-3 (hardcover) | ISBN: 978-0-88150-701-0 (softcover, 2005)